SCRIPTING THE MOVES

Scripting the Moves

CULTURE AND CONTROL IN A "NO-EXCUSES" CHARTER SCHOOL

Joanne W. Golann

PRINCETON UNIVERSITY PRESS

PRINCETON & OXFORD

Published by Princeton University Press
41 William Street, Princeton, New Jersey 08540
6 Oxford Street, Woodstock, Oxfordshire OX20 1TR

press.princeton.edu

All Rights Reserved
ISBN 978-0-691-16887-6
ISBN (e-book) 978-0-691-20001-9

British Library Cataloging-in-Publication Data is available

Editorial: Meagan Levinson and Jacqueline Delaney
Production Editorial: Jenny Wolkowicki
Jacket design: Amanda Weiss
Production: Erin Suydam
Publicity: Kate Hensley and Kathryn Stevens
Copyeditor: Joseph Dahm

Jacket image: Klaus Vedfelt / Getty Images

This book has been composed in Miller Text

Printed on acid-free paper. ∞

Printed in the United States of America

10 9 8 7 6 5 4 3 2 1

For my parents

CONTENTS

ACKNOWLEDGMENTS

WRITING A BOOK is a long and winding process. I am indebted to the community of scholars, educators, and friends who have supported me along the way and contributed valuable insights to this project. Here I name but a few.

This book began at Princeton University, under the guidance of Mitchell Duneier. He took a recovering demographer under his wing and turned me into an ethnographer. His lessons to seek variation, to humanize subjects, and to connect the micro and macro are at the heart of good ethnography and good research. I also thank Paul DiMaggio for his prompt and detailed feedback; Sara McLanahan for her support of my ideas and changing directions; and Thomas Espenshade for his mentorship, collaboration, and friendship through the years.

That was the beginning. My Dropbox folder of chapter files, each marked with a revision date, tells the longer story. It was at a school of education where new ideas for the book took shape. Working at Peabody College, Vanderbilt University opened my sociological eyes to new questions of education policy and educational inequity that have informed and enriched the book. My department has been a warm and welcoming place to transition to faculty life and to write this book. Christopher Loss has been a champion mentor whose advice has always been sound and whose support has been constant. Ellen Goldring as department chair helped me navigate my time and commitments. My wonderful junior colleagues, Adela Soliz, Christopher Candelaria, and Matthew Shaw, were with me in the trenches and continue to be dear colleagues and friends.

I am thankful for all those who read and reread chapters of the book (and sometimes the whole book) and provided feedback. First on the list is Annette Lareau, whose generosity to a practical stranger has extended from an initial lunch meeting to line-by-line feedback (twice) on the book manuscript. I had a dream team of school ethnographers—Maia Cucchiara, Amanda Lewis, and Edward Morris—who took the time to attend my book workshop and help me brainstorm next steps. (I won't forget Amanda's frightful words at the time that the book could be twice as long!) I also thank

Jennifer Jennings, Karen Kozlowski, Mira Debs, David Diehl, Claire Smrekar, Chris Torres, LaTonya Trotter, Rebeca Gamez, Katerina Bodovski, Jennifer Nelson, Jennifer Darling-Aduana, Walter Ecton, Anthony Jack, Jessi Streib, and Shana Starobin for reading drafts and helping to refine arguments.

A special word of thanks goes to my working group, Erin Johnston and Victoria Reyes, who have provided support, ideas, and encouragement every step of the way. Lauren Senesac is hands down the best "scholar's sidekick." Her editorial eye, research assistance, and sense of humor have shaped and strengthened the book. Eunice Koo and Kathryn Li have been kind friends to ask me about the book through the years and listen to my updates.

This book has benefitted from the research assistance of a cadre of bright students at Vanderbilt University, including Richard Hall, Kara Mitchell, Taqiyyah Elliott, Ashley Jones, Anna Weiss, Erin Smith, Lauren Covelli, Margaux Cameron, Taylor Seale, Shihe Luan, Ana Delgado, Jenny Gao, and Alexandra Vierling. Sarah Soliz also provided editorial assistance. Research for this book was funded by the National Academy of Education/Spencer Dissertation Fellowship and Peabody College, Vanderbilt University.

I am most fortunate to have had the opportunity to work with Princeton University Press. Many thanks go to my editor Meagan Levinson for taking on this project and sticking with it. I am grateful for the careful work of the staff in bringing my book to production, including copyeditor Joseph Dahm, production editor Jenny Wolkowicki, and editorial associate Jacqueline Delaney.

Portions of Chapters 3 and 6 were previously published in two of my articles, "The Paradox of Success at a No-Excuses School," Sociology of Education 88, no. 2 (April 1, 2015): 103–19 and "Conformers, Adaptors, Imitators, and Rejecters: How No-Excuses Teachers' Cultural Toolkits Shape Their Responses to Control," Sociology of Education 91, no. 1 (January 1, 2018): 28–45. They appear by permission of SAGE Publishing.

There would have been no book if Dream Academy's students, staff, and families had not welcomed me into the school and been willing to share about their experiences. They allowed me to be a part of their world, and I am appreciative of the kindness and assistance extended to me during my time at the school.

I owe much to my parents and brother, whose love and confidence in me gave me a firm foundation from which to grow. I also owe much to my husband, David, who has supported me on this long and winding journey. He also painstakingly edited the final manuscript. Finally, to my children, Matthew and Catherine, this book is not nearly as exciting as Harry Potter, but it is your mom's first book. I am glad to be finished.

SCRIPTING THE MOVES

CHAPTER ONE

Introduction

"SO THE S is for 'sitting up straight,'" Ms. Anderson, a thirty-one-year-old White teacher with curly, shoulder-length hair and glasses, announced to the students in a clear, crisp voice.[1] She folded her hands together, with her fingers interlaced. "What I'm not doing is sitting like this," she demonstrated, pretending to slouch back in a chair. "Like this," she said, straightening her back. "Try to sit all the way up. Relax your shoulders now." The crop of new Black and Latino fifth graders, seated "crisscross, applesauce" in eight straight rows on the cafeteria floor, mimicked her positions.[2] "I don't have all eyes," Ms. Anderson prompted. Then, she continued on with L for "listening," A for "ask questions," N for "nod for understanding," and T for "track the speaker."

Pointing her two fingers to her eyes, she demonstrated how students should keep their eyes on the speaker. "I should naturally see your eyes following me," she instructed, as she paced around the front of the room. "To make it even better, you can add a little smile." As the students' mouths curled up in smiles, the nervousness in the air seemed to lighten.

"Why do we SLANT? It shows respect. Posture is everything. If I'm sitting like this, it doesn't look academic." She leaned backward on her chair. "SLANTing makes you look and feel smart. It also allows the blood to circulate to the brain more. It lets you listen and absorb and retain. It helps you prepare for the real world. I can't go to my job, my mom can't go to her job, my husband can't go to his job without paying attention."

Here, on the first day of school at Dream Academy, a "no-excuses" school, I observed a lesson in how to pay attention. I was not taken aback by this lesson. In fact, I had decided to immerse myself as a researcher in the school for the year precisely because I was interested in lessons like these.

I first became interested in no-excuses schools—the name given to a number of high-performing urban schools, including KIPP (Knowledge Is Power Program), Success Academy, Uncommon Schools, YES Prep, and Achievement First—when I heard about SLANT. I was struck by its explicitness—it translated middle-class expectations for showing attention into a simple acronym. I nod (a lot) when I engage in conversation, but I certainly do not remember ever having been taught to do so.

When I started studying sociology as a graduate student, I was drawn to the concept of cultural capital because I recognized the importance of cultural know-how in getting ahead. Cultural capital comprises the cultural attitudes, skills, knowledge, and behaviors that give certain groups advantages in institutional settings.[3] It can be thought of as the "taken-for-granted ways of being that are valued in a particular context."[4] As a daughter of Chinese immigrants, I had observed cultural differences between the deferent manner in which I approached my professors and the casual style in which my graduate school peers interacted with faculty, or in how I stumbled through an explanation while my husband, who grew up in an affluent neighborhood, always sounded like he was giving a lecture. I wondered if my peers' seemingly natural ability to make small talk or articulate an argument could be learned.

To be a successful student requires a lot of background knowledge, not just about facts and figures, but also about what is appropriate to say and do. Sociologists of education have argued that schools operate under a set of middle-class, White (dominant) norms that favor children who have acquired the requisite social, cultural, and linguistic competencies at home.[5] For children whose knowledge, skills, and behaviors do not match those expected in the classroom, school can be a disorienting experience. These students can have their actions and intentions misinterpreted by teachers and school administrators, particularly by those whose backgrounds differ from their own.[6] Teachers' perceptions of students have consequences for students' academic achievement, as teachers assign higher grades to those who display skills like attention, engagement, and organization and, conversely, have lower expectations for, and give poorer evaluations to, students whom they view as disruptive, dressed "inappropriately," and lazy.[7] As misunderstandings multiply, young children may come to unconsciously sense that school is not a place for them, and adolescents may actively resist school.[8]

As a sociologist, I had read many studies about the role that cultural capital played in shaping students' experiences and outcomes in school, but I had seen few studies that looked at whether or how this cultural know-how could be taught. That's why I was intrigued when I heard about

SLANT. It literally spelled out what students needed to do to conform to school expectations for showing attention—they needed to sit up, listen, ask questions, nod for understanding, and track the speaker. I thought it was clever. Intrigued, I decided to see for myself how and why no-excuses schools were teaching students to SLANT and whether they were successfully transferring cultural capital to the predominantly low-income Black and Latino students they served.

Yet the more time I spent inside Dream Academy, the more I wondered whether Dream Academy's rigid behavioral *scripts* equipped students with the *tools* to successfully navigate middle-class institutions. To teach what the school considered "middle-class" behaviors, Dream Academy used *scripts*, which I define as detailed and standardized behavioral codes or procedures. Students at Dream Academy were given exhaustive scripts for how to dress, how to complete a homework assignment, and how to clap in an assembly. They were given scripts for how to walk down the hallways and how to sit at their desks. They were given scripts for how to interact with teachers—no eye-rolling, no teeth sucking, no refusing a teacher's directions, and no talking back, even if wrongly accused. The rigid scripts students were taught to follow, however, left little room for them to develop what I call *tools of interaction*, or the attitudes, skills, and styles that allow certain groups to effectively navigate complex institutions and shifting expectations. Would the behavioral scripts the school worked so hard to teach transfer to a different setting? As students reached the targeted goal of college, would they be able to adjust to a less structured environment? Or had no-excuses schools like Dream Academy, in their eagerness to get students to the college door, inadvertently failed to prepare students with the cultural capital they would need for life success and upward social mobility?

Scripting Success at No-Excuses Schools

The language that we use in teaching sometimes is "scripting the moves." You've got to script the moves for students. You have to narrate the experience so students understand exactly what the outcomes are. . . . It's really not that different with teachers. If you want teachers to look thoughtfully at student work, you have to script the moves for them.

—PRINCIPAL, URBAN ASSEMBLY SCHOOL FOR LAW AND JUSTICE[9]

In 1994, David Levin and Michael Feinberg, two young White Ivy League graduates, had recently completed their stint with Teach for America, a Peace Corps–type program that places recent college graduates in hard-to-staff, underresourced schools for a two-year commitment. Eager to do more in the fight against educational inequities, Levin and Feinberg decided to try their hand at starting their first two charter schools, one in Houston and one in the South Bronx. At that point, charter schools were still newcomers to the educational landscape, the first charter law having been enacted in Minnesota in 1991. Charter schools, which are independently run public schools that offer families alternative options to their district school, are now established in forty-five states and serve over three million students.[10] Although they continue to generate controversy, charter schools receive bipartisan support and have become a central component of education policy, particularly because they are seen as a way to help low-income families access better schools for their children.[11] As schools of choice, charters generally are open to any student in the district who wishes to apply and are required by state law to enroll students through a random lottery process. Charter schools are concentrated in urban areas, with more than half located in cities (compared to a quarter of traditional public schools).[12]

When Levin and Feinberg founded their first two KIPP schools, they could not have anticipated their eventual success and impact. For its first eight years, KIPP Academy Houston was recognized as a Texas Exemplary School, and KIPP Academy New York was rated the highest performing public middle school in the Bronx for eight consecutive years.[13] By 2020, KIPP was serving more than one hundred thousand students in 255 schools nationwide.[14] Of the students KIPP serves, 95 percent are Black or Latino; 88 percent are low-income students.[15] The U.S. Department of Education has declared KIPP "one of the most promising initiatives in public education today"[16]—a claim echoed by media outlets including the *New York Times*, the *Washington Post*, *Newsweek*, *Forbes*, *The Oprah Winfrey Show*, and *60 Minutes*.[17]

KIPP would become a model for a group of mostly young, White "education entrepreneurs" starting new charter schools in the 1990s and 2000s and embracing market-based education reforms that emphasize choice, competition, and accountability (see chapter 5).[18] Many of these new charters would come to replicate KIPP's successes. Although charter schools on average have performed no better than traditional public schools on statewide standardized assessments, urban charter schools that follow KIPP's "no-excuses" model have fared better.[19] Over the past decade, a number of methodologically rigorous studies that compare the outcomes of students who apply to the charter school lottery and are not admitted with the outcomes of those who apply and are admitted have found positive effects of no-excuses schools on students' standardized test scores, high school graduation rates, and college enrollment rates.[20]

The term "no-excuses"—a label that has fallen out of favor in most of these schools—comes from two books highlighting high-achieving, high-poverty schools that refuse to make excuses for students' failure, regardless of their race or ethnicity, socioeconomic status, neighborhood, or skill level.[21] This statement might seem unremarkable, but many scholars suggest that schools alone cannot overcome the persistent effects of poverty and family background.[22] The image of the failing urban school is a common one, though this stereotype has been critiqued by scholars as misrepresenting the diversity and assets of urban schools.[23] Yet it remains true that despite many repeated school reform efforts, urban schools continue to face significant obstacles, including staggering rates of teacher turnover, inadequate funding, dilapidated buildings, limited curricular options, and school safety concerns.[24] The low-income Black and Latino students concentrated in urban schools, the result of a long history of segregation and racial discrimination in the United States, thus face "opportunity gaps" that translate into "achievement gaps" that have proved difficult to close.[25] This is why no-excuses charter schools have been celebrated by many educators and policy makers for narrowing long-standing test score gaps.

Because of the unusual academic success of no-excuses schools, replicating them has even been proposed as a large-scale education reform strategy to close the racial achievement gap.[26] In the past two decades, the Walton, Broad, and Gates foundations, among others, have poured hundreds of millions into expanding no-excuses charters.[27] In cities like Boston, Newark, and New Orleans, no-excuses schools have come to dominate charter school options.[28] Even public school districts, including those in Houston, Chicago, and Denver, have experimented with no-excuses practices.[29] But before we too eagerly turn to "successful" charters to remake public education, it is important to take a look inside these schools and closely examine their practices. This is one of the first books to do so.[30]

No-excuses schools typically share a common set of practices, such as an extended school day and school year, frequent student testing, highly selective teacher hiring, intensive teacher coaching, a focus on basic math and literacy skills, and a college-going culture.[31] What is most distinctive about these schools, though, is their highly structured disciplinary system. No-excuses schools generally do not permit students to talk quietly in the hallway, enter and exit classrooms on their own, keep backpacks at their desk, wear jewelry, stare into space, slouch, put their head down, get out of their seat without permission, or refuse to track the teacher's eyes.[32] In the words of the urban school principal quoted at the beginning of this section, these schools "script the moves." They are very intentional in their systems and procedures, dictating to students and teachers how to behave. Although scripting of student behavior and teacher instruction can also be found in traditional public schools, it tends to be concentrated and intensified in no-excuses charters.

Let us take a look at a no-excuses script. To understand the detail and rigidity of these scripts, we can turn to the student conduct section of a student handbook from a KIPP high school.[33] In this section, a comprehensive chart extends for nine pages detailing three tiers of misbehaviors and their consequences. The first tier of misbehaviors includes violations for being off-task, not following directions, disrupting class, sleeping in class, calling out, being out of one's seat, using offensive language, and committing a dress code violation.[34] A closer look at the first few categories clearly illustrates the detailed nature of the schoolwide script for student behavior:

> *Off-task*: Not paying attention during instruction; not doing work; not following along; losing focus. This can also include the following: fiddling w/ tool or object, grooming—doing hair, using lotion, passing beauty supplies around classroom, etc. in class; losing place in book while popcorn reading.
>
> *Not following directions*: Not following a class or school procedure; failure to follow a teacher direction or meet an expectation (i.e., missing a direction, not following class routine like passing papers, putting electronics away, lining up, still writing when teacher has given direction to put pencils down, etc.). *This is non-defiant but rather incompetent or opportunistic.*
>
> *Minor disruption*: Talking, tapping, mouth noises, making faces, poor class transitions, excessive volume (i.e., not talking in whisper voices during T&T), any other potentially distracting *behavior exhibited unintentionally or without malicious intent.*

This KIPP high school makes no assumptions that students know what behaviors are expected of them in school; it spells out precisely what they need to do to comply with school expectations. From one perspective, this chart makes transparent what are typically unspoken behavioral expectations of schools, helping students follow them. From another angle, it is unnecessarily precise and prescriptive, reinforcing racialized patterns of social control, a point we will return to shortly.[35]

In recent years, critiques of no-excuses disciplinary practices have intensified.[36] Yet supporters of no-excuses schools have defended these practices as teaching low-income students middle-class behavioral norms. In *Sweating the Small Stuff: Inner-City Schools and the New Paternalism*, education writer David Whitman describes no-excuses schools as an example of a "highly prescriptive institution that teaches students not just how to think but how to act according to what are commonly termed traditional, middle-class values"—such as punctuality, discipline, and effort.[37] Similarly, in *No Excuses: Closing the Racial Gap in Learning*, education scholars Abigail and Stephan Thernstrom argue that successful new schools for the urban poor not only teach math and reading skills but also change culture and character. In their book, they quote KIPP founder David Levin as saying, "We are fighting a battle involving skills and values. We are not afraid to set social norms."[38] In an editorial on Promise Academy, a no-excuses school in Harlem, *New York Times* columnist David Brooks likewise states, "Over the past decade, dozens of charter and independent schools, like Promise Academy, have become no excuses schools. The basic theory is that middle-class kids enter adolescence with certain working models in their heads: what I can achieve; how to control impulses; how to work hard. Many kids from poorer, disorganized homes don't have these internalized models. The schools create a disciplined, orderly and demanding counterculture to inculcate middle-class values."[39]

Are no-excuses schools teaching middle-class values and skills? Are they transferring valuable cultural capital that their students lack? In this book, I argue that these schools are *not* teaching what sociologists consider to be advantageous middle-class skills and strategies, nor do rigid behavioral scripts afford students the flexibility to learn to deploy cultural capital effectively.

Overview of the Argument

I argue that no-excuses schools like Dream Academy are giving students *scripts* for success but not developing the kinds of *tools* students are likely to need for long-term success. Despite these schools' efforts to get students to college and set them on an upward trajectory, their rigid behavioral scripts do not supply students with the types of cultural capital that middle-class students use to navigate the more flexible expectations of college and the workplace—skills like how to express an opinion, advocate for resources, and interact with different kinds of people in different types of situations. This suggests that what might work for success in K–12 may not work for college success. It also suggests that what might work to teach the official curriculum may not work to teach what scholars have called the "hidden curriculum" of schools.

Along with the three Rs—reading, 'riting, and 'rithmetic—students also learn in school a hidden curriculum of rules and roles through the structure of daily routines and social interactions.[40] Through this implicit instruction, students learn how to think about themselves and their place in society; they learn skills and strategies for how to be successful; they learn how to interact with their peers and authority figures. Sociologists have viewed this socializing function as one of the most important purposes of schools. Standing midway between the family and society, schools transmit to students values, norms, and behaviors that prepare them for their future roles.

Early sociological theorists showed how schools taught norms of independence, achievement, and universalism to prepare all students with the attitudes, skills, and behaviors that they would need to be productive members of society.[41] Later research, however, took a more critical view of schools. Pushing against the idea that schools give all children a chance to learn, these researchers pointed to the ways in which schools are a microcosm of society, reproducing race, class, and gender inequalities. In particular, these scholars argued that through the hidden curriculum, schools differentially socialized students to take on stratified roles in society, reproducing existing social class hierarchies. Students from low-income families were taught to follow rules and fill out worksheets, learning skills like obedience, punctuality, and deference that were necessary to perform low-wage work, while students from more affluent backgrounds were taught to express their opinions and show creativity in their work to prepare them for managerial positions where they would need to demonstrate leadership.[42] Harking back to the student conduct chart we looked at from the KIPP high school, we can see how scripts like these give students little latitude to question authority, bend rules to their advantage, or act spontaneously during the school day. By holding students to these scripts, no-excuses schools, while intending to prepare students for college, continue to teach them obedience, punctuality, and deference—all in the name of social mobility.

More recently, no-excuses charter networks have begun to reflect on the implications of their rigid behavioral scripts. Not only have protests and scandals erupted at no-excuses schools over their rigid disciplinary practices,[43] but these schools also may not be meeting their own metric of success: the college degree. The KIPP network reported that while

80 percent of their students enrolled in college, only 35 percent received a bachelor's degree within six years of high school graduation.[44] A study tracking students from thirteen KIPP middle schools found that they were no more likely to persist in a four-year college after the first two years than comparable students who did not attend these schools.[45] Finally, a national study of KIPP schools found that attending a KIPP school had no effect on a variety of measures of student attitudes and behaviors related to college success, including self-control, grit, school engagement, effort or persistence in school, academic confidence, and educational aspirations.[46] This book offers one explanation for these puzzling results—the school's rigid behavioral scripts may not provide students with the attitudes, skills, and interactional styles to effectively navigate college.

CULTURAL CAPITAL AS TOOLS OF INTERACTION

Culture is a resource. In introducing the concept of cultural capital, Bourdieu recognized that affluent families, besides providing their children with social capital and economic capital, also transferred cultural capital—a less visible form of advantage.[47] Early studies of cultural capital tended to focus on high-status cultural practices, like visits to the museum, knowledge of classical music, and art lessons.[48] Privileged students whose families had the time and money to invest in this form of cultivation were seen as more successful in school, both because they were familiar with the material being covered and because they were evaluated more positively by teachers who shared their status culture. Later studies have broadened the concept of cultural capital to encompass a wide variety of cultural attitudes, preferences, knowledge, behaviors, and goods that signal status within a field.[49] These studies have measured cultural capital as linguistic competence, the number of books in the home, children's participation in organized activities, children's work habits and behaviors, parents' homework help, parents' intervening on behalf of their children, and parents' knowledge of organizational processes.[50] Yet too often studies of cultural capital have treated cultural capital as a fixed commodity, identifying particular behaviors (taking art lessons, having books at home, participating in extracurricular activities) and not looking enough at the flexibility in which these behaviors are enacted.

In an effort to clarify an unwieldy concept, sociologists Annette Lareau and Elliot Weininger redefined cultural capital as the "micro-interactional processes whereby individuals' strategic use of knowledge, skills, and competence comes into contact with institutionalized standards of evaluation."[51] This definition emphasizes cultural capital as a set of strategies used by certain groups to access resources and rewards in institutional settings, making clear that cultural capital must be actively employed in particular contexts, or what Bourdieu calls "fields."[52] That is, it is strategically applied rather than universally enacted. To activate cultural capital, one must possess not just the strategies or skills, but also the knowledge of when and how to use them. The natural "ease" by which children from higher social classes deploy cultural capital to their advantage is not easily imitated. Cultural capital becomes embodied into what Bourdieu called *habitus*, or ingrained and automatic ways of understanding and acting in the world that are durable though not unchangeable.[53] For cultural capital to reap profit, it must be effectively deployed and received.

Following Lareau and Weininger, I propose that cultural capital can be thought of as *tools of interaction* that allow certain groups to effectively navigate complex institutions and shifting expectations. By defining cultural capital as tools of interaction, I highlight its specificity and its flexibility. Like Lareau and Weininger, I emphasize cultural capital as an *interactional* resource that is dependent on the particular institutional context. In this historical moment, middle-class institutions privilege self-confident, assertive, and expressive individuals who advocate for their needs.[54] This reflects a shift over the second half of the twentieth century in middle-class cultural norms from strict discipline and self-restraint to informality, flexibility, and individuality.[55] Thus, the tools of interaction that a college student today needs to navigate the financial aid office or make a favorable impression on a professor are proactive skills—skills like how to negotiate with institutional agents and how to feel comfortable with authority, not how to sit quietly and show deference.[56]

In defining cultural capital as *tools*, I borrow from sociologist Ann Swidler, who first proposed the idea of culture as a "'tool kit' of habits, skills, and styles from which people construct 'strategies of action.'"[57] Culture can be thought of as a set of tools—not one prescribed way of doing something—that we can activate in different situations. Instead of a rigid script to follow, social actors have "a set of heuristics, hunches and shallow (but useful because they work most of the time) *practical skills* that allow persons to best interface externalized structures, contexts and institutions."[58] If we were to make a sports analogy, we could say that to be a successful soccer player, one needs to be familiar with the rules of the game, have the right skills, and know when and how to use which plays. In other words, tools of interaction include (1) knowledge of the system (the "rules of the game"), (2) skills for acting effectively in that system

(including how to innovate and bend rules), and (3) the ability to interpret different situations and pick the right skill to deploy (a "feel for the
game"). While other scholars have made useful conceptual distinctions
between these different components, I include them together as components of cultural capital because they are difficult to distinguish empiri-
cally and each contributes to whether an individual is evaluated favorably
in an interaction.[59]

The cultural capital that middle-class students possess and use to their
advantage in schools and workplaces is a flexible tool, not a straitjacket.
Middle-class students know when to follow rules but also when and how
to deviate from them. Sociologist Jessica Calarco, for example, found that
middle-class children in an elementary school not only followed rules but
also figured out how to strategically bend rules to their benefit, securing
more attention, assistance, and accommodation from their teachers than
did their working-class peers.[60] Affluent students learn how to defer to
authority but also how to be at ease with authority. In his study of an elite
boarding school, sociologist Shamus Khan observed how the privileged
students developed a "sense of ease" through interacting with adults in
both formal and informal situations that prepared them for managerial
positions where they would need to be comfortable interacting with the
custodian or the CEO, in the board room or at the bar.[61]

If we understand cultural capital as *tools of interaction*, we can begin
to see the ways in which no-excuses schools like Dream Academy may
fall short in both *what* kinds of behaviors they are trying to teach (i.e.,
obedience rather than initiative) and *how* they are trying to teach them
(i.e., through rigid scripts rather than through developing a flexible set
of skills).

HOW TO TEACH CULTURAL CAPITAL

Cultural attitudes, skills, and behaviors are often implicitly transferred
through a long period of family socialization, a process that is time-
intensive and costly. Traditionally, schools have not tried to teach cultural
capital to students who are not familiar with dominant norms.[62] As the
role of cultural capital in promoting success becomes more widely recognized, however, institutions and programs that support low-income and
first-generation student success have also made efforts to explicitly teach
cultural capital. College preparatory programs for low-income students
and students of color like Prep for Prep, A Better Chance, I Have a Dream,
and others often include a socialization aspect where students learn norms

for applying to colleges and navigating interactions with peers and faculty on campus.

Despite the growth of these programs, few scholars have examined how they teach cultural capital.[63] Although there have been some studies of how teachers can teach students dominant norms while affirming students' own cultural knowledge and skills, in practice teachers often lack a clear sense of how to implement this kind of culturally responsive/relevant teaching.[64] Additionally, teachers who try to teach students school-appropriate ways of dressing, speaking, or interacting often unintentionally reinforce negative stereotypes about racial and ethnic groups, framing students' culture in deficient ways.[65] Finally, even if Black and Latino students acquire and deploy dominant cultural capital, they may not reap the same rewards as White students given institutionalized racism and implicit racial biases.[66] Sociologist L'Heureux Lewis-McCoy has argued that theories of cultural capital need to take into account institutional reception, particularly the ways in which race shapes how schools respond to different groups' attempts at advocacy and entitlement.[67] For these reasons, some education scholars have distanced themselves from a focus on cultural capital in favor of concepts like "community cultural wealth," which shifts attention to the assets students from nondominant groups possess rather than the dominant cultural capital they lack.[68] Sociologist Prudence Carter has termed the cultural capital of socially marginalized groups as "non-dominant cultural capital."[69]

Although these are good reasons for shifting the lens away from cultural capital, an argument can still be made for explicitly teaching cultural capital to students from nondominant groups. In her influential essay "The Silenced Dialogue," education scholar Lisa Delpit advocated for teaching the "culture of power" (or cultural capital) to students of color in order to help these students access power.[70] Schools do not teach students the culture of power, she contended, because White liberal educators find being explicit about rules and expectations too prescriptive. To tell students that they have to show attention by SLANTing, for example, makes clear the teacher's power over the student. Yet by insisting on the same freedoms for all students that middle-class White parents want for their own children, argued Delpit, schools fail to teach all students the codes they need to acquire power.

Herein lies an important tension in thinking about cultural capital and whether and how it can be taught. To explicitly teach cultural capital is to be prescriptive. High levels of prescriptiveness, however, impede students from acquiring the tools of interaction—tools like assertiveness, initiative, and ease—currently valued in middle-class institutions. Pre-scriptiveness also stands in contradiction to the flexibility required to develop and use tools.

The rigid behavioral scripts used at Dream Academy magnify these tensions. As we've seen, no-excuses behavioral scripts make crystal clear what are typically unstated norms of schools and can make it easier for students to learn school-sanctioned ways of speaking, dressing, and inter-acting. Scripts, however, are also extremely prescriptive, leaving little room for agency or adaptation. A student who is required to SLANT at atten-tion, for example, will not learn when or how to be at ease with authority. A student who is carefully monitored for speaking out of turn will not learn when it is appropriate to interrupt. A student who is told not to talk back, even if falsely accused, will not learn how to negotiate. Because culture is complex and situations are difficult to predict, individuals need interpretative skills to read a situation and choose among alternatives—skills that are difficult to transfer through a rigid script.

Developing entitlement, initiative, and ease requires a degree of auton-omy, flexibility, and egalitarianism. The prescriptiveness of the directives used by no-excuses schools can potentially hamper students from fully understanding and navigating the rules of the game. The rigid scripts the school uses to teach cultural capital may inhibit students from learning the proactive and flexible tools it is composed of. Being a competent stu-dent and, more generally, a competent cultural actor requires more than a script—it requires *tools of interaction*.

CAPITAL OR CONTROL?

Scripts are meant to be useful in teaching students cultural capital to help them achieve success. However, scripts in no-excuses schools sometimes serve more as social control than useful capital. Given the racialized and classed history of social control, any exercise of intense social control over students who have been historically marginalized needs to be considered from a vantage point of power. Such was Brian's take on the school's prac-tices. One afternoon, sitting in an empty classroom during lunch, I inter-viewed Brian, a Latino eighth grader, along with his girlfriend, Angie. As we talked about school rules they didn't like, Brian pointed to SLANT. He saw SLANT as another way for the school to "overpower" students, not a way to help them pay attention. "Now SLANT is another word for power," he insisted. "S-L-A-N-T. P-O-W-E-R. Same five letters of the words." Angie agreed, arguing that you listen with your ears, not your eyes and hands. Students like Brian and Angie found school scripts like SLANT to be an example of the school's extreme control over their bodies rather than a way to help them learn.

Through this lens, we can interpret the rigid behavioral scripts employed by no-excuses schools as in line with a long history of managing poor youth of color through social control, surveillance, and punishment. The poor have long been viewed as intractable, in need of guidance and reform. From the welfare state to penal institutions, the state has a long history of regulating the poor. Through "distorted engagement," sociologist Patricia Fernández-Kelly contends, "[poor] individuals learn to see themselves from early childhood as subjects of regulations and discourses so constrictive and detrimental as to incite mostly manipulation, resistance, and circumvention."[71] While the middle class engages with state institutions with a degree of autonomy and entitlement, the poor are surveilled and controlled. Since the 1970s, neoliberal reforms that have increased personal freedoms and consumer choice for the middle classes have coincided with an erosion of the social safety net and even greater controls on the poor and marginalized.[72]

Race and social control are also intimately intertwined. Sociologist Loïc Wacquant identifies four social institutions throughout history that have been used to contain and confine African Americans: slavery, the Jim Crow South, the ghetto, and the prison.[73] Schools, however, have also become part of what sociologist Victor Rios terms a "youth control complex" of institutions that control and criminalize Black and Latino youth.[74] Beginning in the 1980s and 1990s, schools—particularly urban schools that served youth of color—began to resemble prisons in employing metal detectors, surveillance cameras, and uniformed police officers to establish control. These decades also saw the introduction of zero-tolerance policies that mandated suspensions or expulsions for drug and violent offenses but were applied liberally to more minor status offenses and paradoxically to truancy.[75] An abundance of research has found that the intensification of school discipline has disproportionately impacted Black and Latino students, whose suspension rates soared between the early 1970s and the early 2000s.[76] Studies of school discipline have found that Black males in particular receive more frequent and harsher punishment,[77] are perceived as more threatening and aggressive,[78] and are more likely to be referred for subjective behaviors like making excessive noise or being disrespectful as compared to White students, who are referred for more objective violations like smoking or vandalism.[79]

Too many urban schools in marginalized communities have become places, in sociologist Pedro Noguera's words, "whose primary mission is not to educate but to ensure custody and control."[80] Although the primary mission of no-excuses schools, and many other programs that try to transfer cultural capital, is not custody and control but preparing students with the knowledge and skills for college, overly rigid scripts for behavior risk reinforcing a narrative of low-income Black and Latino students as "out of control" and in need of strict discipline.[81] Discipline, which traditionally has pushed students out of school, excluding them from academics, is now perceived as a vehicle to transform students into more productive learners, an inclusionary mechanism for preparing students with the skills and behaviors to be successful in a middle-class world. The line between teaching cultural capital and reinforcing social control is not easy to draw apart, and in drawing it schools risk justifying the latter in defense of the former. In this way, behavioral practices that are seen as promoting social mobility for students can serve to maintain racial and classed structures of domination and subordination through control of vulnerable populations in vulnerable spaces. As has been made all too clear in recent police shootings, the perpetuation of negative stereotypes of Black and Brown bodies as dangerous and in need of control can have deadly consequences.

Inside a No-Excuses School

At the time of my fieldwork, Dream Academy, a pseudonym I use for the school to protect its confidentiality, leased a brown-brick building at Sixth Street, across from a line of vacant storefronts and next to a Catholic church. The school is compact, with three floors and about a dozen classrooms: the bottom floor houses the seventh- and eighth-grade classrooms; the second floor houses the main office and the fifth- and sixth-grade classrooms; and the top floor contains the music classes and the cafeteria, which doubles as a gym and auditorium. Classrooms are referred to by their college names—Princeton, Penn, Carnegie Mellon—and painted with college colors and logos. The hallways are neat and brightly decorated, filled with college pendants, brightly colored posters of "grit," "self-control," and "gratitude," and exemplary student work. There are no lockers inside the school.

Dream Academy promotes itself as a no-excuses school and adheres closely to no-excuses practices, including an extended school day (seven thirty to four) and school year (mid-August through June), frequent student testing, highly selective teacher hiring, intensive teacher coaching, a focus on basic math and literacy skills, and a college-going culture. Scrolling down Dream Academy's website, we can see these core elements of the model:

Highest Standards

We use a college preparatory curriculum for all students

We have highly structured student conduct expectations

We consistently enforce our student conduct expectations—across each classroom at each campus, at every hour, day and month of the year

Students earn or are denied privileges based on their conduct

We hire an elite professional staff and give them demanding responsibilities to fulfill

Data Driven

We measure everything

We conduct regular student formative assessments to track our progress

We judge teacher performance based, in part, on student test results

We transparently communicate data organization-wide to inform decisions

Tough Love

We have a longer school day—8 1/2 hours—and longer school year— 200 days

We explicitly teach and reinforce our core values of caring, respect, responsibility and honesty

We recognize students and staff for successes before the entire school community

We expect members of our community to acknowledge their mistakes and to apologize to their peers when appropriate

As in other no-excuses schools, instruction is traditional, with a focus on basic skills and the use of techniques like direct instruction, guided instruction, and independent practice.[82] In addition to basic academic classes, students also participate in music, gym, advising, and morning circle—a schoolwide assembly that features chants, announcements, recognition of students and teachers, and a short lesson on character. Five times a year, the school administers practice schoolwide assessments that reflect the content and conditions of the state standardized test. Following these tests, teachers and administrators devote a full day to analyzing student test results and making plans for reteaching areas that students have not mastered.

For a period of eighteen months, beginning in March 2012, I became a regular presence at Dream Academy, which at the time served approximately 250 middle school students in grades five to eight, with 25 to 27 students per class.[83] Founded in the 2000s, it was one of the highest performing middle schools in this medium-sized northeastern city. Like many other deindustrialized cities, the city faced problems of crime, concentrated poverty, and low educational attainment—half of the students did not graduate from the city's public high school. Charter schools in the city had a mixed record of success. In the year preceding my fieldwork, three charter schools in the city closed for discipline problems, low student attendance, and poor student performance. By contrast, Dream Academy had performed well. Over two-thirds of its students passed the state's standardized assessment in math, compared to about one-third of students in the local school district; more than one-half of Dream Academy students passed the state literacy assessment, compared to just over one-quarter in the local school district.[84] Dream Academy was recognized by the state for significantly improving students' standardized test scores, and both its charter renewal application and expansion plan had been approved. Its first graduating high school class boasted a 100 percent college acceptance rate. Given the selection of students and families into charter schools, however, Dream Academy's academic results do not necessary mean that the school was more successful than district schools because it served a different mix of students. Although the cost to attend the school was free and students were selected via a random lottery, students and families still had to apply to the school and commit to its expectations. Because there was no bus transportation available, families had to live in the vicinity of the school or be able to transport their children each day.

Over 80 percent of Dream Academy students received free or reduced-price school lunch; for a family of four, this meant that the students' household income had to be below thirty thousand dollars for free lunch and forty-three thousand for reduced-price lunch.[85] Approximately two-thirds of students were Black and one-third Latino,[86] mirroring the demographics of the city. Families were required to sign a contract committing to the school's expectations and values before their students were enrolled. Contracts between schools and families have become a common feature of no-excuses schools.[87] At Dream Academy, parents promise to bring their children to school on time and ensure that they complete 90 to 120 minutes of homework each weekday night, while students commit to following a stringent set of behavioral expectations. These expectations may be reflected in the low number of special education students (10 percent) and limited English proficiency students (1 percent) served by the school.[88] Although attrition can be high in no-excuses schools, student attrition rates were low, at less than 1 percent during the school year.

The school staff was predominantly young and White, with little prior teaching experience. It included four newlyweds, a handful of first-time full-time job holders, three Ivy League alumni, several graduates from local colleges, and a former executive assistant to the founder of a highly successful tech start-up company. Most teachers were under thirty—the youngest was twenty-one and the oldest was fifty-eight. Mr. Bradley, the White school principal, was thirty-four; Ms. Williams, a Black instructional dean who became principal halfway through my observations, was twenty-nine. (Mr. Bradley planned to serve as principal of the network's new elementary school the following year, so this arrangement gave Ms. Williams time to ease into the role, with the benefit of having Mr. Bradley around to advise.) No-excuses teachers have traditionally tended to be young, with strong academic backgrounds and limited classroom experience, and they often have taken alternative routes into teaching.[89] At Dream Academy, teachers' work hours were considerably longer (seven fifteen to four thirty) than those of teachers in the local public school district (contractually limited to six hours forty-five minutes with a lunch break), and the pay for a novice teacher was approximately 10 percent lower.[90]

Mr. Taylor, the genial Black founder and director of the school, compared its teachers to the individuals one finds on Wall Street or Capitol Hill. It is the same pool of smart, hardworking, ambitious young people, each with a slightly different motivation—to make money, to serve the country, or to make a difference in children's lives. One teacher at Dream Academy applied to the school after watching *Waiting for "Superman,"* a documentary featuring successful no-excuses charter schools. Two left finance jobs to do more meaningful work. Ms. Wallace, one of the students' favorite teachers, came to Dream Academy as a local reporter on an assignment. She was so impressed by what she saw, she decided to switch professions.

My own role in the school was mostly as an observer, following one fifth-grade and one eighth-grade class almost every school day, typically for four to five hours. However, I also engaged with students: sitting with them at their lunch table, assisting them with class work, tutoring them after school, and accompanying them on field trips and to football games. Sometimes I would sit in an absent student's seat or fall into line behind the students as they walked silently through the hallways, trying to get a better sense of their experiences in the school. To better understand the teachers' perspectives, I also regularly observed their one-on-one meetings with their supervisors, sat in weekly staff meetings, and attended the two-week summer teacher orientation. To meet parents, I attended parent association meetings and school activities. Finally, to get a sense of students' preparation for college, I conducted observations at Dream Academy's high school and the local community college where students took dual-enrollment courses. I sought parental permission to interview students, and by the end of my fieldwork I had conducted interviews with seventy-two students. These interviews were typically conducted during lunch in a private room and lasted approximately thirty minutes. I also interviewed thirty-three current and former teachers and twenty-seven parents, with these interviews lasting between one and two hours. All the names used in this book are pseudonyms to protect the identity of my respondents. A fuller discussion of my research methods can be found in the methodological appendix.

Part of the work of an ethnographer is to make the familiar unfamiliar. What follows may feel both familiar and unfamiliar to those who experienced the school year with me. As an ethnographer, my vantage point is different, shaped by the theories I have studied and the different perspectives I had the privilege of observing from. During my fieldwork, I often felt uneasy gazing critically at the school, jotting notes, when everyone else was working tirelessly to help the kids succeed. I admire the teachers and staff and still feel ambivalence in highlighting some of the unintended consequences of the school's practices. My aim in this book is not to point fingers but to think about the larger structures and narratives that are shaping schooling in new and old ways for children in economically deprived urban communities. This book focuses on one no-excuses school, but the concepts and ideas developed in the book extend beyond the scope of no-excuses schools and can be applied to understanding similar processes in other schools and other institutional settings.

Organization of the Book

This book presents an in-depth look into how Dream Academy used *scripts* to demand strict regulation of both students and teachers. It shows why these scripts were adopted, what purposes they served, and where they fell short. What emerges is a complicated story of the benefits of scripts, but also, importantly, their limitations in developing in students the *tools of interaction* they need to navigate college and other complex social institutions: tools like flexibility, initiative, and ease with adults.

The book examines how Dream Academy's efforts to transmit cultural capital through rigid behavioral scripts distorted students' *expectations* about what it takes to be successful (chapter 2), impeded their *skills* for navigating middle-class institutions (chapter 3), and constrained their *styles* of interacting with authority (chapter 4). The book then turns to the no-excuses organizational script and examines how adherence to this script also limits the tools that schools (chapter 5) and teachers (chapter 6) develop.

Chapter 2 introduces the school's behavioral scripts for how to achieve success. Following the incoming fifth graders through new student orientation, we see how students are explicitly taught a detailed set of behavioral codes to follow, including how to complete homework, how to clap at an assembly, and how to walk down the hallway. Though seemingly impossible to follow, these rigid scripts were enforced through a detailed schoolwide system of rewards and punishments and justified as a way to teach students middle-class values and behaviors. Yet when we consider what lessons students learned from these rigid school scripts, we see a divergence between the expectations that the predominantly low-income students at Dream Academy formed about success and those that middle-class students internalize. Taught to make "no excuses," Dream Academy students were pressured to make no mistakes, as the prospect of failure and the weight of success were placed on their shoulders. Middle-class students, by contrast, learn to be successful by sometimes "making excuses"— that is, by demanding accommodations for themselves and bending rules in their own favor.

In chapter 3, we meet students like Alexis who perceptively recognized that their college preparatory school was not preparing them with the skills they needed for college. As students were taught behavioral scripts to keep silent and follow rules, they failed to develop tools critical for college success like expressing an opinion, being flexible, displaying leadership, advocating a position, and making independent decisions. As we visit with students in their college-level classes, we see how Dream Academy's scripts may not have translated well to a less structured college environment where students must take initiative and manage their work independently.

Chapter 4 illustrates how students were given narrow scripts for how to relate to their teachers rather than a broad set of tools for interacting with authority. With the school's myriad rules and constant monitoring, students come to see teachers as out to get them, leading students to become distrustful, resentful, and resistant to authority. Because time and space at the school were so highly structured, students and teachers had little informal time to correct these impressions and develop more positive relationships with each other. As a result, students developed a *sense of antagonism* toward authority rather than a *sense of ease*.

Chapter 5 zooms out to present the history of Dream Academy and its behavioral scripts, weaved into the broader history of no-excuses schools and the charter school movement. We learn how Dream Academy school leaders copied a rigid script to establish order but found it difficult to deviate from this script to address the school's emerging needs. We see how the no-excuses model also spread through copying, both through individual mimicry on the part of charter school leaders and through a strategy of replication on the part of powerful foundations. The spread of the no-excuses script throughout the urban charter school landscape, however, potentially undermines two core goals of the school choice movement: innovation in education and responsiveness to local communities.

Chapter 6 focuses on teachers who also were subjected to the school's rigid behavioral scripts. We see how the school recruited mission-driven and coachable teachers who were likely to be amenable to following school scripts. School scripts support novice teachers in managing their classrooms but do not develop in teachers the tools to adjust their practices to fit their own styles and respond to different student needs. Overreliance on behavioral scripts also can limit teacher autonomy and undermine teacher expertise and commitment. Teachers, however, did demonstrate agency in modifying and resisting school scripts.

Chapter 7 concludes by stressing that cultural capital needs to be seen as flexible, not fixed, not scripted. I offer lessons for teaching cultural capital and, alternatively, for supporting students from marginalized communities by affirming their cultures and recognizing their more pressing everyday needs. I also offer lessons for no-excuses schools and for educational policy. Ultimately, I argue that students, teachers, and schools need flexible tools they can adapt, not rigid scripts from which they cannot deviate.

CHAPTER TWO

Scripts for Success

"OKAY, WHAT GRADE are you in?" asked Ms. Anderson, the instructional dean leading new student orientation.

Seated before her was the new crop of Dream Academy students, attired in white polo shirts and khaki slacks, spaced out in perfectly straight rows on the cafeteria floor. Her question was deceptively simple. When a few students raised their hands and offered "fifth grade," Ms. Anderson shook her head. Fifth grade was the correct answer but not the one Ms. Anderson was looking for.

"Some of you said fifth grade, and that's okay, but that's not why we're here," she explained. "We are not here to make you the fifth graders get to sixth grade. The reason why we are here is to ensure that each and every one of you gets to college and graduates from college."

From here on out, she told the students, they would be referred to not as fifth graders but as the college class of 2024. She pointed to the numbers "2024" now displayed on the projector screen. Banners that read "Class of 2021," "Class of 2022," "Class of 2023," and "Class of 2024" lined the auditorium stage, reminding these middle-school students of the years they would graduate from college.

"Where are you going to college?" Ms. Anderson continued, pointing to her next slide, which was filled with colorful college logos. She mentioned that several of the teachers at the school had attended these colleges. "Every person in this room is going to help you get there," she assured the students.

Having set the new students' vision on college, Ms. Anderson then offered a reality check. The next slide was an infographic of students' progression through the main public high school in the city. For each year from ninth grade to twelfth grade, the icons of students reading books dwindled. "For every fifty students that enter in ninth grade," Ms. Anderson reported, "there are six left who are college ready."

"For that reason, we do a lot of things differently," she continued. "I can assure you that no other student in the city is in school today. I can assure you that you are going to go home and tell mom and dad, the school is so strict. You are going to complain about the amount of homework you are going to have."

As a charter school, Dream Academy does not have to comply with many state and local regulations governing traditional public schools. It can thus extend the school year and implement its own disciplinary systems. The strictness that Ms. Anderson foreshadowed would soon become evident to the students. But before getting to the means by which the school would achieve its ends, Ms. Anderson first focused students' attention on these ends.

Clicking to the next slide, Ms. Anderson showed a graph of average annual earnings by education level.

"So, if you drop out of high school, the average person makes $23,000."

The students, who had been mostly quiet, stirred.

"Now a lot of your eyes got big. You're thinking that's a lot of money. But it is—and isn't."

She explained how high school graduates do a little better, at $30,000 a year. Getting a bachelor's degree, graduating with a four-year diploma, pushes salaries up to $52,200. If you go on after that, get a master's degree, $62,300. A professional degree, $109,600.

"Look at the amount of money you could make."

She added that it wasn't just about money, but also about opportunity.

"We want you over here," she said, gesturing to the higher income bars on the right side of the graph.

In the city where Dream Academy resides, approximately three-quarters of the population are high school graduates but only one-tenth have bachelor's degrees. The median household income is thirty-five thousand dollars, and approximately one-quarter of families live below the poverty line.[1] To beat the odds, Dream Academy has committed to doing things differently than traditional public schools in the city.

As we follow the new students through their first days of orientation, we will get a better sense of how different the school's practices are. Just as students learned on the first day of school that they are not fifth graders but the college class of 2024, they will soon learn new rules for how to do their homework, how to enter a classroom, and how to clap in an assembly. The purpose of cutting students' summer vacations short by two weeks is not to squeeze in additional instructional time but to begin to familiarize students with the school's distinctive culture. To achieve success, students will learn to conform to the school's *scripts*, or detailed and standardized codes or procedures.

After familiarizing ourselves with the school's scripts, we will turn to examine what messages these scripts send to students about success. If these scripts are aimed at getting students to college, the lessons they teach students about how to get there are distinct from those taught at more affluent schools. As we will see, while the predominantly low-income Black and Latino students who attended Dream Academy learned to make no excuses and earn their way, their middle-class White counterparts actually learn to make excuses and bend the script to their own advantage.[2] Students with different opportunities and obstacles may take very different pathways to success, but the message that Dream Academy sent to its students placed on them a heavy burden to achieve and a sense of blame for falling short.

Teaching the Script

On the projector screen at the front of the cafeteria were displayed two words: "NOT ALLOWED!"

Warm but strict, Ms. Scott, a biracial woman in her forties who was the head of discipline at Dream Academy, had been tasked during new student orientation with introducing the school's rules and consequences. She started with proscriptions for food and drink.

Gesturing toward the images of food displayed on the projector screen, Ms. Scott gave a quick explanation for each item: Soda ("Soda is not allowed at all"). Sunflower seeds ("People spit them everywhere, put them in books, so nasty"). Candy ("Candy gives you cavities, makes your brain work slow. We've got to get you to college"). Hot chocolate ("We're trying to stay away from caffeine"). Donuts ("Why do you think we can't have donuts? They have a lot of sugar"). She warned the students that teachers would take and throw away the items if they saw them.

Prohibiting sugary foods is not an uncommon practice in schools. More distinctive was the next set of expectations about behaviors that would not be tolerated.

After covering more typical categories like harassment, bullying, and intimidation, Ms. Scott continued on: "Not allowed: eye-rolling." She directed the students to give her their best eye roll. Looking around at the students sitting on the floor and staring at her, she teased, "Now people are acting like they don't know how to roll their eyes. Maybe this group just doesn't roll their eyes. That's good because it's not allowed."

After eye-rolling came teeth sucking. To make a teeth sucking sound, you press your tongue against the roof of your mouth, with the tip of your tongue against your teeth. Then you inhale slightly and release the tip of your tongue to make a loud sucking sound. Teeth sucking is considered a form of disrespect. On the count of three, Ms. Scott let the students have at it. The kids let out a flurry of "tsk" sounds as they sucked their teeth. This time, Ms. Scott was impressed. "You know how to do that one," she applauded. "Get it out of our system now so go ahead and suck your teeth." After a few moments, she asked them to stop. Still hearing sounds, she said more sternly, "We didn't get 100 percent. When I say stop, everybody stops." She paused. "Nope, I still heard one person over here and one person over here."

"Refusing to follow directions—not allowed." Ms. Scott explained that if a teacher told you to move your seat, you were not allowed to say that you didn't want to move.

"Talking back—not allowed." Even if students felt unfairly accused and wanted to defend themselves, Ms. Scott told them that "you're just not going to do anything."

As Ms. Scott ran through these rules on the second day of student orientation, students learned that Dream Academy would indeed be different from their prior schools. Schools often make general statements about being respectful or not running in the hallways, but as sociologist Hugh Mehan has observed of schools, "the criteria used to evaluate students' behavior are seldom stated in so many words."[3] In contrast to most middle schools, Dream Academy was very intentional in communicating to students its rigid behavioral expectations—down to forbidding eye-rolling and talking back. In fact, this was already the second time that students had been told about the school's rules.

The first was during their home visit in the summer, when two staff members called on the home of each family of a newly enrolled child. The purpose of the visit, as written in the five-page home visit script, was to "explain how we are different than other schools" and to assure parents that "we will implement *every single element* of the program we describe to you today" (see table 2.1). Mr. Taylor, the Black founder and director of Dream Academy, believes that home visits are the most important thing the school does because they make clear school expectations for

Table 2.1. Home Visit Script

Introduction

- Introduce self. Ask parent: "would you mind turning off your cell phone, TV, radio, etc."
- We meet with all of our families to explain how we are different than other schools. We want you to have a clear picture of our expectations so that you can be successful.
- In the past some parents did not realize how seriously we implement our program and they ended up leaving our school because they felt we were "too strict."
- We can assure you that we will implement *every single element* of the program we describe to you today.
- Dream Academy is not for everyone so we ask that you listen carefully and ask any questions you may have to make sure that we are the right school for you.

High and Clear Expectations

- We expect more than other schools.
  - We have the hardest working students in the City so if you come to our school, you will have to work harder than you ever have before.
  - Our expectation is that you will attend and graduate from the top colleges in the nation, therefore, you will receive 90 min to 2 hours of homework every night (we will share more on homework later).
  - We do not tolerate bullying or fighting of any kind.
- We expect you to always be prepared for and focused in class:
  - You must be prepared for class with your pencils (NO INK PENS), notebook and other required materials.
  - You must be very organized.
  - You must SLANT (Give SLANT handout and model the actions)
  - **S**it up straight with your hands folded in front of you
  - **L**isten
  - **A**sk questions if you do not understand
  - **N**od for understanding
  - **T**rack the speaker
  - SLANTing is respectful and helps our students to focus and develop listening skills. (As an example, show students what it's like for them to be talking and have you not looking at them.)

Building Community

- **School-Parent-Student Contract**—Go over School-Parent-Student Contract. Presenter reads key points of School and Parent section, child reads student section. Model and explain everything that has not yet been covered. Get signatures.
- We are a school of choice. It is not for everyone. We do not think our program is the only way to educate students, but it is our way. There may be rules or policies you do not agree with but please know we do not intend to change because we have clear data to prove our strategies work for most of our students. If you disagree with our policies you and your family will need to determine if this school is the right fit for you.

Source: Excerpt from the Dream Academy Home Visit Checklist.

families. When families find themselves frustrated by school rules, they are reminded that they agreed to them in their own living rooms. In this way, these visits become a means for getting families to understand and accept the school's scripts.

During one home visit I attended with two White teachers, we met with a Black father and his incoming fifth-grade son. Mr. Sudano, one of the teachers leading the visit, began by asking the father to turn off the television and then explained that the school does things "completely differently" from the public school his son had attended and how "we understand that it's not for everyone." For most of the time, Mr. Sudano spoke directly to the son, who listened attentively and nodded from time to time. The teachers explained that students received at least ninety minutes of homework each night, compared to the thirty minutes the son reported doing now. They then demonstrated how to SLANT (sit up, listen, ask questions, nod for understanding, track the speaker) by folding your hands and looking at the speaker. Mr. Sudano praised the son for looking at him when he talked even though this was a strange setting, with him sitting next to him on the couch. At the end of the visit, the son was sent out to review the school's behavioral contract, which he signed and returned. He was instructed to stand up and read the contract, which he read without flaw. While the son was out of the room, the teachers talked to the father about his responsibilities as a parent: to make sure there was a quiet space for his son to study, to "sweat the small stuff" in checking over his son's homework ("tell him to rewrite a problem if it's messy"), and to respect the teachers and voice concerns. They told him it was going to be hard. "For me?" he asked. "For your son," Mr. Sudano corrected. Mr. Sudano explained that many kids found it difficult in the first weeks to adjust to the homework expectations and to the strictness. "They call it jail," he noted. The father did not appear too concerned. He asked where to sign the parent contract.

Throughout the first week of new student orientation, school staff would reiterate these expectations. During one orientation session, Ms. Williams, a Black teacher who was later promoted to principal of the school, reviewed homework expectations with students. Walking up and down the center aisle of the floor while snapping at students for attention, she emphasized that Dream Academy followed the same expectations as students would experience in college. After showing a short clip from the cartoon show *Arthur*, she explained how successful students would need to be like Arthur and burn the midnight oil in completing their homework. They would receive ninety minutes to two hours of homework "Every.

Single. Night." She told students that it wouldn't be a big deal because "you know homework is preparing you for what?"

"College," the students chanted.

"Homework is preparing you for *what*?"

"College!" they repeated more loudly.

"Homework is preparing you for *what*?"

"COLLEGE!"

Ms. Williams went on to explain that it was not just about completing homework any which way. At Dream Academy, homework had to be four things: neat, complete, on time, and best effort. Ms. Williams explained that "neat" meant that homework could not be turned in "stained, crinkled, or folded up." Connecting the school's scripts to college, she declared, "Let's take it back to college. Your college application cannot have dinner stains on it, holes from your pencil or pen." "On-time" meant that the homework had to be turned in during homeroom. "Complete" meant that students had to answer all parts of all questions and had to write their full heading at the top of the page. "Best effort" meant that they had to show their work, write in complete sentences, and call their classmates or the teacher if they were having trouble with a question.

If students followed these directions, they would receive 100 percent on their homework. If they did not, they would receive a zero—to which Ms. Williams added, "oh no," indicating that these students were not going to get a zero. She had students repeat "oh no" three times. She then told students that if they turned in homework that was not neat, complete, on time, and best effort, they would also receive a same-day detention.

As with the expectations for student behavior, we can see how the expectations for homework are also precise. To be a successful student at Dream Academy and to succeed in college, students learned that they would have to conform to an exacting script. Throughout orientation, students learned new scripts for disposing of their food at lunch, passing in papers, and keeping the bathroom clean. To move through the building, students learned to walk in silent, single-file lines, their bodies facing forward and their hands to their sides. To enter classrooms, they lined up outside and entered silently when the teacher gave permission. Then they were to "silently stow belongings, proceed to your desk, write your homework in your planner." This was to be followed by working on their Do Now, a short assignment that was used to focus student attention and maximize student learning at the start of class. If students needed to get out of their seats during class, they were taught to use hand signals to ask permission to use the bathroom (a fist with the thumb tucked between the middle and pointer finger) or request a pencil (one finger down), a drink (one finger up), or a tissue (three fingers together). At the end of the class, the teacher would dismiss students who were in SLANT position to pack and line up.

To minimize distractions, students were allowed no water bottles, no electronic devices, and no cell phones.[4] Uniform rules were also particular and scripted. As described in the student handbook, the school uniform consisted of a long- or short-sleeved polo shirt emblazoned with the school logo and khaki pants that could not be overly loose or tight, cargo-style or skinny leg. Students had to wear solid white or solid black socks and solid black shoes without "off-black or other color patterns, stripes, logos, laces, lips, toes, heels, eyelets, parts of the sole or any other parts of the shoe or sneaker."[5] Bracelets or necklaces were not allowed, and earrings had to be smaller than a nickel. Only one watch could be worn. Excessive makeup was prohibited, as were facial piercings and tattoos.

While the brunt of the school's scripts fell on students, teachers also had to adhere to strict regulations—as I saw when I was given a copy of the teachers' script for new student orientation. An eight-page, single-spaced document directed teachers as to what they were supposed to cover in their presentations and where they were supposed to be stationed if they were not presenting. The bathroom procedures alone were nearly half a page, detailing where each teacher should be during the break, what order students would be allowed to go, and how students should behave while waiting, moving through the halls, and forming lines.

This form of micromanagement, called "discipline," is an expression of power that is insidious and more difficult to see than sheer force. Discipline, according to social theorist Michel Foucault, rose in the eighteenth century as a form of total control meant to improve efficiency and productivity for the organizations that impose it.[6] Foucault provocatively argues that this new form of discipline, first adopted by prisons looking to control and rehabilitate criminals, subsequently spread to modern institutions like hospitals, the military, and schools. In much the same way that the modern army teaches young men and women exacting procedures for how to speak, march, and carry a gun, Dream Academy reorients its students to how to show attention, request a tissue, and walk through the hallway. The parallels between the military and Dream Academy are not lost on teachers or students. New student orientation, after all, is called boot camp.

Enforcing the Script

A script may be written in a handbook or in a contract, but we know that organizations and individuals frequently deviate from official practice. What is striking about no-excuses schools is the degree to which they try to enforce their rules and procedures, not only during the first weeks of school but throughout the school year. Early in new student orientation, I received a glimpse of how closely students would be monitored at the school.

On the second day of orientation, after the students had filed into the cafeteria, Ms. Anderson called out a list of about twenty student names. These students were directed to Eastman, the music room named after the premier Eastman School of Music. The remaining students were told to sit at the cafeteria tables, which had been pushed to the side the day before so that students had space to sit on the floor.

"There's a reason you all are sitting here," Ms. Anderson announced to the students seated in the cafeteria. "The ultimate reason is that you all want to get to college. Another reason is that you did a fantastic job yesterday of following our instructions; particularly, you fixed your behavior without attitude, without issue, consistently trying to do your best."

She told these students that they had earned their first privilege at Dream Academy: their seats.

To celebrate this accomplishment, Ms. Russo, the White music teacher, came forward to teach the students the "roller coaster" cheer. Putting her hands out flat at waist level, she moved them up with a "ch-ch-ch" sound, as though a roller coaster were inching up its initial climb. Then she swam her hands down in waves, imitating a roller coaster ride, while making a "woo-woo-woo" sound. The next time around, the students joined in the celebration.

Celebrations at Dream Academy were also scripted. Over the course of the next weeks, students would learn a dozen or so celebratory cheers, including two snaps and a fruit loop, the seal clap, and the gym teacher's favorite, the Jersey Shore, a cheer that involved putting your fist in the air and chanting, "Yeah, buddy." These cheers added what the school called "zest" to the otherwise draconian rules. On an early visit to a different no-excuses school, I had observed similar chants and celebrations at a morning assembly. Surprised by the students' enthusiasm, I had told a friend who had been a teacher at a no-excuses school how impressed I was by the students' engagement. He corrected me: "They have to show enthusiasm." These ritualistic celebrations were also part of the school's scripts.

After the brief celebration, Ms. Anderson continued on more seriously. "Now I will say that some of our teammates did not earn their seats yesterday," she announced. "That doesn't mean that they are any less than us. We need to find ways to support our teammates who haven't earned their seats yet. By modeling good behavior."

The afternoon before, I had sat in on a meeting where the teachers had discussed which students should not earn their privilege of sitting in a seat. During the day, the teachers had been tasked with monitoring student behavior and taking note of the students who were not complying with the school's behavioral expectations. Now they came together to make recommendations. As I listened, I jotted down their evaluations:

"Chris—had to speak to him two to three times. He refused to track."

"Moses—he was twirling around." There was some debate over Moses, with one teacher advocating for him, noting that he had attention-deficit/ hyperactivity disorder (ADHD).

"Justin—he was lost in the sauce." One teacher protested that "he was so sweet about it, wasn't deviant in any way," but he was added to the list.

"Enviasia." She kept eating after lunch.

"Bianca." She was not tracking. "Was she defiant?" asked Ms. Scott. "She wouldn't stand in line," replied a teacher.

"Tyrone." He was the first to run and jump when Mr. Bradley, the school principal, said to listen.

The list went on—Craig decided it was nap time at lunch; Carla showed defiance by crossing her legs; Hosea was told to stop eating—after which, he looked at the teacher and bit his apple. Melissa brushed her hair. Camille had a bad attitude. There was a short discussion on Camille, as Ms. Scott pushed the group that "a bad attitude" was not behavior-based. But the teachers noted that she had also rolled her eyes, had to be spoken to several times about tracking, and talked about wanting to go back to her old school. She was added to the list.

As I listened to this discussion, I was struck by the degree to which students were watched and assessed. Though it was given gently and with encouragement, the message that students received was clear: they were under the school's watchful eye. There would be no twirling, jumping, or eating out of turn at Dream Academy. When the students who had not earned their seats returned to the cafeteria, they were directed to sit on the floor in front of the first row of tables, their deviance visible to their peers.

Education writer David Whitman has noted that no-excuses schools "sweat the small stuff" in contrast to typical inner-city schools that "pick their battles."[7] This sweating-the-small-stuff approach resembles the "broken windows" crime control strategy adopted by large cities like New York, Chicago, and Los Angeles in the 1990s, in which police targeted minor signs of disorder (e.g., littering, loitering, graffiti, and panhandling) in an effort to reduce serious crime.[8] At no-excuses schools, broken windows are things like heads on desks, side conversations, and eye rolling. These schools demand that students adhere to a meticulous set of behavioral standards—or be punished with consequences. To ensure that teachers administer consequences, Dream Academy distributes to teachers "monthly performance metrics," which display the number of infractions and detentions assigned by each teacher over the past month. To be rated highly on the "Sweating the Small Stuff" section of the teacher evaluation rubric (see chapter 6), teachers are expected to assign infractions at a rate consistent with other teachers.

Over the course of the school year, teachers at Dream Academy assigned a total of 15,423 infractions to the school's approximately 250 students. Students on average received 60 infractions over 188 days, or approximately 1 infraction every 3 days. Six students, with an average GPA of 3.9, managed to slip by without a single infraction over the school year; on the other extreme, one fifth-grade Black boy, with a 1.36 GPA, accumulated 295 infractions. Teachers had little choice but to enforce the school's rigid behavioral scripts because they too were evaluated on their adherence to them.

In line with the school's sweating-the-small-stuff approach, students received infractions for very minor misbehaviors. The most common infractions during the school year were for not submitting homework, not following directions, talking at inappropriate times, and submitting incomplete homework. Other infractions included serious class disruption, rowdiness/horseplay, difficulty packing/lining up, head down on desk, and not tracking the speaker. During the school year, the school had very few major infractions, such as fighting, major graffiti, and bullying.

Table 2.2 presents the frequencies of different types of infractions assigned over the school year, divided by category.[9] The school had a three-tiered behavioral code.[10] Category 1 offenses were for minor misbehaviors like making unnecessary noise, putting a head down on a desk, or being off-task. Category 2 offenses were for more serious misbehaviors like not following directions, not submitting homework, and displaying minor disrespect. Category 3 offenses targeted what the school considered "very serious" misbehaviors like leaving the classroom without permission, skipping detention, and displaying serious forms of disrespect.

Table 2.2. Frequencies of Student Infractions by Category

Category 1	Frequency
Violation of cafeteria rules	3
Violation of food/beverage policy	8
Not tracking speaker	24
Saying "shut up"	57
Difficulty unpacking/getting started	65
Violation of hallway rules	76
Unprepared for class	79
Difficult packing/lining up	87
Making unnecessary noise	160
Head down on desk	175
Out of seat without permission	183
Minor disrespect	278
Off task	358
Minor dress code violation	574
Talking at inappropriate times	1,687

Category 2	Frequency
Littering	4
Minor graffiti	10
Name calling	72
Roll eyes, suck teeth, stomp feet	82
Gum chewing/objects in mouth	150
Tardy	205
Talking back: "What? It was not ME!"	328
Serious class disruption	412
Incomplete homework	1,265
Not following directions	2,653
Homework not submitted	5,399

Category 3	Frequency
Bullying, harassment, intimidation	1
Spitting on someone	1
Major graffiti	3
Exhibitions of intimacy	4
Fighting/assault	5
Inappropriate displays of anger	9
Threatening	32
Talking to bench student	36
Forgery/falsification	38
Inappropriate language	62
Skipping detention	62
Throwing objects	72
Talking back: "Get out of my face!"	86
Rowdiness/horseplay	117
Leaving supervision without permission	120

If these misbehaviors seem inconsequential, the punishments were not. Nearly three-quarters of the recorded infractions resulted in detention. As Black fifth grader Tyrone complained to me, "Just because you mess up on a few things doesn't mean you have to serve a one-hour detention just because you forgot to put your heading on your paper, like that shouldn't be a major consequence." Detention lasted an hour and took place in the third-floor cafeteria, where sometimes forty to fifty students were spaced out across the tables and expected to work silently on their homework. Teachers rotated to be on "detention duty" and were monitored for how detention went, reprimanded if too many students were assigned additional infractions during their watch. Students were required to serve detention on the same day as their offense; at the end of the day, teachers read through a printed detention list to inform students who would be staying late. Those who skipped detention were given another detention or placed on "bench," a more serious consequence.

Started by the KIPP (Knowledge Is Power Program) schools, the first of the no-excuses charters, "bench" derives from the KIPP practice of "porch," named after the first KIPP mascot, Big Dog, and the motto, "If you can't keep up with the big dogs, stay back on the porch." KIPP students who were "porched" had to wear their shirts turned inside out, could not interact with their peers, had to ask permission from teachers to enter and exit rooms, and could not participate in lunch or gym class with their peers.[11] At Dream Academy, bench had similar consequences. To identify themselves to their peers, benched students had to wear yellow shirts all day (a pile of which Ms. Scott kept in her cubicle). Benched students were not allowed to talk to other students (students who talked to a student on bench were benched themselves), had to eat lunch separately, could not participate in gym or after-school clubs or activities, and had to serve detention.

Benched students at Dream Academy also carried a clipboard with individualized goals to be met, such as "Refrain from making any unnecessary noise or gesture in class/hallway" and "Refrain from making any sound or gesture that could be considered disrespectful." To earn their way off bench, students could get no more than two "no's" on their clipboard for the day from their teachers, who circled "yes" or "no" at the end of each class to indicate whether the student had met the goals. It was the students' responsibility to obtain these signatures; if they failed to ask, despite their protestations, they would continue to be on bench the next day.

Bench was used as a consequence for category 3 "very serious" misbehavior, but at Dream Academy, this included infractions like spitting, making noise during a fire drill, and using profanity. Approximately half of Dream Academy students were benched at least once during the school year. At the extreme, one sixth-grade Black girl was benched twenty-seven times.

Ms. Scott had the final say in assigning bench to students and letting students off bench. Each morning, she gathered together the bench students to give them their yellow shirts and clipboards. When we spoke, however, Ms. Scott told me that consequences work only for certain students and only to a certain extent. Unlike most of the school staff, she had grown up in poverty and had experienced her fair share of school discipline as a child. As a child, she found that consequences like sitting in a room by herself writing out the dictionary did not change her behavior. Meeting a teacher who believed in her motivated her to turn things around. Still, she supported the school's strict approach and believed in the importance of consistent and clear expectations for students. Much of the staff likewise believed that a sweating-the-small-stuff approach was critical to the school's success. For Mr. Taylor, his own failures in establishing control at his first charter school, which we will review in chapter 5, led him to adopt a model that was much more prescriptive than he had originally imagined necessary. In place of the "educational malpractice" he had witnessed, he opted for tight control, a detailed script for success.

As we've seen, however, Dream Academy's staff understood its rigid behavioral scripts not only as a way to establish control, but also as a way to prepare students for college and their future success. As Ms. Williams said in an interview, "When I say to parents why we do what we do, it's not—we've got to keep your kids in order. I'm not a corrections officer. This is not a jail; this is not a prison." Instead, school staff framed their behavioral practices as a way to transmit cultural capital, or the cultural attitudes, knowledge, skills, and behaviors through which middle-class students gain advantages in institutional settings. The school's scripts were seen not as contradicting or inhibiting the school's dedication to opening opportunities for low-income Black and Latino students but as supporting students' preparation for college and upward mobility.

Explaining the Why

Seated in student desks arranged in a circle, the teachers studied a two-page chart photocopied for them from a book. The chart was titled "Hidden Rules Among Classes." On the chart were columns labeled "Poverty," "Middle Class," and "Wealth" and rows with categories such as possessions, money, food, clothing, time, and driving forces. The chart provided descriptions for each of these categories for each social class. For example, the driving forces for poverty were described as survival, relationships, and entertainment; the driving forces for the middle class were listed as work and achievement; and the driving forces for wealth were defined as financial, political, and social connections.

The book under discussion during the August teacher orientation was Ruby Payne's *A Framework for Understanding Poverty*, a book widely used in staff development and multicultural education courses to inform educators on how to engage with the "culture of poverty." The "culture of poverty," an idea first proposed by anthropologist Oscar Lewis, refers to the idea that poverty creates its own subculture—one characterized by a short time horizon, poor work ethic, and feeling of powerlessness, among other traits.[12] This culture of poverty is seen as keeping families in poverty across generations. Critics of this concept have argued that it "blames the victim," presenting poverty as a group pathology, rather than contextualizing poverty within systems of power and privilege, policies and practices. The poor and marginalized are viewed not only as disadvantaged but also as deficient and depraved, their poverty a result of their own lack of effort, poor choices, and flawed culture.[13] Payne's book has also been subject to criticism for reinforcing culture-of-poverty ideas.[14]

Leading the discussion, Mr. Bradley, who is White and had grown up in a blue-collar family, talked about how Payne's book helped him understand a lot of things they did at the school. For instance, the school's rigid behavioral scripts, while they might seem extreme to an outsider, were intended to teach middle-class culture to the school's high-poverty student population. "School is the only place where students from poor families can learn the hidden rules of the middle class," he explained. Most of the teachers expressed their agreement with this perspective. Only Ms. Larkin, a twenty-three-year-old White teacher new to the school, pushed back: "Our country is based off a middle-class educational system. At the same time, what about the middle class makes it the penultimate [*sic*]? Don't we want to embrace where students come from?" Reversing the culture of poverty argument, she asked, "Don't we have a poverty of culture?"

Ms. Rivas, one of the school's few teachers of color, stepped in. "I am going to agree with this framework. I grew up in poverty, the parents are not there," she said. She explained how it wasn't because the parents did not want to be there, but it is the school's job to show students that they have more choices for their future. She explained how she goes out of her way every day to show students how she also conforms to middle-class norms. While she likes to be comfortable and wear sweatpants, she explains to students how she has to look professional for work.

"Students need to be taught the hidden rules of the middle class—the language of power, the culture of power," Ms. Williams agreed, referencing the work of education scholar Lisa Delpit, who argued that students from nondominant backgrounds should be taught the "culture of power" so they can access power.[15]

In this discussion, we see invoked several distinct perspectives on teaching cultural capital. Mr. Bradley and Ms. Rivas here articulate an assimilationist framework of conforming to middle-class norms to be individually successful in a middle-class world. Ms. Larkin, in line with more recent work on culturally sustaining pedagogies, challenges schools for only valuing middle-class norms rather than embracing a diversity of cultural perspectives.[16] In referencing Delpit, Ms. Williams takes a middle ground, seeing the learning of dominant cultural capital as a pathway for marginalized groups to acquire power and disrupt existing power structures. Although this discussion raised nuanced viewpoints on teaching cultural capital, a simpler rationale was typically used by teachers and staff to justify Dream Academy's rigid behavioral scripts. In "explaining the why," as the school called it, teachers and staff argued that the school's relentless rules and practices prepared students with the types of skills they would need to succeed in college and in the workplace. Why did students receive detention for arriving one minute late to school? Because it helped them develop time management skills. College applications would not be accepted if they were one minute late. Why were there silent hallways? Because self-control would get kids to and through college. As Ms. Anderson explained to me, "But I think that the way you can eliminate a lot of [student frustration] is through rationale, and repeated rationale, and explaining why it is that we're doing what it is that we're doing repeatedly, and in a way that's meaningful for children."

These "explanations of the why" became a simple way to justify to teachers and students the use of extreme social control, which is racialized, classed, and gendered. As sociologist Ann Ferguson has shown, tight regulation of students' bodies disproportionately falls on poor Black boys who are perceived as threatening and lacking self-control.[17] Black girls are also perceived as loud, aggressive, and hypersexualized and needing to be controlled.[18] Any reservations teachers may have felt about the school's tight control over the bodies of students of color, however, were moderated by their belief that they were teaching middle-class skills. For example, when I mentioned to Ms. Costello, a White math teacher, that some students felt that teachers were too picky, she responded that it was okay to be particular about things that were important. "Everything that we do and everything that we pick on, there's a standard for it in the outside world," she replied. "So yeah, maybe like telling a student they have to have their shirt tucked in might seem nitpicky to somebody, but to me, once you go to the real world, you have to dress a certain way and look a certain way and be neat and be presentable and so you're really just teaching a bigger life lesson." Ms. Rivas, who the previous year had felt that the school was "too militant" and its procedures "demeaning towards the kids," came around to understanding and defending the school's rationale.

But are no-excuses schools like Dream Academy teaching middle-class attitudes, skills, and behaviors? Are they transmitting cultural capital? In the remainder of this chapter, we will focus on how the school shaped the attitudes and expectations students developed about achieving success; and in later chapters, we will turn to how the school's scripts shaped students' skills and interactional styles. I will argue that, despite the school's intention to teach cultural capital, the lessons students received diverged considerably from those taught to middle-class kids.

Making No Excuses

"So, this morning we watched an individual who had every motivation to make excuses. If he didn't make excuses, you shouldn't either," Mr. Bradley exhorted the fifth- and sixth-grade students gathered one March morning at circle time. "Our Mount Kilimanjaro is getting that college degree. Let's think about this, let's show grit."

Circle is an assembly time where students and teachers gather twice a week to prepare for the school day (the fifth- and sixth-grade classes gather on different days than the seventh- and eighth-grade classes because of space constraints). Circle time included brief character education lessons, recognition by teachers of students' acts of character, daily announcements, and a concluding call-response chant. These morning assemblies were a more celebratory time and helped to build school community; however, they were also a space where students continued to be regulated. During morning circle, students had to stand with their homeroom teams in silent, straight lines along the perimeter of the room, so that circle was actually a square formation, which the school found more orderly, as one student noted to me while giving me a tour of the school. During circle time, homeroom teachers were tasked with closely monitoring student behavior. It was here where many students began to accumulate infractions—often because they were fidgeting or talking.

On this day, the students had just finished watching a short clip of Kyle Maynard, a quadruple amputee, who had climbed Mount Kilimanjaro. It was one of those *60 Minutes*-type specials that went through his life story, from his baby pictures to an interview with his sister to his telling the interviewer how he had lost dozens of wrestling matches in high school before finally winning one. At one point, Kyle looks directly at the camera and says, "My message is a pretty simple one: it is to make no excuses."

"Everyone is going to face obstacles," Mr. Bradley emphasized, picking up on the video's theme. "Not doing well in math, obstacles at home. Every excuse that we make keeps us from the things we want in life." His message was clear: If Kyle, a man with no arms or legs, was able to climb Mount Kilimanjaro, the students could put in the effort required to persist through a strict environment and get their college degree. Though students were meant to learn that they must not make excuses for why they could not be successful, this understanding of "no excuses" as taking responsibility for one's future differs from the no-excuses philosophy from which no-excuses schools like Dream Academy derive their name.

First used in the titles of two books featuring high-achieving, high-poverty schools, the term "no excuses" refers to the idea that schools should make no excuses for student failure, regardless of students' race or ethnicity, socioeconomic status, neighborhood, or skill level.[19] That is, *schools* and *teachers* must take responsibility for ensuring that their students succeed. Much in line with this "no-excuses" philosophy, Dream Academy states on its website that it is committed to taking responsibility for ensuring that all students are prepared for college. The school refuses to make race, poverty, or low academic skills an excuse for why students can't achieve. Ms. Melendez, a first-year Latina special education teacher, accurately understood this "no-excuses" philosophy as meaning that "where [students] came from or where they grow up doesn't necessarily mean that they're not capable of doing great things in life." This mindset runs counter to the low expectations that are often placed on students of color.[20] Studies have found that teachers' low expectations for low-income students and students of color can become a self-fulfilling prophecy whereby teachers simplify instructional content and focus on classroom management, offering students few opportunities to learn.[21] By contrast, teachers' high expectations can positively shape students' educational aspirations and academic performance.[22]

If "no excuses" is *supposed* to be about the school making no excuses for student failure, it *ends up* being about the school accepting no excuses from students for deviating from the school's rigid behavioral script. When I asked teachers in interviews what it meant that Dream Academy was a no-excuses school, I heard a variety of interpretations that emphasized the personal responsibility of the student to follow the school's expectations rather than the collective responsibility of the school to ensure that students were successful. These definitions put the burden and responsibility on students to adhere to the school's meticulous scripts for conduct:

> *Teacher 1:* My students can't make up an excuse nor can teachers. So why didn't you bring your homework in? I left it there. That's an excuse, that's not acceptable. So why are you laying down on your desk? Because I'm tired. Well, that's an excuse. So not to make excuses about anything, and I think it is to develop that responsibility in the student to the point where they can function and they can do things and they can follow rules and expectations just without even thinking.
>
> *Teacher 2*: From what I understand, it's just no excuses. You don't hand in your homework, you're in detention kind of thing. Sweat the small stuff, all that kind of stuff, right?
>
> *Teacher 3:* You know, you're holding people to high standards and you're, you know, not letting them make excuses for it, and you're picking out the small things and pointing them out and making people correct them, and you're holding people responsible for their character and their actions and their education.

Instead of putting the onus on schools and teachers to provide the extra supports to help all students achieve, the no-excuses philosophy was reinterpreted in the context of the school's behavioral script to mean, as reflected in the third teacher's words, "holding [students] responsible for their character and their actions and their education." This perspective attributes the failures of urban schools to low-income Black and Latino children who are seen as lacking the right attitudes and values (like hard work, diligence, personal responsibility) to be successful and sees success as holding these children to tighter expectations. One veteran White teacher at the school explained the school's reasoning behind their behavioral practices in this way: "I think when we first started, [we assumed] the students knew nothing when they got to us. And that we were kind of molding them into what they needed to be. Like we didn't assume that they knew their manners. We didn't assume that they knew the rules. We didn't assume they knew how to talk to teachers or talk to each other and things like that. And so that was kind of, you have to assume that there's no consistent parenting."

Sociologist Eduardo Bonilla-Silva has characterized these types of explanations as a form of "cultural racism" where racial bias is disguised through cultural explanations.[23] Such explanations are considered racist because they attribute the poor outcomes of racial/ethnic groups to deficit characteristics of the groups (their lack of appropriate skills, behaviors, and values) rather than institutionalized racism or differential resources. Teachers assumed that students and their families lacked the right attitudes and behaviors when Dream Academy attracted those families who had the time and resources to learn about and apply to the school. Because the school did not market itself, students often learned about the school through teachers who singled them out as strong students and encouraged them to apply. Additionally, families and students had to be willing and able to comply with the school's behavioral policies. Parent-teacher conferences boasted participation rates over 90 percent. Even teachers acknowledged that there was a big difference between the families at Dream Academy and at previous urban schools where they had worked—as one teacher put it, parents here showed up and were supportive. In his book on Success Academy, a no-excuses charter network in New York City, education writer Robert Pondiscio similarly found that one of the reasons for its success was its selection of more invested and stable families. Although children were admitted randomly through a lottery process, Success Academy held a series of mandatory welcome meetings prior to the first day of school that weeded out nearly half of the initial families.[24]

Moreover, sociologist Jessica Calarco has found that working-class parents already emphasize to their children "no-excuses" problem solving—to work hard and not bother others with requests for accommodations. Middle-class parents, by contrast, take a "by-any-means" strategy, encouraging their children to negotiate with their teachers and bend rules to their benefit.[25] Middle-class parents use these strategies themselves, lobbying teachers and administrators to *excuse* their children from homework, ask for special accommodations, and get their children out of punishment. If the school wanted to teach middle-class expectations to its students, oddly enough, it should have taught them how to effectively *make* excuses.

To be certain, Dream Academy's leaders were aware that a no-excuses philosophy was not about holding students fully responsible for their success. On Dream Academy's website, it explains "What 'No Excuses' Is Not": "It does not mean placing the burden for success solely on the shoulders of students. It does not represent a school setting lacking in caring and consideration for family needs. And it does not represent a school where the adults fail to recognize the significant challenges associated with preparing students for college within communities." Yet despite this recognition, the messages that teachers and students received from the school's relentless behavioral expectations spoke otherwise. Rigid scripting allowed for little flexibility because to do so would be to permit students to make excuses. This led teachers to gloss over legitimate excuses, hiding the structural issues that shape students' behaviors and actions.

Take the case of Leah, a Latina girl who struggled with arriving to school on time and was at risk of being retained in eighth grade another year. Dream Academy's policy was that if a student accumulated more than twelve unexcused absences, he or she would be retained in the same grade for another year. Three unexcused tardies counted as an unexcused absence. When I first met Leah, she was writing a note during class asking her mom to allow her to transfer back to her old public school because she was stressed from being late all the time and worried she would be retained. She argued that it would make it easier on her mom not to have to transport the four children, one of whom was autistic, to different schools and promised to make honor roll at the public school. Leah's lateness was a consequence of her family situation, the quality of neighborhood schools that had led her mom to place her in a charter school, and the lack of transportation provided by Dream Academy. It had little to do with her character. But in a school that refuses to accept excuses, her arriving to school even a minute late was understood as her personal responsibility (for which she would also serve an after-school detention as all unexcused lateness resulted in an automatic detention). This lesson is communicated clearly to students. When explaining the school's lateness policies during the new student orientation, Ms. Wallace told students, "Even if it's mom's fault, grandmom's fault, we are no excuses. To be tardy is to show disrespect." If the school instead were shouldering the responsibility for making no excuses for student failure, school staff might take responsibility for providing transportation to students instead of punishing students for arriving late.

Or take Manuel, a reserved Latino eighth-grader whom I interviewed one day at school when his classmates had gone on a snow tubing trip. He had not been able to attend because he had accumulated too many infractions, most of which were for missed homework. At Dream Academy, students had to earn their field trips by demonstrating good behavior. He sat across from me in the empty classroom and was noticeably upset. As we talked, it became clear that Manuel, the eldest of three brothers, felt at age fourteen that he had "far over what I'm supposed to do." This made completing his homework difficult. He explained to me that after school, he volunteered as a tutor at the Boys & Girls Club, worked helping his grandfather's friend install carpets and helping his father load boxes in a warehouse, and assisted around the house, cooking for his brothers and cleaning so his mom would not feel stressed when she returned home from work. He then did his homework from nine o'clock until midnight. Sometimes, he did not begin his homework until eleven, completing it by flashlight under his covers until one or two in the morning. "It's like, they don't get what a student goes through every day," he told me. "Sometimes your family has to come before your education or . . . you have to go before your education because if something happens to you, then it's gonna affect you in some way or form, physically or mentally."

I asked him if he had tried to talk to anyone at school about the difficulties he was facing finishing his homework. He said he had tried to talk to one of his teachers, but while she expressed sympathy, she emphasized to him that "school is important right now 'cause if you don't have an education, you can't get nowhere in life." At his old school, his teachers were more flexible and would lighten his homework load if he told them that he had a sports game or other obligation, but at Dream Academy they did not accept excuses. Using a middle-class strategy of seeking accommodations, Manuel told his teacher about his struggles to balance his home responsibilities with his schoolwork. However, he was told that his schoolwork needed to come first. He was sent the message that the way to achieve success was not to bend rules but to make no excuses and rigidly follow the school's scripts.

In many ways, no-excuses schools create an alternate universe for students, one that promises upward mobility if students will only follow the school's scripts for success. Students are asked to "overcome" their backgrounds and assimilate into dominant culture, a process sociologist

Angela Valenzuela calls "subtractive schooling" because it does not build on students' own cultural resources.[26] But it is not easy—and perhaps not prudent—to insulate students from their home worlds. It risks not recognizing the ways in which students are affected by out-of-school factors and can potentially be detrimental to students' sense of identity and feelings of connectedness. Instead of seeing students' out-of-school demands as "excuses," one could see them as assets. Critical race scholar Tara Yosso argues for the need to recognize the "community cultural wealth" that nondominant students bring with them to school.[27] Manuel, for example, could be viewed not as lacking the right priorities but as possessing what Yosso calls "familial capital"—a sense of commitment and caring for one's community.[28] Moreover, Manuel could be recognized for the many responsibilities he takes on and the array of skills he has developed through his tutoring, working, assisting his neighbors, caring for his younger brothers, cooking, and cleaning. Students like Manuel often take on much more responsibility than their middle-class White peers, yet they are seen as needing to stop making excuses and start assuming greater personal responsibility.

Earning over Entitlement

As the students entered the classroom, they waved their hands in the air, their voices amped up. One boy slammed his book down on his desk. "We had mad fun," another exclaimed. "We watched movies."

Strutting their way into Ms. Anderson's fifth-grade classroom were the handful of students who had not earned that October's field trip to the aquarium. Between the four lower-school classes, I had counted thirteen boys and three girls left behind at school, all Black except for five Latino boys.

These students had indeed watched movies that morning. One of their assignments was to watch *Harriet the Spy* and take notes on signs of disrespect given to Harriet.

Ms. Anderson paid little attention to the students' antics. Sitting at the front desk, she turned her attention to the rest of the class, asking them to share highlights of the trip. Eager hands shot up. "I pet a blue lobster." "I fed a stingray." "I pet a shark." "I saw a blue leopard stingray." "A shrimp was jumping on my hand." As the day's activities filled the air, the students who had boldly entered soon fell silent.

It had been a fun field trip. For many students, it was their first time visiting the aquarium and their first ride on the train. The latter was as exciting as the former. Typical school rules were relaxed. There were no silent straight lines or hand signals, and students spent the day leisurely exploring exhibits in small groups. In the group I assisted with, students fell behind or walked ahead, and occasionally bumped into an unsuspecting visitor, but they mostly followed directions. No one was sent home, despite initial warnings.

After the students reminisced for a few minutes, Ms. Anderson turned to the students who had not earned the trip. She acknowledged that while they might have had fun, it was important to earn field trips. There would be another opportunity in about a month's time, a Friday night social at the school.

Field trips, which expose students to new experiences and enrich the curriculum, can be considered an entitlement that all students deserve, as they are in most schools, not a reward that must be earned. The same can be said of other privileges students had to earn, including their seats, as we saw earlier. In addition to an extensive consequence system, Dream Academy had a point system where students earned up to one hundred points per week. Each day, they could earn twenty points: ten points for coming to school on time and turning in homework and ten points for meeting all school and class expectations. At the end of the week, before dismissal, students received a printout of the points they had earned. (Because teachers did not always communicate clearly to students when they had lost points during the week, there would often be some back-and-forth between students and teachers over infractions listed on this sheet.) Dream Academy's point system is a variation of the paycheck systems found in many no-excuses schools where students earn and lose "dollars" based on their behavior. These paychecks can be used to purchase items from a school store or to receive special privileges. Conversely, if paychecks fall below a certain threshold, students receive consequences like detentions and even suspensions.

At Dream Academy, points earned students various privileges. Each marking period, students who earned a seventy-five weekly point average and made honor roll (a B or higher average with no failing grades) earned a status card that granted them privileges like eating lunch with students from other classes, immunity from whole-class punishments, and exemption from homework detention. There were also point thresholds for earning field trips, school socials, and special dress days. One of the first big goals for students was to earn their school shirts. Students new to Dream Academy began the school year wearing a white polo shirt; in November, those who had earned sufficient points and demonstrated appropriate behaviors were rewarded with the school's navy blue polo, which was conferred in a ceremony that one student described as like the Olympics. These students earned the privilege of representing the school by wearing the school's colors.

As students learned to adhere to the school's demanding scripts in order to gain privileges, they developed what I call a *sense of earning*. Students with a sense of earning work hard, make no excuses, and believe that they are responsible for their own success and culpable for their bad choices. Students with a sense of earning learn that they must earn privileges, even basic ones like school seats and school shirts. As Jada, a Black fifth grader, put it, "You gotta earn the shirt, you gotta earn your seat, you gotta earn everything. Everything earn, earn, earn, earn or you don't get it."

Earning can be motivating, helping students comply with the school's behavioral script. When I asked two Black fifth-grade girls, Queenie and Jasmine, about a time they were happy or excited at school, they talked about qualifying for a field trip. "I started jumping up and down," said Queenie. Jasmine recalled how she was on the brink of being disqualified for a field trip and explained how she was "so happy because I had to work so hard not to get one more infraction." She also felt anxious, however, about getting another infraction because it was not hard to earn an infraction at the school. "Like I told you, all you have to do is walk into the classroom. You got an infraction," she explained to me. "And like for me, I got plenty of infractions. I got 102 and but at least I don't got the most in the class. This boy named Richard, he has very the most. He's got 280 infractions because he just gets it soon as he walks through the door, he be on the bench the whole time."

A *sense of earning*, however, contrasts with a *sense of entitlement*, which sociologist Annette Lareau has identified as a middle-class mindset. Middle-class families foster in their children a sense of entitlement whereby their children feel deserving of other people's time and resources.[29] Children with a sense of entitlement believe that others are partially responsible for their success. Through their self-advocacy, entitled students gain advantages for themselves, from extra attention in preschool to classwork assistance in elementary school to a grade bump in college.[30] Moreover, it's not only middle-class families who teach their children to have a sense of entitlement. Schools also cater to middle-class White families, positioning them as "consumers" whose needs ought to be attended to rather than "beneficiaries" who should be grateful for the privilege of attending the school.[31] Thus, while the idea of working hard and succeeding through one's own efforts is a familiar American theme, the messages about earning sent to children from different racial and social class backgrounds are often distinct. If a sense of earning is communicated to students through rigid scripts and rewards and punishments, a sense of entitlement is developed through individuating attention, accommodation, and negotiation.

Even if all students were sent the same message about earning their way, it's important to recognize that the playing field is still uneven. The idea of meritocracy—that anyone can achieve the American Dream so long as they work hard and show disciplined effort—is based on the assumption that all children start with equal opportunities and all families have similar resources. Scholars have criticized the "myth of meritocracy" for fostering a "context-neutral mindset" that ignores or minimizes the structural obstacles that make it difficult for certain racial and socioeconomic groups to climb the social ladder.[32] For affluent White students, believing that they have earned their way through hard work legitimates social privilege.[33] For low-income students of color, conversely, believing in a meritocratic system puts students in the precarious position of deriving their self-worth from their achievements. A study of low-income students of color, for example, found that sixth graders who believed the education system to be fair or meritocratic were more likely to show declines in self-esteem and demonstrate risky behavior across their middle-school years than their peers who believed that certain groups of students had inherent advantages.[34] Students who believed in a meritocratic system blamed themselves for their perceived lack of success over time.

We can see these assumptions about meritocracy and worth begin to play out at Dream Academy. I noticed that all but four of the students who had not qualified for the field trip to the aquarium wore plain white polo shirts, meaning that they also had not earned their school shirts. Already, these students, mostly Black boys, could be identified by their peers in multiple ways (wearing a white shirt, not participating in the field trip, wearing a yellow shirt if benched) as failing to perform to school expectations. Not only is this hierarchy of worth shaming;[35] it also ignores the reality that not all students are equally able to follow the school's exacting behavioral scripts. Mr. Taylor readily admitted that "this is not a model for everyone." As he put it, "So, people who can attend to the teacher really well, who can walk in straight lines really easily, who can sit still and do homework for long periods of time, we work really, really well for those people. For the people for whom that's not their natural state of being, it's really, really, really difficult." Mr. Taylor knew of families who medicated their children for ADHD so their children could be successful in the school, although the school did not encourage it.

Students who are frequently disciplined are often those who have the greatest academic, material, and social-emotional needs.[36] Recent research on adverse childhood experiences (ACEs) has found that students who display significant behavioral problems at school often have experienced trauma—such as abuse, neglect, or household dysfunction.[37] These students need safety, support, empowerment, and voice, not punishment and humiliation, which can trigger previous traumas, as one study of Black males in a no-excuses high school found.[38] In her first year, Ms. Wallace, the teacher who had switched careers from journalism, used to take students' behaviors personally. Now she understands that their behaviors often have little to do with her and her actions. "There's just so much else that is behind certain behaviors and I get that now," she reflected. Through her students' writing journals, she has learned about the traumatic experiences many of her students have been through. Students have also felt supported in sharing their own stories. "It lets you see what we go through and why we come to school mad, upset or other things," one student wrote for a class exercise on the process of journaling. Another student wrote, "The journalizing experience allows all students' stories to be heard. We all go through something that someone needs to hear."

In addition to disregarding differences in students' experiences and developmental needs, an emphasis on earning also fails to acknowledge teacher bias. As a multitude of research on school discipline has shown, Black boys are disproportionately targeted and punished at school for behaviors that are frequently ignored for White students like displaying an "attitude" and showing disrespect.[39] Black girls are also punished for being loud and assertive.[40] Consistent with racial trends in school discipline, Black boys at Dream Academy accumulated the most infractions. On average, Black boys accumulated 93 infractions over the course of the school year, compared to 69 infractions for Black girls, 47 for Latino boys, and 34 for Latina girls. The school had few White students; the three White boys averaged 42 infractions over the school year, and the two White girls each received 31 infractions over the school year.

Studies have found that low-achieving Black males are the demographic group most likely to receive consequences in no-excuses schools,[41] and that these students are more likely to leave these schools.[42] One study of thirty KIPP schools found that approximately 40 percent of Black males left the schools between sixth and eighth grade.[43] To support Black boys in the school, especially those who consistently accumulated infractions, Ms. Johnson, a White teacher who had worked at the school since its founding, started a mentoring program specifically for them. Almost every Saturday for the entire school year, she transported in her van sometimes more than a dozen boys to football games and treated them to dinner. She organized open gym time for them at the high school. Her efforts took up a tremendous amount of her own time and resources, but she found that not everyone was supportive. "And so, I mean, some of the teachers kind of, I think, got frustrated because I was giving them what they didn't deserve," she explained to me. "And even some of the students were like, well, they don't deserve it, they act up. Or they talk back to you." Interestingly, these teachers and students had internalized the school's message of earning and felt it unfair that she was giving these Black boys special privileges.

Ms. Johnson pointed to the students' drop in infractions as evidence that her approach of mentoring worked better than the school's approach of earning rewards and consequences. She saw changes in the attitudes and behaviors of the boys she mentored, a result she attributed to the camaraderie the boys developed among themselves and the space they had to be vulnerable with each other. By the end of the year, one of the students she took under her wing—a tall, lanky boy who had been retained twice—earned a school field trip for the first time in his five years at the school.

Grit

On a Friday afternoon in May, the two eighth-grade classes crowded into "MIT," as the classroom was named, for the middle school graduation speech competition. The winner would give the speech at Dream Academy's recommitment ceremony, a college-like graduation that marked students' passage to high school. The black wooden science tables had been pushed to the edges of the room in a U shape with students crowded around. Ms. Wallace, who was leading the event, called students to attention.

"So, expectations," she began. "We do not get up out of your seats and move around the room because it's way too tight." She warned students not to interrupt someone's speech. "No comments, no criticisms. If you like what you hear, use a nonverbal and then we can all snap at the end." Snapping was a school-sanctioned form of applause. She passed around index cards to the students on which they were to rate the top eight of the ten speeches presented.

Ms. Wallace called the first speaker, a Latino boy who came to the front of the room holding a piece of notebook paper containing his speech. He read his speech, which talked about how he had attended private school for a year, but his mother was working all day and the tuition was hard to pay, so he came back to Dream Academy. He said how he strongly disagreed with the school's terms, but learned to "play by the rules." To close, he exhorted his classmates that "when you become doctors and basketball players, know you come from the best school in [the city] that accepts nothing but excellence." The students snapped in response.

Upon request, Ms. Wallace read the essay for the next student, a Black girl who seemed embarrassed to share in front of her classmates. She described in her essay how "sixth grade was a living hell for me" and "seventh grade was going to knock me down hard" but eighth grade was "magnificent."

The next student, a short Black boy who dreamed of being a World Wrestling Entertainment wrestler, spoke about how he kept screaming, "I'm free, high school here I come!" He recounted how the students had to "run up the Rocky Mountains."

As I sat listening to the speeches, the same themes repeated themselves. Students talked about how "hard work and persistence will pay off tremendously"; "it was all about counting down the years, months, weeks, days, hours, minutes, and seconds until . . . freedom"; "this is not the end of a tedious journey; this is the beginning of a wonderful adventure"; "through five years, I always said I hate this school but I love this school with all my heart." What became apparent was that school for these students was a long hard road, and getting to graduation—even middle school graduation—was a formidable accomplishment. To make it through this school required grit.

"Grit" has become the new catchphrase in education, a term resurrected by psychologist Angela Duckworth, author of the *New York Times* best-selling book *Grit: The Power of Passion and Perseverance*. She defines grit as the ability to persist toward long-term goals: "Grit entails working strenuously toward challenges, maintaining effort and interest over years despite failure, adversity, and plateaus in progress. The gritty individual approaches achievement as a marathon, his or her advantage is stamina."[44] In her research, Duckworth shows how grit can help explain who persists through boot camp at West Point, who makes it to the National Spelling Bee finals, and who gets high grades at Ivy League schools.[45]

No-excuses schools have embraced the idea of teaching grit in part as a response to seeing that their graduates were not doing as well in college as they hoped. When KIPP began tracking their first cohorts of students, they noticed that almost all of their students were accepted to college, but only about one-third of them graduated from college in six years. This number was not insignificant—it was four times higher than the national college completion rates of low-income students, but it was well below the 75 percent goal KIPP had set for itself, a rate on par with that of high-income students.[46] As the KIPP leaders reflected on what distinguished college graduates from noncompleters, they landed not on academic preparation but on strong character.

This began KIPP's courtship with character education. With the help of Duckworth, David Levin, one of KIPP's founders, worked to incorporate teaching character in his schools. Duckworth's graduate school advisor, Martin Seligman, had written an "800-page tome" that identified twenty-four character strengths, which Levin eventually whittled down to a more manageable seven: optimism, zest, grit, curiosity, social intelligence, gratitude, and self-control.[47] Shortly after, the New York City KIPP schools implemented the first Character Report Cards, rating students on these seven character strengths. Levin liked the idea of teaching character because it wasn't about middle-class values. "The thing that I think is great about the character-strength approach is it is fundamentally devoid of value judgment," Levin is quoted as saying.[48] "Character" provided an uncontroversial way to teach students "middle-class" norms and behaviors. It wasn't about devaluing kids' home cultures and telling them that they had to be someone else to succeed. It was now about character—research-proven ways to make them more successful.

Even though Levin liked the idea of teaching character because it was value-neutral, these schools' efforts to resocialize students into behavioral norms are value-laden. Like the culture of poverty argument, these efforts are undergirded by assumptions of the attitudes, behaviors, and skills that Black and Latino students in urban schools lack. When I asked Mr. Bradley about Dream Academy's efforts to teach character, he explained that teaching character enriched the school's focus on regulation. It also empowered kids, he continued, because many of their students come from homes where there is negativity, where excuses are made. The school wanted to change that.

We can see these assumptions about character deficits seep into the school's character lessons. One April morning during circle time, the seventh- and eighth-grade students were given a lesson on grit. Standing shoulder-to-shoulder with their hands to their sides and their toes on the line, the students directed their attention to the projector screen at the front of the room. The clip being shown, from one of the *Rocky* movies, showed Rocky and his grown-up son walking the streets at night. When Rocky's son asks his father to drop out of an upcoming fight because he's afraid his father will lose and ruin both their reputations, Rocky stops and lectures his son: "The world ain't all sunshine and rainbows. It's a very mean and nasty place, and I don't care how tough you are, it will beat you to your knees and keep you there if you let it." He then goes on to say that life is not about how hard you hit, but how hard you can get hit and keep moving forward.

After the clip ended, Rocky's quote was displayed on the screen for students to ponder. Mr. DiCarlo, the White teacher leading the morning's lesson, asked the students how this quotation related to grit. Raising their hands to be called on, students offered, "the world is not going to cater to you"; "you get down one day, you gotta keep pushing through"; "if you don't prove yourself, the world is going to squash you."

Next, Mr. DiCarlo asked the students how the quote related to them. A few hands went up. One student noted that it was "how you can take a punishment"—to just take it and keep going. Mr. DiCarlo called on another student.

"Nobody else can control your life," the student offered. "You pass or fail depending on you."

Mr. DiCarlo liked this sentiment and reiterated it: "You succeed or fail based on you and nobody else." He told them to remember this "as you go through life and today."

"It's a simple thought," Mr. Bradley affirmed, stepping in to conclude the character lesson. "If success were easy, everyone would be driving BMWs, have a big house, everyone would be successful. It's not about ideas, how smart you are, it's about grit."

In this mini-lesson on grit, several messages were sent to the students. First, there are many obstacles they will have to push through. Second, their persisting through these obstacles will determine their success or failure. Third, their success or failure is their responsibility alone. To get the BMW and big house, students will need to show grit and take personal responsibility for their outcomes. What is missing here, of course, is any mention of the opportunity structure that makes it easier for those born to certain families in certain neighborhoods to drive BMWs and have big houses. One criticism of teaching grit is that it promotes an individualistic mentality (success depends on effort alone) and attributes the problem of failure to one's character (not enough determination or grit), ignoring structures like racism and sexism.[49] "In a society marked by profound racial and class inequalities, it is difficult to believe that character and merit—as color-blindness advocates would have us believe—are the prime determinants for social and economic mobility and a decent standard of living," wrote critical education theorist Henry Giroux. "The relegation of racism and its effects in the larger society to the realm of private beliefs, values, and behavior does little to explain a range of overwhelming realities—such as soaring black unemployment, decaying cities, and segregated schools."[50]

Students at Dream Academy were not taught to understand the larger structures that shaped their path to success; instead they were told to show grit and push through. It is thus not surprising that stress was a by-product of being in an environment where expectations were high and excuses were few. A few weeks into my fieldwork, I sat down at lunch with a group of three Black eighth-grade girls who seemed to be constantly getting in trouble. Lunch was one of the only times during the school day that students could freely talk with each other as there was no recess and hallways were silent. I asked the girls whether they liked the school and immediately got back three "no's." When I inquired why, they talked about not liking the discipline, the disrespectful way teachers talked, the homework, and the rules—like walking in a straight line in eighth grade or wearing yellow shirts when they were benched. One of the girls conceded that she did learn a lot here, more than she might learn somewhere else. "But it's not worth the stress," she insisted. Pointing to her hair, she explained that it started falling out only after she came to this school. Her friends agreed. The school had recommended they see a therapist; one of the girls had already been tested and referred to the Big Brothers Big Sisters program.

Even for those students eager and able to comply with the rigid scripts of the school, the pressure not to make a mistake could be overwhelming. Well-behaved students experienced pressure because they tried so diligently to follow school rules. One day after school, I interviewed Sydney, a Black eighth grader who was mostly quiet in class. She told me she was reluctant even three years later to reflect back on her first year at the school. "It was like I was freaking out the first year," she told me. "I just could not take the pressure in the beginning. I was so scared." She recounted how she would receive homework detentions after spending so much effort completing her assignments because she had forgotten to put her name on the assignment or accidentally skipped a problem. Sydney felt tremendous pressure not to make a single error in a no-excuses school culture. Sydney eventually eased up on herself, but only after her mother explained that everyone makes mistakes once in a while.

Ms. Deliz, the mother of a fifth-grade Latina student, Kay, had to take even more drastic action. She ended up keeping her daughter home for two weeks in November because Kay was under so much stress. Afraid of "messing up," Kay felt extreme pressure to do well because her teachers singled her out as an example of good behavior. After two or three days of Kay not wanting to go to school, her mom asked her what was wrong. Ms. Deliz recounted, "She said, 'Mommy, I just can't. It's too much. It is too much to take.' You know, I just take her out of school and let her calm down and then that's okay, you'll be back at school. So . . . my husband went to school, spoke to the teachers, and then let them know it. You're putting too much pressure on her. Like just lean back a little bit on her, you know. She is a good girl. If you put too much pressure, they going to rebel too." Although she supported the school's strict approach, Ms. Deliz felt that the school needed to take into account different student personalities, including her daughter's sensitive nature, shyness, and need for positive affirmation. To resolve the issue, she and her husband ended up approaching the teachers. Interestingly, Ms. Deliz and her husband, who hold middle-class jobs, successfully used the "by-any-means" middle-class strategy of intervening on behalf of their daughter.

While students were taught to show grit by playing by the school's scripts and suppressing feelings of anxiety, frustration, fear, or worry, it is important to note that Duckworth talks about grit as passion and perseverance. What motivates someone to pursue a long-term goal despite obstacles is developing a passion that sustains interest and effort. Developing a passion takes initiative and self-motivation, a different attitude toward success than the effort to comply with school expectations.[51] Teachers recognized that allowing students greater flexibility helped them develop interests and skills. As Ms. Lopez, a Latina teacher, noted, "When you allow them to just sort of loosen back a bit, they're incredibly creative." This is consistent with findings that "deeper learning" occurs when students have larger blocks of open time and more agency over their learning—findings that conflict with the no-excuses model.[52] Dream Academy's rigid scripts for behavior allowed little time or space for students to make their own choices and pursue their own interests. As we will see in chapter 4, in place of the concerted cultivation that middle-class families and schools encourage, Dream Academy operated with a sense of urgency where no time could be wasted.

Students at Dream Academy already had grit. When I asked teachers to describe their students' strengths, they talked about their students' perseverance. "Just thinking of what they go through on a daily basis is really like quite exceptional, you know," stated Ms. Lopez in articulating the students' strengths. "I mean they really work hard. I think all of the students do mostly." Mr. Sudano, the teacher who had conducted the home visit, saw students' grit in facing obstacles both inside and outside of school:

> By far the strength is the grit. Their ability to every morning wake up and already be way behind in so many different levels: economically, financially, socially—to every day, wake up, get out of bed, and know that they're going to go into a school that's extremely disciplined, extremely hard and it's not going to be easy. And then do it two hundred days out of the year. And try to do their best every single day. And know that they're going to make mistakes and know they're going to have detention and do it over and over and over again.

But if students were able to keep persevering through the school's behavioral scripts, what was the cost, both at present and in their future, especially if they did not succeed in getting their college degrees, high-paying jobs, and fancy cars? Would they blame themselves? Moreover, what if these students were given an opportunity to direct their energy not toward complying with the school's strict practices, but toward developing a passion for learning? Ms. Costello saw great potential if students could direct their grit toward their education:

> I mean, I think the kids here are just so smart and they have a really big, like, big capacity and enthusiasm to learn. And I love that. I mean, I think that they're just strong kids. I think many of them come from tough backgrounds, tougher than me. And so, they're strong and they're used to persevering. And so, if you teach them how to persevere through their education—like they're just used to persevering in life— so if you can teach them how to put that into their education, there's just so much room for them to be amazing. Like I think the kids here are brilliant. I really do. And I see how much they can learn and how much they grow as people.

Instead of seeing her students as needing to learn how to not make excuses and how to show grit, Ms. Costello saw her students as possessing incredible character and intellectual strengths. If students' grit were directed toward learning algebra or mastering the violin, she wondered, what would be the possibilities?

Dream Academy's scripts were not altogether negative. High academic expectations and clear and consistent guidelines for behavior can be motivating, teaching students to work hard and aim high. Grit, if properly understood, can help students develop self-efficacy and perseverance. However, overly rigid scripts place the burden of earning and achieving on students. It is students like Kay, who had to stay home for two weeks, and Manuel, who missed the snow tubing field trip, who suffer the everyday consequences of a highly rigid, no-excuses school environment. The burden is not insignificant. Beyond the daily stressors, students learn lessons about themselves and the reasons for their success or failure—lessons that risk communicating to them that they are personally responsible for their outcomes and obscuring the profound structural constraints that shape the opportunity structure. These lessons to make no excuses and earn their way, moreover, stand in contrast to lessons that middle-class students learn—that they are entitled to rewards and can bend the script in their own favor.

CHAPTER THREE

Tools for Success

ONE AFTERNOON, I sat down with Alexis, a bright, outspoken Black eighth grader who had a knack for writing and for accumulating infractions. A student at Dream Academy since the fifth grade, she reflected on her experiences:

> I didn't like it 'cause I was so young when I came here, and it was strict. It still is strict, and I didn't like that. They were just so picky. Like they were asking me so much . . . 'cause they want to get us to college, but that's not how they be acting in college. In college they are—they're not strict. In college, you can do whatever you want. So this is a college preparatory school, so we should be able to do whatever we want, but we're not. So, technically it's not a college preparatory school because you're not prepping us for college—you're disciplining us, like you don't have detention in college. You don't have to wear a uniform in college. You don't have to walk in straight lines in college.

With two stepsisters in college, Alexis knew that college was much less structured than high school. She therefore questioned whether the school's rigid behavioral scripts would prepare her with the skills she needed to succeed in college, identifying a contradiction between the school's prescriptive practices and the flexibility of the college environment.

Alexis was right in recognizing that being a successful college student requires a different set of tools than she was being taught in middle school. Unlike in K–12 settings, where there are clear tasks, high structure, and frequent feedback, colleges give students significantly more independence to manage their time and learning.[1] They also expect students to be proactive educational consumers who ask for help, advocate for themselves, and seek out institutional resources. Because middle-class students are often encouraged by their families and schools to take initiative and assert their needs, their cultural skills match those expected in college.[2] Low-income and first-generation college students, by contrast, may face difficulties adapting to the college student role. Not comfortable with speaking up in class, attending a professor's office hours, or asking for a paper extension, these students may fail to seek out help when they struggle.[3]

As a self-proclaimed college preparatory school, Dream Academy's central mission was preparing all of its students with the knowledge and skills for college success. Dream Academy was successful in getting its middle school students to think about college and in getting its high school graduates to apply to, and be admitted to, college. But as we will see, Dream Academy's rigid behavioral scripts did not encourage students to develop the types of cultural capital that higher-income students use to gain advantages in college. Cultural capital, which I have defined as *tools of interaction*, comprises the attitudes, skills, and styles that allow individuals to navigate complex institutions and shifting expectations. These tools include skills like how to express an opinion, be flexible, display leadership, advocate a position, and make independent decisions. These skills are important for college success, valued in the twenty-first-century workplace, and foundational to participation in a democratic society though, as I will note, not always equally rewarded across race.

In the last chapter, we saw how Dream Academy staff justified their rigid behavioral scripts as a way to teach cultural capital. In this chapter, we will see how Dream Academy's rigid scripts, in reality, impeded students from developing tools of interaction. As we visit with Dream Academy students in their college courses and hear about the experiences of Dream Academy graduates, we also will reflect on the potential consequences of Dream Academy's scripts for students' perception of, and success in, college.

Expressing an Opinion

For Ms. Williams, success means teaching students to effectively communicate with adults. As a Black student at a predominantly White high school, Ms. Williams did not feel as though she could express herself. "I always felt that I was constantly being oppressed," she recounted to me. Although she had a very high GPA, she was not pushed to take Advanced Placement and honors classes, or to apply to selective colleges. Her experiences with racism motivated her to attend a historically Black college, where she learned how to use her voice. At college, her classes were discussion-based and used active, experiential learning, as she conveyed to me: "How they teach, what they teach; they push you to critically think and analyze and give you all parts of the story, not just one part of the story."

After college, Ms. Williams worked as a teacher in a high-poverty urban school for four years, the first two with Teach for America. When a job opened at Dream Academy, she took it to make an impact on the city where she had grown up. With a no-nonsense demeanor and an ability to communicate clearly with students, Ms. Williams quickly advanced to a leadership role in the school, being promoted to principal halfway through my fieldwork. Her primary goal is to empower students to use their voices. "We want to get kids to that social justice and social change avenue," she explained. "However, we can't get them there until they start to recognize how powerful they really are, how powerful their voices are, how powerful the choices that they make are." Her perspective is consistent with that of radical education scholars like Paulo Freire and Henry Giroux, who suggest that schools can be sites of resistance and liberation.[4] These scholars see schools as consequential not only for promoting individual economic mobility but also for developing in students the skills necessary for larger-scale collective change.

Although Ms. Williams was committed to teaching students how to communicate, Dream Academy's structures and practices often made this task challenging. In contrast to Ms. Williams's college experience, instruction at Dream Academy was traditional and teacher-centered. The lesson plan worksheet that new teachers had to submit each week to their supervisors for feedback and review followed a rigid script: a five-minute Do Now (a short handout or question to get students working right away), a review of the Do Now, direct instruction, guided instruction, independent practice, and an exit ticket (an informal assessment to check student learning during class). During the Do Now, independent practice, and exit ticket, teachers often used online stopwatches to count down the silent work time. Group work and discussion were not absent from the school day, but new teachers—particularly those struggling with student behavior—were told to establish order before experimenting with more innovative teaching strategies.

"You know, I sometimes struggle because you want to be the structure and the school for everyone but it just doesn't work that way," Mr. Bradley, the school principal, reflected during an interview. "[The no-excuses model is] very structured, obviously. It's very, you know, direct instruction, guided practice, independent practice, and there's not a whole lot of room for deviation from that." While some studies suggest that a direct instruction model has benefits for low-income students and students who face academic difficulties,[5] such a high level of structure may not afford students opportunities to engage deeply with their learning and develop their own ideas and interests.[6] For example, Mr. Jackson, a Black parent of a seventh grader, found that his daughter struggled to ask questions in her math class because the teacher wanted all hands down when he was giving instruction. Although students had an opportunity to talk after the lesson, he felt that "by that time, the child probably has forgotten or is having a problem with something else." In this case, the school's attempt to make teaching more efficient by having direct instruction time uninterrupted by questions denied students the opportunity to have their questions addressed or the space to wrestle with uncertainties. Mr. Jackson also noted that his daughter would clam up because she felt that her teachers were constantly on her case about her behavior.

Dream Academy regulated not only bodies but also sound. Because of the school's strict parameters for when students could talk—both in class and in other spaces in the school—students learned to hold back their opinions. Even when able to talk, Amir, a Latino fifth grader, learned he should talk only when his teacher asked him for a response. "Self-control is when you're able to talk, when you know to talk at the appropriate time," he explained. "And it's important because you can get a really bad consequence and I do—I really show self-control because I don't talk at all in class, and I talk when the teacher tells me when I have to talk or answer a question. And otherwise I don't talk in class." Brandy, a Black eighth grader, also learned to keep silent in order to avoid punishment: "But then, when I came here, it was like okay, I just have to sit like this forever. You just stay there and be quiet and not even speak. So it took me a long time, but then I got used to it. Like, I know if I don't, then I'm going to get a consequence, which is worse." Under the school's sweating-the-small-stuff approach, students often received consequences for talking to another student in class during silent work time or instruction time. This led students like Tyrek, a Black eighth grader, to feel that their input was not valued. "Like they don't even let us say any—like how we feel, our opinion," he observed. "They never let us state our opinion. If we state our opinion, we get detention."

When I asked Ms. Williams how she reconciled her personal philosophy with students feeling like they were not heard, she insisted that it was not the fault of the system but that individual teachers needed to take the time to listen to students and not shut them down. In a system where teachers also had to follow the school's rigid structures and pace, however, it was not easy to slow down and encourage student voice.

Parents like Ms. Simmons appreciated the school's strict rules and saw a benefit in students learning to show self-control. To prepare students for the future, where "your boss is going to sweat the small stuff," she thought it made sense to train students early. "You have to get them ready for life," she said. "And it's not realistic to expect that you can do what you want when you want to and how you want to, and be successful at the same time. Even the most successful people in the world in a meeting have to know when to shut up, you know." As a Black woman who had not attended college and worked processing health claims, Ms. Simmons saw the school's rules as preparing students for future jobs where they also would have to restrain themselves and follow specific rules. Her view echoes that of neo-Marxist scholars Samuel Bowles and Herbert Gintis, who famously argued that school structures reflected workplace structures in order to socialize students into work-appropriate behaviors and norms. However, Bowles and Gintis also argued that schools socialized students differently according to their social class positions, teaching working-class children obedience, deference, and punctuality to prepare them for working-class jobs, while teaching middle-class students creativity, independence, and assertiveness to prepare them for managerial positions.[7]

Given that Dream Academy was preparing its students for college and upward mobility, the school arguably should have been encouraging expression and assertiveness rather than silence and self-control. Jobs that require a college degree typically encourage worker input and grant workers greater autonomy to voice their opinions. Open communication is the norm in many newer firms seeking to break down traditional hierarchies.[8] Colleges also expect students to voice their opinions and participate in class discussion rather than keep silent.

Angie, a Black student who had previously attended Dream Academy, provided students with a glimpse of the interactional skills students would need for college when she came back to speak about her experience as a first-year student at one of the nation's elite boarding schools. A handful of students at Dream Academy participated in community programs that helped prepare them for private high schools. During the school's morning circle, she encouraged students to be open-minded because "they teach a bit differently at her school." She explained that the students at her school "teach each other" by sitting around a table and having discussions. "You learn different skills and you learn them differently, and they may think differently than you," she told the students. Although it took her some time to adjust, she liked having the opportunity to use her voice. "I love the method—I grabbed on to it. It makes you realize that your opinion matters." For Angie, learning to use her voice was an important skill for being successful in the college-like, discussion-based seminars she experienced at the boarding school.

Showing Flexibility

Flexibility is a key aspect of cultural capital, as I have earlier argued. The cultural capital that middle-class students use to gain resources in schools and workplaces is a flexible tool, not a straitjacket. Because situations are ambiguous and expectations are shifting, individuals need to be able to interpret a situation and choose among alternatives—skills that are difficult to transfer through a rigid script. While middle-class students learn to interpret situations and to act accordingly, Dream Academy students learned to act the same way in every situation.

Consistency in school rules and procedures is a shared goal of no-excuses school leaders.[9] School leaders believe that a schoolwide, consistent disciplinary approach benefits teachers and students by making expectations and consequences clear. In its charter, Dream Academy describes common procedures and expectations as a key feature of the school's approach: "Through using a set of common procedures in all classrooms—class rules, how to enter the class, where to see the day's homework, how to write the homework in students' daily planners, how to respond to questions, what signals to follow to become silent, how to read the daily lesson objectives, etc.—we train students to expect certain things in a classroom." When procedures are consistent from day to day and from teacher to teacher, the school believes that students will more easily internalize expectations. "It becomes a routine where they just do it and they don't have to think about it," Ms. Scott, the student affairs dean, explained. "But when it's wishy-washy, it leaves too much for them to have to think about and process."

No-excuses schools prize consistency over discretion, and even effective teachers who can manage their classrooms in alternative ways are directed to follow school systems. As Ms. Williams argued, "Your discretion depends on whether you're emotional that day, whether you're tired that day—discretion doesn't work." As principal, she implemented a "ladder of consequences" that all teachers were required to follow. For every minor infraction, teachers were expected to assign a consequence, progressing up the ladder for each subsequent infraction: (1) whole-class reminder, (2) student warning, (3) loss of points or lunch detention, (4) after-school detention, and (5) phone call home. While a common set of expectations can be clear and fair to students and reduce individual teacher bias, a schoolwide behavioral code does not teach students how to adjust to different teachers and different expectations.

Let's return to the problem of student expression. As discussed, Dream Academy had clear rules for when students could speak and when they had to stay silent. To reinforce rules about not calling out in class, one homeroom teacher even came up with a contest in which students would be awarded a pizza party if they did not call out in class for an entire day. A student was given a clipboard to keep track of how many times her class-mates called out. The first day, the class had forty-seven callouts by lunch. Although the students did not succeed in meeting these expectations, they received the message that they were to stay silent and always raise their hands if they needed to speak. Such scripts reflect the official school requirements for student comportment but deviate from the actual skills that lead middle-class kids to negotiate advantages in classrooms. Studies have found that although teachers tell students to raise their hands, they tend not to reprimand students for calling out and interrupting and, in many cases, reward them for these behaviors with attention and engage-ment.[10] These studies also have found that middle-class and upper-class students are much more likely than working-class and poor students to engage in help-seeking—and this begins as early as preschool.[11] Thus, although it seems on the surface that "good students" sit quietly, middle-class students actually figure out when and how to be heard, a skill that is encouraged both in their families and in schools.

We need to recognize that these strategies have differential returns by race. Studies have found that teachers rate Black students' classroom behaviors more negatively than White students' behaviors and punish them more severely for minor disruptions.[12] Indeed, one ethnographic study of four first-grade classrooms found that Black students were less able to interrupt the teacher and assert their opinions than White stu-dents, as they were frequently reprimanded by teachers for the same types of help-seeking or knowledge-displaying behaviors that were rewarded or overlooked in their White classmates.[13] In a country where young people of color are scrutinized more than White kids, there is a sentiment that their behavior needs to be twice as good. Students of color are not granted the same flexibility as White students. At the same time, learning how to be flexible and bend rules is a skill that some parents also regarded as important for their children to learn.

Ms. Owens, a Black mother of a fifth-grade girl and a teacher herself, understood the need to be flexible. As someone active in her teachers union, she recognized the importance of being able to read a situation:

> You can't let anybody silence you. You have to be creative. But there's a way of doing things. And we have a running joke in my house. I learned it from mother. You know, we have to learn to be diplomatic. Having other people see it your way, not just you making someone see it your way, but having them see it your way. . . . You have to be able to finesse it to a point where you know when and how to say it, whether you're in your classroom talking to your teacher or whether I'm on my job talking to my principal, or you know, where you're on your job talking to your boss.

Ms. Owens understood that to win others to your side, you have to be diplomatic. To do this, you have to understand the expectations of those with whom you are interacting as well as the norms of the situation. Sociologist Hugh Mehan described competent students as those who understand the social context they are in and can activate skills and behaviors that are appropriate to that context.[14] "Learning that certain ways of talking and acting are appropriate on some occasions and not others, learning when, where, and with whom certain kinds of behavior can occur," Mehan argued, is what makes for effective participation in the classroom.[15] Competent people are those who can "generate and coordinate flexible, adaptive responses to demands and to generate and capitalize on opportunities in the environment."[16]

Ms. Owens offered a metaphor that well illustrates the difference between rigid scripts and flexible tools. In describing her vision for her daughter, she compared a palm tree with an oak tree: "I want her to be more of a palm tree. I want her to be able to bend and be a little flexible. I don't want that sturdy oak because it keeps hitting up against that and it's just like it has no give, it has no bend. That's a problem for me to deal with because I want her to be firmly rooted, I want her to be that solid tree but it sways a little bit in the wind. It is not gonna snap." Dream Academy, in her eyes, was creating oak trees—stiff, straight, rule-following kids. But when the oak tree gets hit and hit, it might just snap. She wanted her daughter to be more like the palm tree—flexible enough to bend, not break. A script from which one cannot deviate does not equip students with the flexible tools to innovate and bend rules to one's benefit.

Displaying Leadership

Midway through practicing with the violin section, Ms. Thurmond, a seasoned Black music teacher who tended to be less stringent with school rules, stopped suddenly.

"What the heck?" she exclaimed, uncharacteristically. She hit her music stand so hard that her sheet music floated to the ground.

She cast her attention on a Black male student who returned her glare timidly and looked apologetic. I hadn't seen what he had done, but Ms. Thurmond told him that "what you are doing is annoying."

The girls sitting in front chuckled at their teacher's uncharacteristic display of anger.

"You're all followers," Ms. Thurmond snapped at them. By calling the students "followers," Ms. Thurmond seemed to associate the students' laughter with their siding with the misbehaving student rather than taking the matter seriously.

"We ain't followers," one girl protested.

"I told my mom, everyone calling us followers," a second chimed in.

"We all followers—we follow directions," a third added, twisting Ms. Thurmond's words to assert that they were indeed followers in this school because they followed directions.

Picking up on this new line of thought, another student called out, "You all Mr. Taylor's clones." Flipping the script, she accused the teachers of being followers because they followed whatever Mr. Taylor, Dream Academy's director, said. Earlier in class, Ms. Thurmond had indeed told the students how she had consulted with Mr. Taylor about whether the students could speak quietly to each other in class when she was working with each instrument section. She had received permission to do so. It struck me as surprising that she would have asked for permission and lent credence to the students' charge that the teachers were just following the directions of their superiors.

Ms. Thurmond took out her cell phone and walked to the door. Now silent, the students waited to find out whose parent was being called. At the sound of the name of a Black boy in the class, the students looked at each other in surprise.

"I was just laughing, not talking," the accused boy protested.

"Yes, you were laughing," Ms. Thurmond replied.

"Call my mom," another student boldly offered.

"Excuse me, don't tell me what to do," Ms. Thurmond said.

"Or me," said the student.

"It's like the center of class is over here," Ms. Thurmond scolded. "I'm the instructor."

"You calling us followers again?" another student called out.

At the end of class, Brian, a Latino student, threw Ms. Thurmond's sheet music in the air in what she described as an act of retaliation. Speaking with him alone in the corridor after class, she explained to him, "This is what I meant by followers." Reminding him that he had asked her to be his mentor, she told him, "It was childish, stupid. You're supposed to be a leader." After he apologized, she told him he needed to do more than that. "You will get people to focus. People will follow you," she told him. "You're not hurting me. You're hurting yourself. I have a job, an education—I'm not being hurt. Students don't hurt their teachers. You got a fifty in class. You hurt your grade."

While Ms. Thurmond was trying to teach Brian to be a leader—to think for himself instead of going along with the crowd—her efforts were hampered by a system in which students did not have much room for leadership. As the students were astute to observe, they were told to be followers in the sense that they were required to follow the school's myriad prescriptions for their behavior. As Siani, a Black eighth grader, put it, "Most of these kids that are here are, like, followers 'cause they don't have a mind of their own because this school is, like, it tells you what you're supposed to do." In a school where students were constantly told to follow the school's behavioral script, being a leader often meant going against the rules.

Aniya, a Black girl at the school who described herself as "energetic, honest, outspoken," "very kind," and "a little sneaky," showed strong leadership qualities. Unlike most students I spoke with, Aniya felt she could express herself in school: "Yeah, I have to. There's no, like, I can't, I got to. I'm going to. Like, you can't say I can't express myself. I'm going to express myself." Her tendency to speak her mind got her in frequent entanglements with her teachers—she nearly got expelled in fifth grade and was held back in seventh grade for her poor behavior and grades. Studies have found that Black girls who defy traditional White feminine standards of being submissive and quiet are perceived by teachers as loud, obnoxious, and defiant.[17] Social control is not only racialized and classed but also gendered.[18]

Aniya had internalized messages that her assertiveness was a bad thing. "But, I mean, one reason I'm a leader is 'cause I was bad," she told me one afternoon. "You know, the people look up to people that's always bad." She looks up to smart people, and has her mind set on attending the historically Black college attended by her favorite teacher, Ms. Williams.

"I don't look up to the bad people, they just irrelevant," she said. "They're doing the same thing I'm doing. I'm trying to do something else."

Her best friend, Keke, likewise learned that giving her opinion was the wrong thing to do in school. Keke had been retained "for my attitude and my tardiness," as she described it, and had repeated seventh grade. By the time Keke reached eighth grade, she found herself speaking out less frequently to avoid detention. At the end of the year, she won the most improved student award. Keke reflected on her change in behavior over her middle school years: "I used to fight back or whatever because I don't . . . like to be told what to do. I want to be the leader. But sometimes I need to let the teacher be the leader 'cause they're the ones here before me, and they're the ones taught what they are now teaching me. I don't like the way some people talk to me. . . . I like getting the last word so I will always fight back and give my opinion when it's really not needed." Keke understood her talking back as a way to assert herself and show leadership, yet over time she learned to step back and let her teachers step forward.

Brian, Aniya, and Keke were taught to show leadership not by using their voice and defending themselves, but by holding back their opinions and conforming to the school's rigid behavioral scripts. In this way, the school did not encourage the types of leadership skills that middle-class students use to gain advantages in college and the workplace. These types of skills are also critical for navigating risky environments. Ms. Lewis, a mother of a Black seventh grader, used the language of "followers" when she spoke to me about her worries for her son. She had seen the city grow more dangerous since she had graduated from the city's schools, and feared that her son might succumb to negative peer pressure: "I don't want [my son] to be a follower and then follow the wrong person and then something might happen to him," she said. "All it takes is just one time and you just never know what can happen, so that's my main concern for him. I want him to be his own person."

We will see how leadership skills can be valuable for future success by turning to the story of Ms. Wallace, one of the students' favorite teachers.

Advocating a Position

In second grade, Ms. Wallace led her first protest. "I still remember the chant to it and I got all the girls in like second, third, and fourth grade and we marched and we marched and we chanted and we handed out posters," she reminisced. "And everything was fine but then the bell rang and I said, we continue."

The girls continued marching on, under the direction of their leader. Eventually, the teacher and principal got every girl in a line. Starting at the back, they asked each girl, "Were you a leader or a follower?" Each student said follower. They asked them whom they followed. The students replied, "Lara Wallace." Finally, they reached Ms. Wallace. She knew what they were going to ask. Preempting their question, she said, "Yes, I'm a leader because this was wrong."

Little Lara Wallace was protesting the unfair treatment of girls. At recess, the boys had not been letting the girls play basketball. The day before, she had complained to her teacher, who told her that basketball was not for girls and handed her a piece of chalk to go draw a hopscotch board. "I didn't even know how to draw hopscotch," Ms. Wallace griped. "I don't think I've ever played it. But it was, like, so insulting." That night, with the help of her parents, she made posters and brochures and glued them onto yardsticks, ready to lead the students in protest.

"It's moments like those where, I don't know, like to shut a kid down like that. Kids are smart," she asserted. "They're smarter than we are, and they can sense a lot of things 'cause they're not jaded. So, when you show them unfairness or just like power 'cause you can, it's just, I don't know, it can really affect them."

Ms. Wallace, even as a young child, was given an opportunity to voice her opinions and take leadership. Supported by her parents, she defied her teacher's authority and organized her classmates together. This assertiveness has served her well, first as a reporter for the local newspaper and then in getting her job at Dream Academy. When she first applied to Dream Academy, she was interviewed but turned away because she didn't have any teaching experience. The rejection did not stop her. A month later, she returned to the website and saw the same position open. She emailed Human Resources, made her case again, and was brought in for a second interview. Again, it was a no. "Get a job somewhere else, just get some experience," they told her, feeling uncertain that she could manage a classroom. Three weeks later, she emailed them again, asking, "How does one gain experience if you're not given the chance to get experience?" She pleaded, "I really think I can do something here." In the middle of the August teacher boot camp, they called her and asked, "Can you start tomorrow?"

Encouraged since childhood to be assertive, take initiative, and show leadership, Ms. Wallace was able to negotiate her way into a job for which the school administrators felt she was underqualified. Like Ms. Wallace, middle-class kids use their cultural capital to negotiate more opportunities for themselves—whether an extension on a paper, a placement in an honors course, or a job opportunity.[19] These students learn to take initiative and bend rules to their benefit.

Ms. Wallace provides an interesting comparison with Aniya. In fact, when I asked her how she would have fared at Dream Academy as a child, she remarked, "No, I would not have done, no—I would have been Aniya." Like Aniya, she was a student who felt comfortable speaking up. "I just had a lot of energy and I could never like shut up and I have no problem like talking back," she recalled. "Like if I thought something was not fair or I felt like my voice wasn't being heard or I didn't understand a decision, I had no problem expressing that and usually probably not in the most respectful way." Because of her outspokenness, she doubted whether she would have been able to be successful at a school like Dream Academy where she would have had to conform to a rigid script.

"You know, and some kids can fit themselves into that box even if they're not that flexible," she said. "And others can't. I don't know if I could. Like the silent lines, like I don't know."

"You would have led a protest," I suggested.

"I would have led a protest, yeah, like, this is wrong," she agreed. "Like there's something wrong with this."

Ms. Wallace likely would have gotten into more serious trouble in second grade (and later on, in high school, when she was arrested twice) had she been Black or Latino, not White, as has been made all too clear in racial disproportionalities in discipline, arrest, and incarceration.[20] Studies have found that Black boys and girls are perceived as older and less innocent than White children and thus are subjected to more severe punishment and force.[21] Black parents are well aware that their children need to learn to carefully navigate interactions with authority figures; their failure to do so can have deadly consequences given the history of structural racism and police brutality in the United States.[22] At the same time, developing self-advocacy skills can help students of color feel empowered to challenge discriminatory practices and assert their desires, needs, and rights.[23] Learning how to advocate for a position is also critical for civic engagement and political change.[24]

Making Independent Decisions

Alexis, the student we met at the beginning of the chapter, believed that the school did not trust students with even the smallest things—walking through the hallway, making appropriate clothing choices, or keeping backpacks at their desk—whereas students worked hard to follow school rules and complete hours of homework each night, trusting the school's promises to get them to college. "They don't trust us to do the right thing and that's not cool," she commented. "Why would you—we trust you with our education but you don't trust us to make the right basic [choices]?"

The school's strict rules and tight regulations made many students feel they were treated like young children who could not be trusted even to walk down the hallway. The hallway rules, which stipulated that students must walk with their classes in straight, silent, single-file lines, were intended to minimize fights and make transitions to class more efficient. Because the school was so small, however, students did not have far to walk between classes, sometimes only directly across the hall. Yet teachers still lined up students at the end of each class and escorted them to their next class. When I was talking with two Black eighth-grade girls about what school rules could be changed, they highlighted the hallway rule. "Our school's real small, so it's like, I want to know where they think we're gonna go—like we're gonna hop down the hallway?" Siani commented. "Like the classes are really right there." Her classmate Kayla agreed: "I think we would be mature enough to be able to talk to our friends in the hallways. Like we need to get maturity, too, as we grow older."

Mr. Taylor acknowledged that the school's strict practices did not prepare students for the freedoms of college. But he also saw freedom as risky for the students they served. Unlike middle-class students who could make mistakes, kids at Dream Academy had less room for error. "The challenge I have is that, for too many of our students, the freedom equals failure," he told me. "It doesn't equal freedom and then the ability to succeed within that freedom." Mr. Taylor was not ready to trust students to take leadership and make good decisions for themselves because he recognized that the stakes were high for these students. However, without the opportunity to make their own choices, students cannot learn to make independent decisions and show self-control.

Self-control is the ability to resist urges, temptations, and desires and to regulate behaviors, thoughts, and emotions.[25] In many ways, Dream Academy's strict behavioral code developed in students a sense of self-control. Students felt that Dream Academy's high expectations for student behavior, paired with consequences, kept student behavior in check in a way that suspensions at previous schools had not. "Okay, the difference is like the behavior—the standards," explained Reggie, a Black eighth grader. "'Cause I have friends that go to [the local public school] and they basically do whatever they want. They fight all the time and everything.

You might get suspended but you always come back, and you do the same thing over and over again. And they don't do nothing." Black eighth grader Lechelle had been sent to Dream Academy by her mom over a year prior because she had not been improving her grades and behavior at her previous school. "I just had a bad attitude all the time so I used to get in trouble a lot," she said. At Dream Academy, she found herself trying to do her homework more, being less disrespectful to her classmates and teachers, and arriving to school on time. She spoke about how "bench," a punishment where students had to wear a yellow shirt and could not speak to other students or participate in activities like gym, acted as a deterrent. "A lot of people don't want to be on the bench so it makes you calm down," she explained.

There is a difference, however, between self-control that is initiated by oneself and self-control that is in response to an authority figure. As grit psychologist Angela Duckworth notes, there is a difference "between two classroom scenarios: an orderly classroom in which students are encouraged and taught to exercise self-control, and another where students are merely conforming to rules for fear of punishment. Children who willingly comply with directives from adults are easier to manage than those who do not, but compliance should not be confused with fully autonomous, self-initiated regulation."[26]

In other words, the "self" part of self-control is key. Learning to follow rules is a different skill than learning to self-regulate—those students who are following rules to avoid punishment are not necessarily developing a sense of control over their behavior. Take the following incident that happened on a Friday in January. This near fight, the only one I witnessed during my year and a half at the school, seemed to have come out of nowhere. Only moments passed from the time I swiveled in my chair to investigate a commotion to when I stood by the classroom door watching students try to restrain Aniya. Ironically, the incident centered around a discussion of self-control.

"It's your presentation; I can't do this for you," Ms. Armstrong told her homeroom team. "You're not showing self-control, and you're presenting on self-control."

Ms. Armstrong, a White first-year teacher who was overseeing one of the two eighth-grade homerooms, was encouraging students to work on their self-control skits during team time. Team time was a relatively unstructured part of the day when students often worked to prepare presentations for the morning circle competitions. For these competitions, students developed and performed creative skits, chants, and dance sequences to illustrate the character trait the school was trying to teach that month.

This month's topic, for the second time, was self-control. The school had decided to extend its lessons on self-control another month because they believed students needed the extra practice. The students had put together two videos of themselves talking about self-control—whether they had it and how they learned it—as well as a self-control rap. But on this day, instead of rehearsing together, groups of students were scattered around the room. Two students had their backs sprawled across the desks. Two boys banged on their desks, continuing the rhythm of the rap after their peers had finished performing it.

At the front of the class, Aniya was actively engaged in rehearsing the presentation. Showing her leadership skills, she tried to quiet down the class so they could run through the presentation again with the timer. As they were about to begin, a loud noise from the back corner of the room interrupted the practice.

I turned to see what looked like a large pad that had fallen to the ground.

"Shut up," Aniya yelled to the girls in back.

"I wasn't talking," responded Alana, a Black girl who generally did not attract much attention to herself in class.

"Shut up," Aniya repeated.

"I wasn't talking," Alana replied, sternly.

This back-and-forth continued for a minute until Aniya started walking toward the back of the room, insulting Alana by calling her hair "nappy." Alana rose from her seat.

Aware of the escalating tension, I walked over to Alana, while Ms. Armstrong approached Aniya. The girls headed to the door. Alana left the room, while some of the other students in the class held Aniya back as she tried to open the door to follow her. To my relief, Ms. Wallace soon appeared at the door's window, promptly extinguishing the confrontation. She directed Aniya to take a walk outside to cool down, and then returned the other students back to their seats.

Outside in the hallway, Alana stood, her lips firmly together. "I'm fine, I'm fine," she repeated as two of her friends asked her how she was and told her she was brave. When the class was dismissed to lunch, Ms. Armstrong apologized to Alana.

One way to view this altercation is as an isolated incident that stemmed from Aniya's frustration with the class for not practicing the skit. Aniya was a student who struggled with self-control and admitted to having difficulty controlling her anger. The school leaders' take, however, was that Ms. Armstrong was a common factor in these types of incidents. In a leadership meeting later that day, the school staff discussed how Ms. Armstrong needed to better anticipate student behavior and intervene if things were going awry. From their standpoint, the fight was the result of a novice teacher not being able to handle the more unstructured environment of team time. Ms. Armstrong's apology to Alana affirmed her own understanding that she could have done more to intervene.

If fights ensue once controls are lifted, however, this is consistent with a view that students are not developing self-control; they are learning to control themselves only when they are being tightly controlled. Other examples confirm this conjecture. School staff, for example, observed how a little change in procedure altered the school culture. Mr. Bradley saw visible changes in student behavior when the school implemented special events like "crazy sock day," where students were allowed to wear any kind of sock they wanted instead of the prescribed solid-colored socks that were part of their uniform. That such a minor change in rules would invite noticeable changes in student behavior gives one the feeling that students are in a pressure cooker where opening the lid can incite an explosion. Mr. Bradley told me that he can predict how the school day will go by how well homeroom runs. If teachers are on top of things in homeroom, students behave well through the day. When teachers are tired or sick, students' behaviors deteriorate. Ms. Scott also has noticed these changes. When she is not feeling well or is not fully "sweating the small stuff" during her cafeteria duty, she finds that students take advantage and get into more trouble. "Even when we're not consistent, like there is a definite difference in the children's behavior when we're not on top of our game," she said.

When the school had an adventure-based learning group lead a few activities with the students, they found that students had difficulty adjusting back to the school structures after being in a less structured environment. "We tried to do . . . this like fun character learning, but I mean, it ended up being a lot more problems than it was really worth because, you know, you try this loosey-goosey approach, and the kids get sent mixed messages," Mr. Bradley recalled. "You're trying to sweat the small stuff, and then you let the, you know, it's a free-for-all for the next hour and a half, and inevitably there was always problems during it."

The school's rigid scripts for behavior established an orderly learning environment, which was critical to meeting the school's goals. These controls, however, also limited the school's ability to develop in students the types of tools needed to know how to independently manage their freedoms. Ms. Larkin, a first-year White teacher who disagreed with many of the school's practices, worried that the school's strict controls were not preparing students to make choices in the absence of immediate consequences. She reflected,

> It almost makes me feel like we—is that how we view people who are in urban schools? Like, we have to be so absolutely strict and tight. We have to—we have to—just be so overpowering. I constantly worry about these kids needing someone to tell them when they're wrong and when they're right, because the consequence system is so overwhelmingly powerful at our school, right? Silent hallways. And it's, like, how are they ever going to develop as people if they can't talk to each other? We don't let them talk at all. And SLANT, like—I just would love to have a rug and let them lay on a floor with a book, right? Could you imagine if I did that?

Ms. Larkin did not want to issue a detention when students did something wrong but instead preferred to talk students through the issue: "Why did you do that? How can we fix this?" She wanted to help students learn to make real choices for themselves and develop a sense of control over their own behavior.

What's interesting is that many students at Dream Academy actually assume more responsibilities at home than their more affluent peers yet are trusted with fewer at school. While feeling treated like a kid at Dream Academy, Alexis wakes up at five o'clock every morning to vacuum her room. "I think my mom tries to teach me to be independent, which is why she doesn't baby me," she reflected. "I think she wants me to like learn how to fend for myself."

Ms. Deliz, the mother of the fifth-grade girl who stayed home for two weeks because of her stress, taught her daughter to be self-sufficient. "If something happens to me today, God forbid, and I pass, she could run this household all by herself," she commented. "She knows how to cook breakfast, lunch, dinner. She knows how to take care of her brothers. She can give them a bath. She's a very independent young lady. She do her own things. She do her wash. She folds, everything. She does it on her own." Ms. Deliz stressed independence with her daughter because she had to learn this lesson herself at an early age when her mother fell ill and she had to raise her sisters.

By requiring students to follow a rigid script for behavior, the school failed to recognize students' strengths—that they could be trusted with

significant responsibility—and to develop in students greater independence. The problem with not trusting students to make their own decisions was that students were hardly afforded the opportunity in school to
practice self-initiated self-regulation.

Preparing for College

One May afternoon, I met with two former Dream Academy graduates
at a local diner for lunch and ice cream. When I arrived at one o'clock,
they were seated and had ordered me a water. The two Black girls, who
were friends, were chatty and were talking about looking for summer jobs.
Kylah, an only child who lived with her mom and dog, had worked for the
past two years at Auntie Anne's Pretzels at the mall but was still being paid
minimum wage. Bianca, who also lived with her mom, had secured a job
at a packaging store but the job had not yet begun.

Kylah and Bianca were members of Dream Academy's first sixth-grade
class and the school's first graduating high school class, which boasted
an impressive 100 percent college acceptance rate. Both girls had just
completed their first year of college, Kylah at a local four-year college
and Bianca at a small liberal arts college. These schools weren't their top
choices for college, but they had received partial scholarships to attend.
Dream Academy had required each student to apply to twelve colleges
based on students' GPA, interests, and colleges they had visited with the
school. Both girls had received a number of college acceptances. I had
reached out to Kylah and Bianca because I was curious to hear how Dream
Academy had prepared them with the skills they needed in college.

"College was definitely . . . having fun, any day of the week," replied
Kylah when I asked what college was like. She found that she had a lot
of free time with classes not taking up much time. The first semester, she
described herself as "a square," going to class, eating, doing her homework,
and sleeping. She had been surprised to hear students coming into the
dorms late at night when she was already in bed. By the second semester,
however, she had adjusted. She started coming back to her dorm between
midnight and two o'clock. Laughing, she turned to Bianca, "You will be so
proud of me. This one night, I came in at five A.M.—on a Tuesday!"

Bianca also found her routines at odds with the expectations of college. She was surprised that one of her classes ran until nine thirty, which
was past her bedtime. Although she described herself as "quiet," she had
an outgoing roommate, also a student from Dream Academy, and ended
up partying with her. "You just want to go out and do whatever," she said.

Although Kylah and Bianca successfully navigated their first year of college, both girls had already switched their majors to elementary education because they had difficulties in their math and science classes in their originally intended majors. Bianca had a 2.7 GPA. She struggled in her math class and also in an English class where she didn't keep up with the essays the teacher assigned. "So like, you could do it or not do it, it don't matter," she explained about the essays. "But then at the end, we had to do our portfolio. I felt like, Wow." Although she managed to write all the essays, she received a C in the class and felt "kinda disappointed." Other students have struggled more. Bianca's roommate, who was a Dream Academy graduate, left the college after one semester. Another one of their high school classmates became a "street pharmacist" (a drug dealer), precisely the kind of future Dream Academy had been working against.

"I feel like at [Dream Academy], it kind of babied me too much," reflected Kylah. "Because now that I'm in college . . . I'm an individual in a big pond. No one's going to cross me, if I'm late to class, like, I'm late. I'm late."

It is not easy to pinpoint what impact the tight controls used by no-excuses schools have on students' college experiences. Success in college is also dependent on students' academic preparation and outside-of-school factors, making it hard to disentangle the influence of one factor from another. To the extent that no-excuses schools are not helping students learn to make their own decisions, advocate for themselves, and take initiative, however, they may be unwittingly undermining their own goals of preparing students for the expectations of college. In KIPP's college completion report, the network observed that successful college students "are strong self-advocates who proactively problem solve, [are] able to communicate with professors about scholastic concerns, identify challenges in areas such as financial aid or housing, and know where and how to ask for help."[27] The KIPP schools, which sent most of their students to college, saw only about one-third of them graduating from college in six years.[28]

No-excuses schools may also be presenting a distorted image of what college is like. Dream Academy's emphasis on strictness and self-control shaped students' understanding of what it took to get to and be successful in college. Ava, a Black fifth grader, did not think the school was too strict because "they're just trying to make it comfortable for what college is gonna be like." When I asked her what she thought college was like, she replied, "I think college is gonna be strict and really hard."

During music class, I asked Kiara, a Black eighth grader, if she liked the school.

"No," she immediately replied, and proceeded to list off the rules that they were required to follow.

"Why do you think the school is so strict?" I inquired.

"They always say they want us to go to college, but we're only in middle school," she answered. "Self-discipline, self-control will help us get to college."

Surprised at her response, I asked, "Why does the school think those things will get you to college?"

The student sitting next to her chimed in, "They probably did it."

He imagined that the teachers had gone to similar schools as this and looked uncertain when I expressed my doubts. As these students' responses illustrate, the school's rigid behavioral practices led students to develop the wrong impression of what college was like. Not knowing for themselves, they literally took teachers at their word when teachers said that the school's strictness was preparing students for college.

Students began to question this vision of college as strict and unforgiving as they gained more exposure to college. After visiting a college, Zayna, a Black eighth grader, had some of her misperceptions about college corrected: "I mean, don't get me wrong in college, yes, you have to be quiet, but you don't have to be quiet when you're going into the dorms. Because I've seen colleges where you can talk a little bit in the, um, in the hallways because sometimes there's couches for you to sit on, so what, they think you're just going to sit down and read a book? So you can talk a little bit. I mean, I understand if we're loud but if it's like a normal tone and normal volume, I think it should be acceptable." Because Dream Academy required students to be silent so much of the time, Zayna had assumed that colleges did this too. She was thus surprised to see couches in dorms, which made her realize that students must be able to talk, at least a little. This led her to question whether some of the rules at school might be "a little extra." The juniors and seniors, when they started learning about college through visits from college admissions staff and visits to different campuses, also had similar revelations, recognizing that they would be granted much more independence than they were used to at Dream Academy.

Ms. Indrigo, the high school's White college counselor, voiced doubts that the school was sufficiently preparing students to make this transition. "You know, I think partially it's their fault because they haven't learned to manage their freedoms, but it's partially our fault because we don't give them any, so when we give them some, they go crazy," she reflected. "And so my biggest fear is that these kids are going to go to college and go crazy and like party all the time and not go to class." She explained how the high school was trying to give students an opportunity to get a taste of college by offering juniors and seniors dual-enrollment classes at the local community college, where they could take a class for both high school and college credit. It was the first time the community college was offering dual-enrollment classes to high school students from the city, and the college wanted this pilot program to be a success.

Classes were held at the college on Monday and Wednesday afternoons. Students were responsible for transportation to the college and received college identification cards and email addresses. "You can go there and be college students and wear jeans," Ms. Indrigo had told the students when introducing the program to them. Because it was a pilot program, the students would be taking classes together but would be taught by a college instructor and might have regular college students taking classes alongside them. They had a choice of taking Math 101, English 101, or Psychology 101.

During one dual-enrollment math class I observed, the instructor, a middle-aged White woman, began class by reviewing homework with the students, the vast majority of whom were from Dream Academy. I noticed that a couple of students had changed out of their Dream Academy uniforms: one boy was now wearing a T-shirt and headphones; another was in a black tank. Students were snacking on Starbursts, Cheetos, and Cherry Coke. The instructor, whom the students called Ms. P, asked the students if they had any questions from the homework. Only one Dream Academy student, a Black female, asked her to do a question on the board. After reviewing the problem, the instructor reminded students that they were responsible for keeping up with their homework. "Did we discuss our friend BOB?" she asked the class. "Back Of Book. You are now in college. We expect you to check answers in the back of the book yourself before class. Do a few problems and check." Unlike their high school teachers, she explained, she did not collect and check homework. College professors assigned odd-numbered questions because those answers were in the back of the book, so students could check for themselves. "We discussed how college students can have enough freedom to take responsibility for their own learning, right?" she asked the students. "Yes," they echoed back. "If it's a game—not doing homework because I'm not collecting—it may not be the best game to play," she warned. She looked askance at a Black boy sitting in front who had said he had forgotten his homework. Through the rest of the class, a few girls attentively followed along and answered Ms. P's questions. One girl spent the class scrolling through her phone. The boys stayed mostly quiet. I noticed about five tables where students had not brought in the textbook to follow.

In a dual-enrollment psychology class, this one with only a handful of Dream Academy students, I observed similar dynamics, with Dream Academy students mostly not taking initiative for their learning. The instructor, also a middle-aged White woman, asked how many students had logged into the course's online portal. Only a few hands went up. Shandra, a diligent Black Dream Academy student, was one of the students—she said she had accessed the portal but didn't know what to do. The instructor lectured the class on how there were sixteen assignments in the portal, and students were already behind. Later in class, she asked if any students had found an article about a research study that she had asked them to bring in. None of the Dream Academy students had. Shandra mentioned that she had found an article but had forgotten to bring it to class. Like Ms. P, the psychology instructor did not monitor students' work or give out immediate consequences if they failed to follow instructions; she expected students to take responsibility for their work. Students like Shandra were showing initiative and learning to manage their freedoms, but other students were not.

When I spoke with a group of juniors, I saw this same variation in experience. Fiona, a Black student who aspired to an Ivy League university, told me that her Psychology 101 class was "not hard at all" and that she and her classmates had been "really good at keeping up with the notes and making sure that we do what we're supposed to do, and, you know, getting good grades." When I turned to ask Richard, a Black student, how he was keeping up in his class, he replied differently:

> I take English 101 and, you know, it's not what I expected at all, you know, 'cause I mean, going to the class, you know, we sit down, teacher talks to us and she gives our assignment and then she's on to the assignment. And whether or not you choose to do the assignment, your choice has no consequences. You just watch your grades suffer. I mean, she won't even say anything to you. She'll be like ready to go to the next assignment. The only thing she'll do is just give you back your failed assignment. Well, actually, she won't give back anything 'cause you didn't do it.

He found it more difficult to adjust to college expectations where he did not receive an immediate consequence for not doing his work. Ms. Indrigo had noticed this trend too. She told me that while some of their students were doing well, others were "not doing their homework, 'cause no one's collecting it and they're not getting detention for it." This trend was very similar to what Bianca had experienced her first semester of college.

The high school principal, Ms. Stewart, a young, energetic Black woman who had graduated from an elite university, recognized that students needed to be prepared for the less structured expectations of college. In an interview, she articulated her vision for the high school. "I have a vision for high conduct and I have a vision—and this is what doesn't really always mesh well with no excuses—but I have a vision for the gradual release of structure," she reflected. "I want the kids to leave here at the end of twelfth grade as young adults, and not as adolescents. And so I'm trying desperately to find the way to maintain our structure, and at the same time enable them to leave as young adults." She admitted to not knowing how to resolve this tension. Like the middle school, the high school continued to rely on strict behavioral scripts that were reinforced through rewards and consequences. Part of the perceived need to keep tight structures was because the high school had new students who entered from other middle schools and were not familiar with Dream Academy's expectations. However, the school also faced resistance from its own students. During the ninth grade orientation, the students who had attended Dream Academy's middle school were pulled aside and lectured by their teacher and three of their classmates for "acting a mess" and being "blatantly disrespectful," knowing school rules but not following them, and acting as a poor example for the new students.

In this chapter, we have seen ways in which Dream Academy's tight scripts for behavior failed to instill in students the tools of interaction to help them navigate college and other middle-class institutions. The school's emphasis on conformity seemed to counteract the types of critical thinking skills that are crucial to success in college. In the next chapter, we will turn to how the school's scripts shaped how students learned to interact with authority.

CHAPTER FOUR

Ease and Antagonism

FOR MS. WASULIK, her one year teaching at Dream Academy was the most difficult of all her previous teaching experiences. She had applied to Dream Academy after watching *Waiting for "Superman,"* a documentary film that highlighted the successes of no-excuses charter schools. By the end of the year, however, she questioned her teaching abilities. Despite having received a Teacher of the Year award at her former school, a "second chance" charter school in the same city that targeted kids with behavioral or academic difficulties, she applied to nonteaching positions after leaving Dream Academy.

Ms. Wasulik, a White woman in her early forties, found it difficult to build positive relationships with students at Dream Academy and felt like the students did not trust teachers. In all her years of teaching, she explained, she never before had encountered students so defensive and hypersensitive, a reaction she connected to the school's rigid scripts for student behavior. "I feel like I'm picking them to death," she told me. "Like the ugly duckling." Just like the ugly duckling who is constantly teased and picked on by the other animals, Ms. Wasulik felt that students, subjected to teachers' constant surveillance of their behavior, also grew irritable. Although she supported the school's disciplinary practices, she recognized that "there is an extreme to that, too."

In this chapter, I will suggest that the school's rigid behavioral scripts shaped not only the expectations and skills students developed, as we saw in chapters 2 and 3, but also the ways in which students perceived and interacted with authority. Learning how to relate to authority is a skill and form of cultural capital. Cultural capital, as previously discussed, can be thought of as *tools of interaction*—attitudes, skills, and styles that individuals use to gain advantages in institutional settings like schools. As

institutional gatekeepers, authority figures hold access to key resources—
they decide whether someone will be hired or fired, they support or deny
requests, and they make evaluations. Knowing how to interact with these
authority figures is a valuable form of cultural capital. For instance, sociologist Anthony Jack showed how affluent students as well as the "privileged poor"—low-income students who had attended elite high schools
and acquired this form of cultural capital—proactively made connections
with college faculty and staff, securing numerous benefits including letters of recommendation, on-campus jobs and internships, introductions
to visitors, and advice on navigating college.[1]

In his study of St. Paul's, an elite boarding school, sociologist Shamus
Khan found that students developed "a sense of self and a mode of interaction" through their time at the school.[2] He calls this form of cultural capital a *sense of ease*—a disposition somewhere between presumption and
reverence. Through interacting with their teachers in a variety of formal
and informal settings (such as in the classroom, in the dormitory, in the
dining hall, and on the athletic field), these privileged students learned
how to interact with authority in flexible ways, a skill that prepared them
for future leadership positions where they would be interacting with different types of people in different settings. Students learned to engage
their faculty formally at seated meals, casually before class, and playfully
as they hung out at their teacher's apartment, sprawling on the couch and
joking with their teacher about the beer in his fridge. As Khan notes, students who learn to adopt a sense of ease act as though hierarchy does not
exist.[3] In a study of fifty-five American boarding schools, sociologists Peter
Cookson and Caroline Persell similarly found that as students progressed
through school, they acquired a style of behavior that concealed their privilege and helped them interact with others with ease.[4]

At Dream Academy, students learned different lessons. Although
teachers were supportive of students—for example, they were expected
to be available to assist students with homework until nine o'clock each
night—their constant monitoring and punishing of minor student behaviors led students often to find themselves at odds, rather than at ease, with
their teachers. Instead of acquiring a broad set of tools for interacting with
authority, students at Dream Academy were given narrow scripts for how
to interact with their teachers. These scripts taught students to defer to
authority but had the unintended consequence, in many instances, of pro-
voking students to become defiant toward authority. These scripts thus
did not prepare students with the ease that makes affluent students seem
less formal and less distant than their low-income peers and helps them

build rapport with college professors and future coworkers. Instead, many of the low-income students of color at Dream Academy developed what I call a *sense of antagonism*, where they became distrustful, resentful, and resistant to authority.

Student Resistance

For the past twenty minutes, students had been working in small groups on math worksheets matched to their skill level. As the end of class was nearing, Ms. Wasulik reminded students of the class expectations.

"What's the expectation? Silence. Yesterday you were all a hot mess."

Ms. Wasulik displayed the classroom's "exit procedures" on the smart board. At the beginning of the year, each teacher was required to create detailed entry and exit procedures for how students should enter and leave the classroom in order to ensure a smooth transition and maximize learning time. Ms. Wasulik had been advised by her supervisor to reset expectations to tighten transitions out of her class. This was the reason why, on this April afternoon, she was asking a student to read the exit procedures aloud. As the student read, Ms. Wasulik interrupted several times to correct student behavior and assign consequences:

> I will pass out the homework one column at a time. (Ms. Wasulik wrote the initials of two students who were talking on the board.)

> Only when you have been given your homework are you to silently get up and get your backpack. ("At this time, I can't take questions," Ms. Wasulik told a student raising his hand.)

> Return to your seat and silently pack up. (She put another initial on the board. "That's your warning," she told two students who are talking. "Please stop banging, Justin.")

> Sit in S position. ("What is S position?" a student called out. S position, which all students knew, referred to SLANT, sitting with hands folded on the desk and eyes on the teacher. Ms. Wasulik replied, "You've been here since fifth grade.")

In this exchange, we can see that as Ms. Wasulik tries to reinforce class expectations, students actively resist by talking, banging on their desks, and calling out. We can also see Ms. Wasulik's attempts to assert her authority by giving out consequences. She writes students' initials on the board, which is their warning. If students receive a check mark next to their name, they lose their behavioral points for the day. Points, as we saw in chapter 2, earned students privileges like wearing the school's shirt and attending field trips.

Ms. Wasulik explained to the class that they would follow these exit procedures so she could better monitor their behavior. Glancing over to her side, she noticed a student erasing the blackboard.

"Thank you for doing that," she told him. "But the expectation is to sit in your seat."

"I thought the expectation was silence," he replied.

"You're right, it's both," she conceded. "Why do we do this? So we can be more successful when we leave here. So you can be fabulous in your next class."

Ms. Wasulik began to run through the exit procedures. As she was directing a row of students to grab their backpacks, the Spanish teacher who was using the room afterward entered. The teacher reprimanded Zayna, a Black girl sitting in the front row, for talking. Zayna, typically a student who caused little trouble, tried to defend herself.

"Step out," the teacher responded.

"Can you say please?" replied Zayna.

"No, step out."

"So, I'm not stepping out."

The class burst into laughter. Zayna's standing up to the teacher had emboldened the rest of the class. The volume in the room increased and desks began to shift and tilt in the air. The teacher asked Zayna for her mother's phone number.

Ms. Wasulik now entered the conversation, speaking in a harsher tone.

"You think you're all funny. I can call all your mamas too. You don't disrespect anyone in this school, not yourself, not anyone in this school," she said. "Zayna, I'm not impressed by your behavior, you're an ambassador of this school." Student ambassadors were carefully selected for their academic and behavioral excellence because they acted as representatives for the school, giving school tours and helping out at school events.

Initials flew on the board. By the end of class, five students had lost their points and eleven had received warnings, the vast majority of these occurring in the last minutes of class.

Dream Academy appeared orderly and had few fights, but students constantly were engaged in subtle forms of resistance like the ones displayed during Ms. Wasulik's class. When a teacher's back was turned or a teacher did not enforce rules consistently, students quickly took advantage. They combed each other's hair, sneaked into backpacks, tore up papers, took off their shoes, displayed colorful socks, pretended to sit without being on the chair, leaned their chairs back on two legs, erased names off the infraction list on the board, and stealthily played games like passing a packaging air pillow around the room while avoiding the teacher's notice. Moreover, students became sticklers to the rules themselves, obeying them in law but not spirit. For example, if a teacher put forth the expectation of no talking, students tapped on their desks or hummed. As sociologist Erving Goffman wrote of tightly controlled institutions like prisons and mental asylums, "Where enthusiasm is expected, there will be apathy; where loyalty, there will be disaffection; where attendance, absenteeism; where robustness, some kind of illness; where deeds are to be done, varieties of inactivity . . . each in its way, a movement of liberty."[5] Resistance became a way for students to express themselves in an institution where their identities were severely constrained.

Students are not passive actors but have their own agency to resist and modify school practices. Students resist authority in all types of schools, but as Ms. Wasulik had noted to me, students seemed particularly reactive at Dream Academy. As we will see, this was not a hostile overreaction but the product of being in a school environment where teachers were granted little flexibility to deviate from the school's rigid behavioral scripts.

Different explanations have been proposed for why low-income students and students of color engage in acts of resistance at school.[6] One explanation of student resistance suggested by sociologist Frederick Erickson is that students withhold assent when teachers and schools lose their legitimacy. In other words, if students do not trust their teachers or do not believe that school rules are fair, they will be more likely to resist. Further, Erickson argues that in order to follow authority figures, students need to believe those authority figures have good intentions, that their own best interests will be taken into account, and that authority figures are respecting their identities.[7] Even if cultural differences between teachers and students exist, students will not necessarily resist school if trust is maintained.

Researchers have found that students support strict disciplinary policies *if* they perceive school rules and teachers as fair. In schools where consequences are viewed as unfair, strict disciplinary policies are associated with negative academic outcomes and higher student resistance.[8] Thus, while students in stricter schools may behave better, the opposite may hold in cases where school discipline is not perceived as legitimate. "For discipline to be effective, students must actually internalize school rules," sociologist Richard Arum writes. "This internalization occurs much more readily when school discipline is equated with the legitimately exercised moral authority of school personnel."[9] Being strict is foundational to a teacher's gaining authority; however, being *too* strict can result in losing legitimacy.

In the incident in Ms. Wasulik's class, we can see how students may have questioned the fairness of school rules and the legitimacy of teacher authority. Ms. Wasulik's resetting of exit procedures near the end of the year may have felt oppressive and unnecessary to these eighth-grade students, reinforcing their feelings of being treated like little kids. It was in the instances when teachers tried to exert greater control that I saw student resistance increase. Zayna's outburst was prompted by her being given a consequence when several other students were also talking during this time but were not called out. When students felt like they were unfairly accused, they often protested. By the end of class, we saw rising tensions between students and teachers, with Ms. Wasulik shifting from her friendly banter to a clear disciplinarian role and the students shifting from individual acts to collective resistance to their teachers' authority.

In the next sections, we will examine in more detail how the school's rigid behavioral scripts undermined teacher legitimacy by making students at times feel unfairly targeted, wrongfully accused, and disrespected. We will see how racial dynamics between the largely White teaching staff and the school's Black and Latino students exacerbated these tensions. We will also see how the school's sense of urgency allowed little unstructured time for students and teachers to develop more positive relationships with each other. As a result, many students began to develop a *sense of antagonism* toward their teachers opposite to the *sense of ease* learned by their affluent White counterparts.

Picking On Everything

No-excuses schools "sweat the small stuff." Under a sweating-the-small-stuff approach, authority is exercised over "a multitude of items of conduct—dress, deportment, manners—that constantly occur and constantly come up for judgment."[10] "Picking on" students is part and parcel of a sweating-the-small-stuff model, but teachers' constant attention to minute student behaviors led to the unintended consequence of students feeling unfairly targeted and aggravated, viewing their teachers as out to get them. "Oh, my God, it just irks me," complained Tyrek, a Black eighth grader. "They like try to—it seems like they're trying to push you overboard. They want you to go to the extreme."

One of the primary tasks of teachers, besides executing their lesson, was to constantly remind students of the school's behavioral expectations and monitor them for compliance. Teachers like Ms. Anderson, whom we met earlier in new student orientation, were adept at continually narrating expectations for student behavior and scanning the classroom for compliance, all without interrupting the flow of their lesson. On the half day of school before Thanksgiving, I watched Ms. Anderson correct the behavior of several students and assign three consequences within minutes of her entering the classroom.

"I need everyone to sit correctly in their seats," Ms. Anderson began as she walked in. "Luis. Luis." Luis sat with his legs turned to the side. "David, I need you to focus and work." Turning to her coteacher, Ms. Anderson thought aloud, "I'm getting a little nervous that during team time today, we're going to have to have a silent team time." A few minutes later, she changed her strategy from a threat to positive reinforcement. "Let's forget about who's talking and focus on our math drill like so many of our teammates are doing," she encouraged. "A lot of people are doing the right thing." Giving out a verbal warning and then a detention, Ms. Anderson announced, "Brandon, that's a one, I'm sorry, a two." Gesturing to a girl slouched over, she continued, "Shaniya, sit up. Shaniya, sit up." Catching two students talking, she gave out two more warnings. "Micah, that's a one, stop. Grace, that's a one, stop."

Ms. Anderson was so accustomed to scanning for behavioral infractions that when she went to interview at a no-excuses charter school in the state to which she was moving the following year, she described having a visceral reaction to teachers ignoring students' noncompliance with school expectations. "It made my skin crawl," she recounted. She was so uncomfortable that she eventually said something to the assistant principal who was showing her around the school. "I say, 'Are students allowed to wear hats in the building?' 'No.' 'Are students allowed to wear—have their phones clipped to their belts?' 'No.' I watched a child have both the things clearly visible, and probably about eight adults, including the assistant principal, who was about two feet from the child, not address it at all." This experience made her realize how habituated she had gotten to monitoring for and picking up on minor student behavior.

Ms. Anderson, however, admitted that she can sometimes become overly focused on catching student misbehavior. While the Catholic school she attended herself had rules but "didn't really push them," here it was natural to push rules because "you're always scanning; you never stop looking." She gave an example from earlier in the day when she picked a

fight with a student who was fanning herself, first with a paper and then
with her hand. Without air conditioning, the school was very warm on this
last day of May, and it was reasonable that the student would be trying to
cool down:

> I'm sitting there, and I'm like, "Why am I—I'm telling Grace to stop
> fanning herself, but it is ninety-five degrees in this classroom; why am
> I picking a fight over this?" You know, it's, like, it's just—and I think
> that's kind of the double-edged sword of a no-excuses environment, is
> that it's pushing me to pick up on everything, and call out everything,
> and notice everything. Whereas, in some cases, logically, it's like, let
> me step back and think about this for a second. Why am I fighting this
> battle again? You know, and I think that that's one of the hardest parts,
> is walking that fine line.

In hindsight, Ms. Anderson recognized that she should not have reprimanded Grace for fanning herself on this ninety-degree day, but she was
so used to noticing any slight deviation from school policy. As a result,
Grace received a detention.

Ms. Russo, a White teacher in her mid-twenties, also felt she sometimes
went too far in monitoring her students. She told me that she was the "joke
of the school" her first year at Dream Academy and thought she was going
to be fired because she struggled so much with classroom management.
Over time, though, she had internalized the school's behavioral practices
to the degree that she described herself as "obsessed" with securing full
behavioral compliance. As an example, she explained how she needs to
see all students holding their violin on their legs in rest position before
they play: "I think I've become a little crazy with some stuff. You know,
like I feel like I become obsessed over things. Like in orchestra class, if the
whole class isn't in rest position I freak out. Like rest position—really I
yelled at—I raised my voice at a student who was just playing too fast—like
a little fifth grader. Like, you're going too fast. And it was a lot—my tone
was much harsher, and I'm, like, oh my gosh, I'm crazy." Because it takes so
much energy to ensure students are following every rule, the work of discipline can come to dominate teachers' attention. Focusing exclusively on
the means, teachers can forget the ends. Sociologist Robert Merton calls
this *goal displacement*. "Activities originally conceived as instrumental are
transmuted into ends in themselves. The original purposes are forgotten
and ritualistic adherence to institutionally prescribed conduct becomes
virtually obsessive."[11]

Obsessing over student behavior can keep all students on task. Both Ms. Anderson and Ms. Russo ran a tight ship and produced results: consistently high test scores from Ms. Anderson's students on the state's math exams and awe-inspiring performances from Ms. Russo's students. On one December evening, families packed into a local college theater for Dream Academy's winter concert. The front of the stage and banisters had been lined with glittery red and white garlands, and the three microphone stands each had been adorned with a holiday ribbon. Large gold, silver, and red stars rested against the side of the stage. The students look transformed in their white dress shirts and black bottoms; one boy sported a black-and-white polka dot bow tie. The highlight of the evening was Ms. Russo's sixth-grade orchestra. As they concluded each of their pieces, they held the last note, then lifted their bows together in perfect unison, and kept their bows steady in the air until Ms. Russo's hands dropped down to shouts of approval from family members. The pickiness that Ms. Russo had exacted from her students had yielded much fruit, to great effect.

So much focus on consistency and regulation, however, can produce adverse consequences. Subject to constant nagging for seemingly harmless behaviors, students received the impression that their teachers were picking on them or out to get them. "If you don't put your name on your homework, you get a detention," said Brandy, a Black eighth grader. "If you are one minute late, you get a detention. If you breathe really hard, you get a detention. When we get too loud, they get mad." By constantly attending to student behavior, teachers aggravated students and amplified situations. For example, during one class, Ms. Anderson walked over to Damien, a Black fifth grader who had slid his shoes off and put his feet on another chair.

"First of all, put your shoes on," she told him.

"Can you leave me alone?" he responded. She pulled the chair out that he had rested his legs on. "Oh my God, can you just leave me alone?" he repeated. She directed him to push his chair in closer to his desk, and he begrudgingly inched it in.

"That's what you lose credit for, the little outbursts," Ms. Anderson replied. She fetched his "bench" clipboard and started writing something on it. He said that he already had lots of days on "bench," a punishment where students had to wear a yellow shirt and lost privileges for the day including speaking to other students (see chapter 2). Again he put his feet back on the seat. She came over and pulled the chair out from under his feet.

"Can you just leave me alone?" he snapped.

"No, I can't leave you alone," she said matter-of-factly. "It's my job to get you to college."

"My stomach hurts," he complained.

"Your stomach doesn't hurt that much, otherwise you wouldn't be here." In a louder voice, she warned him, "Don't even think about putting your feet on the desk."

Damien, who had difficulty sitting still in class, responded sharply to Ms. Anderson when she corrected his behavior. While he spoke in a sharp tone to Ms. Anderson, had he been left alone, he may not have reacted so negatively. This interaction resulted in Damien's staying on bench for yet another day; to get off bench, students needed to have their teachers check off on their clipboards that they had demonstrated appropriate behavior in class.

Black eighth-grader Alexis recounted to me an incident in which she had lost her temper because her teacher had kept prodding her. Earlier in the day, at lunch, she had gotten into an argument with another student because he did not say hello to her. When she jokingly accused him of not acknowledging her, he became offended. She thus entered her next class upset. Admitting to a short temper, she tried to calm herself down by putting her head down on her desk, but her teacher started "poking me, yelling my name." She explained,

> That's actually gonna make me want to snap on you even though you didn't do anything. . . . If a child is just quiet, not messing with anybody and they're mad, like you should respect that 'cause I'm not disrupting your class, I'm just trying to sit down, trying to recollect myself. But yet you all come over here and mess with me and then get mad saying I'm disrupting your class when you just disrupted me trying to calm down. Because like when I'm mad, people know when I'm mad. You can just tell without looking at my face, you can just tell my body language. But yet these teachers just keep on pulling at you.

Instead of reading her body language and knowing to leave her alone, her teacher felt compelled to follow the school's rules and not grant her a minute to be off-task. In this way, her teacher was not giving her the opportunity to practice self-control, as discussed in chapter 3. During my time at the school, I observed teachers refusing to allow students who said they had a headache to leave their heads down on the desk, or prodding to attention students who looked like they were staring into space. As we will see in chapter 6, some teachers did modify and resist the school's scripts; however, overall, they were given little discretion in enforcing them. The inflexibility of teacher practice led to overbearing teacher behavior.

Ms. Larkin, the first-year teacher who questioned whether students were learning to self-regulate, felt that her students behaved better when she refrained from constantly nagging them. She tried to create a classroom environment that was "productive and calming for the kids, instead of aggravating them, punishing them." She found that students responded to her approach to discipline:

> And I feel like, constantly, the kids are so angry, you know? I feel like, in so many ways, I need to make up for the other classes because they're so stressed out usually when I get them that unless I do something funny and silly, you know, it's going to be a rough class. . . . Of course, like, at the start of the year when I was trying to . . . just adhere to these rules, I had so much more difficulty. I had students just not even want to talk to me, so mad, you know? And now I have those same kids that I just— they want to spend time with me. And they want to—they come into my classroom and they're happy.

Teachers, however, had limited means to modify the school's rigid behavioral scripts. Teachers like Ms. Larkin were reprimanded by their supervisors for not following the school's approach, which was seen as necessary for maintaining consistency and order.

Feeling Unfairly Accused

A second unintended consequence of the school's close and constant monitoring of student behavior was that it led students, at times, to feel unfairly accused. When rules are ubiquitous, students become keenly aware of the rules and the processes by which they are enforced. Immediately after teachers issued a consequence, it was not unusual to hear a student protest: "What did I do?" or "It wasn't me!" At times, these reactions were aimed to provoke, but in many situations students felt that their teacher had made a mistake. Yet in nearly all the interactions I observed, teachers instructed students to defer to their authority even when students disagreed with the teacher's judgment. Moreover, students who argued with their teachers often increased their consequences from talking to showing disrespect to the teacher, as we saw in the interaction between Zayna and her teacher at the start of the chapter.

Shariece, an eighth grader, described this cycle:

> Say, for instance, you get in trouble and you got the freedom of speech to explain it, what you did, what you didn't do. When it came to Ms. Wasulik, she didn't care, like, she'll go based on what she thinks she saw or heard and you wasn't able to explain what you actually did or said. And when you did try to explain it, she had this three-strike system: it was warning, points, and then detention, then call home. And if you tried to explain to her what you did, then she'll just put you on next strike, saying, "I know what I saw" or "I know what I heard." She assumed a lot of things.

Shariece compared teachers' not giving students the chance to defend themselves with the "freedom of speech" guaranteed to the accused. The connection she made between schools and citizenship is one that many education scholars have also reflected on. Schools have long been viewed as critical to sustaining democratic society by producing citizens who can express their opinions, deliberate a point of interest, and advocate for themselves. A number of educational scholars have raised concerns that the strict controls and limited interaction in no-excuses schools reduce opportunities for students to develop these active citizenship skills.[12]

Without an opportunity to defend themselves, students could find themselves wrongfully punished. This sense of unfairness could be personally distressing. I observed this one April afternoon as I was sitting in the teachers' offices. Sarah, a Black sixth grader, had been sent down to see Ms. Rivas, who had been taking over some of the student affairs responsibilities. Students were sent to Ms. Rivas for serious behavioral incidents that resulted in benching. Sarah explained to Ms. Rivas that she had gotten permission from one of her teachers, Ms. Scaduto, to use a wet rag for gym class because she was hot, but another teacher took the rag out of her hand and threw it out. At the school, students were not allowed to have any items on them except those required for class.

Ms. Rivas asked Sarah if she had explained to the teacher that she had been granted permission to use the rag. Sarah affirmed that she had.

"Were you yelling when you said it?" Ms. Russo inquired.

Sarah demonstrated how she had spoken, not in an offending voice. She told Ms. Rivas that the teacher threatened her.

"A detention is not a threat," Ms. Rivas countered.

"To me, it is, she made me feel—all the teachers be straight mean to me for no reason," exclaimed Sarah. "I hate this school."

"If you talk, I bet this won't happen. . . ."

"They make me mad. They be yelling at me first."

"Would you yell back at your mom?"

"No."

"These are the ones who will help you get to college."

"No, they're giving you detention for no reason," Sarah insisted. "If you don't have a pencil, you get a detention. If you don't stop saying, 'it's hot,' I'll give you a detention."

Sarah told Ms. Rivas that she would get witnesses to validate her story. At this point, Ms. Scaduto arrived at the cubicle and explained that she had allowed Sarah to keep the towel over her head.

"You gotta be trusting me, too," Sarah pleaded. "I said the same thing."

Ms. Scaduto explained how Sarah had gotten very upset, that it was understandable, but Sarah kept making very disrespectful comments under her breath about the teachers and the school. Ms. Scaduto looked over at Sarah. "If you had just talked . . . ," she began.

"But she was helping somebody, she wasn't even listening," cried Sarah. "She jumped in and just started yelling."

"You completely shut down," said Ms. Scaduto. "You didn't learn anything."

"She's right," Ms. Rivas affirmed. "You need to let me have a chance to help. All you had to do is say something."

"This school's hot, this school's horrible," cried Sarah. "I wouldn't send my kids there."

She broke down in tears. Another teacher who was working in the office came over to give her a hug, also asking if she spoke in an appropriate way with the teacher. Although consequences were not fun, she added, they were not a big deal. It was like when she speeds and gets a ticket.

Sarah's emotional reaction to being wrongfully accused and then given a detention for trying to defend herself illustrates the personal toll that teachers' mistakes can have on students. In the moment, the teacher, busy with other students and keeping an eye out for rule breaking, may have raised her voice at Sarah instead of listening to what she was saying. Teachers, short on time and tasked with patrolling student behavior, sometimes overstepped their boundaries, leading students to feel disrespected. But when Sarah tried to explain her situation, she lacked the self-control to do so in an appropriate way and thus was benched for speaking disrespectfully. Ms. Rivas and Ms. Scaduto, while trying to teach Sarah how to communicate effectively with authority, did not acknowledge Sarah's feelings of injustice at being wrongfully accused. While this was only one incident, Sarah had developed a negative impression of the school and teachers from the many interactions in which she felt picked on and given consequences "for no reason."

Racial differences magnify these tensions, with Black and Latino students perceiving White teachers exerting arbitrary power over them. It is impossible to understand school discipline without attending to the history of racialized social control in the United States, extending back to slavery.[13] Students were keenly aware of how race colored their interactions and unfair treatment. In my classroom observations, I heard students mutter "racist" under their breath at teachers who they believed were unfairly punishing them. During one class in which a White male teacher, in lieu of showing a movie, had students write out a full-page apology note for not behaving appropriately, a group of Black boys mumbled to me that their teacher was racist and asked me whether I could teach the class. On another occasion, a Black girl accused another White teacher of being racist because she was assigned a detention for talking when other students were also talking.

One afternoon, as I was sitting in the teachers' offices, Ms. Harvey, one of the school's four Teach for America teachers, all of whom were White, recounted an incident that had happened earlier. "I was hysterically crying," she told me and the teacher sitting next to her, noting that she does not cry often. She explained how she had called the mother of one of the Black boys in her class because the class had been misbehaving that day. When she gave the phone to the student to talk to his mom, as teachers sometimes would do, the boy cried and told his mom that his teacher had disrespected him. The mom then proceeded to scold Ms. Harvey for disrespecting her son by yelling at him when other students in the class were also talking. "I don't know what college you went to but the one I went to didn't teach us to yell at kids," Ms. Harvey relayed the mother's words. The mother then told her, "You're different than the children here. You will never be able to understand them, maybe you should consider that." Ms. Harvey told us that the Black school secretary, on hearing this story, jumped in to translate what the mother meant by "different": "You're White, I'm Black." Ms. Harvey told us she was shaking while on the phone, and was still visibly upset.

Ms. Harvey, who on that day was wearing a hot pink long-sleeve button-down shirt with her blond hair pulled back in a side ponytail, *was* different from many of the students she taught. She grew up in what she described in an interview as a "very comfortable" living situation, where she "never had any needs," and from a young age, and early on, became a "perfectionist" who studied a lot and performed well in school. In the interview, she explained that it was hard for her to understand some of her students' behaviors "because in how I was raised, in my household, that was not allowed, and I was taught that from an early age, so I never tried it. And when I have a student screaming in my face, or cursing at me, or bumping into me, that is what really gets me over, and I'm not always able to keep my composure the way that I should." Ms. Harvey, unfamiliar with her students' personal lives and befuddled by their behaviors, could not connect her students' experiences with her own, attributing them to differences in her students' upbringing rather than the students' resistance toward the school's scripts.

We can understand how Ms. Harvey, who was working seventy-hour weeks between the school's demands and her Teach for America classes, was hurt by this parent's critique. As I will discuss in chapter 6, no-excuses schools intentionally recruit *mission-driven* and *coachable* novice teachers because they are seen as more willing to adhere to school scripts; these predominantly young White teachers, however, typically have had limited prior experiences interacting with racially diverse students and may be ill-prepared to address issues of race and racism.[14] Studies have found that White teachers often take a color-blind perspective, invoke deficit thinking about their students, and take on a "White savior" attitude that draws on a narrative of rescuing students of color from their families and communities instead of recognizing students for their assets and strengths.[15] Teach for America also has been criticized for taking a market-based approach to education reform that attributes the failures of traditional public schools to bureaucracy and mismanagement, not preparing its teachers to understand the structural roots of educational inequality.[16] As we can see, Ms. Harvey had not been prepared to recognize how her own implicit biases may have shaped her interactions with her students nor to understand this parent's critique. At the same time, this parent was right to be frustrated at her son being inappropriately disciplined by a young, White, inexperienced teacher who lacked the cultural competence to understand and respond effectively to student behavior and perceived mistreatment. Culturally responsive classroom management methods ask teachers to recognize how the broader social, economic, and political contexts shape institutional practices and attend carefully to how their own biases shape their work with culturally diverse students.[17]

To their credit, Dream Academy leaders did recognize that not giving students an opportunity to defend themselves was a serious problem. They tried to ameliorate this by instituting the "W sign," standing for "When can we talk?" Students could raise three fingers in a W sign when they wanted to talk to a teacher about a disciplinary matter; the teacher was supposed to write a pass for the student to come back later in the day for a conversation. The W sign, however, did not provide an effective solution: some teachers ignored the sign, did not have free time to meet with students, or grew frustrated with students misusing it.

Troubleshooting the W sign was a topic raised in multiple staff meetings. In one staff meeting, Ms. Williams, who had become principal, urged teachers to "please just acknowledge the W sign." She explained that it was important to "give students an outlet to communicate." Teachers in the meeting, however, pushed back. One teacher explained how "it's honestly been driving me crazy" because she had two students who used the W sign every single day. She described the W sign as a "crutch for them." Another teacher talked about how her students put the W sign up for problems they could solve on their own. Ms. Williams acknowledged that some students had little self-control and would use the W sign inappropriately, but "we can't really disregard it no matter how silly it seems." Ms. Anderson agreed. "The purpose is to give them voice. I am hesitant to put limits on it." Despite the school's efforts to give students some voice, the W sign failed to alleviate students' concerns and did little to address the underlying problem of the fairness of school rules.

Feeling Disrespected

"You are absolutely silent," Ms. Rivas instructed the eighth-grade class lined up in the hallway outside of her classroom. "I'm looking right now and I'm appalled at what I see. You should be on the second full square and you should be forward-facing and your hands should be at your side." The class, shuffling in from lunch, now worked itself into a straighter line. At Dream Academy, students moved through the hallways in single-file lines, walking on a particular row of tiled squares on the floor. Since summer orientation, school leaders had emphasized the importance of entering the classroom silently and encouraged teachers to have students "do it again" until they met expectations. Today, the redo process was taking longer. "It is not that difficult," Ms. Rivas repeated to the students in an exasperated voice. "Don't be upset when you get a consequence because I'm giving you an opportunity to demonstrate self-control and fix your own behavior." Suddenly, a loud burp interrupted the silence, followed by peals of student laughter.

A short Black girl standing in front rolled her eyes at me and let out a more muted burp. I could hear, but not identify, the sources of the other sounds—coughs, throats being cleared, more burping. Not hopeful that the class would fall in line, Ms. Rivas began sending individual students into class to begin silent packet work. Now fifteen minutes into class, nine students remained in the hallway. "Those of you who want to stay out here and act ridiculous, you can proceed to stand," Ms. Rivas lectured them. A boy tried to speak, but she quickly cut him off, "You need to keep your mouth shut. You are being treated like a baby just because you can't exhibit self-control." Two hands sprung into the air. "I didn't ask any questions, hands down." One of the students dropped his hand but kept his arm raised. "I said hands down." "It is down," he replied. "Arm down." In slow motion, he dropped his arm to his side.

Incidents like these, where students and teachers were pitted against each other in a power struggle, were not uncommon at Dream Academy. Ms. Rivas, moreover, was a warm teacher who was strict but not extreme in measure. In this interaction, she did not yell at the students, and she explained her reasoning calmly. Yet she told students that they were "act[ing] ridiculous," that they needed to "keep your mouth shut," and that they were being "treated like a baby." These kinds of comments were disrespectful to students. Students, in turn, reacted by engaging in minor acts of resistance, not complying with Ms. Rivas's demands for silence and forcing her to waste nearly half of the instructional time on that day.

In addition to feeling picked on and unfairly accused, a third source of student frustration and resistance toward their teachers came from feelings of being disrespected. Students felt disrespected when teachers got "too personal." Examples of teachers getting too personal included yelling, getting in a student's face, tapping or touching them, snapping fingers at them, and making sarcastic remarks. When I interviewed two Black eighth-grade girls, they articulated this complaint. "All right, these teachers be thinking they our parents," Shariece explained. "They holler at us and they get in our faces. That gets me mad." Her friend, Kia, added, "And they snap at us like we dogs." She demonstrated, "They do this [snap], they be like [snap]." At Dream Academy, teachers snapped to get students' attention because it was a quick and nonverbal way to redirect students, but students took this action as disrespectful. Kia complained that she received a detention for telling her teacher, "You don't come in somebody's face and snap in their face, what is wrong with you?" In his study of Black males who had attended a no-excuses high school, education scholar Ramon Griffin found that teachers' condescending tone and close proximity to students when speaking to them in some cases retriggered students' previous traumas. He argues that vulnerable students who have suffered trauma need affirmation and support, not "a culture of stress, bullying, belittling, disproportionate discipline, fear, envy and favoritism" experienced by the students in the no-excuses school.[18]

Students pointed out the double standard that the school held around behavior. The school expected them not to yell while their teachers yelled at them. Teachers punished students for displaying an attitude, when teachers also lost their cool and spoke in an unprofessional way. If the school expected students to control their temper, then students expected teachers to follow this same expectation because teachers were older and more experienced. As Alana, a Black eighth grader, told me in an interview, "What I don't get is when, all right, when a student disrespects a teacher, it's a whole entire adventure and problem, but when the teacher disrespects the student, it goes straight to consequence [for the student]."

Sociologist Elijah Anderson has written about the centrality of respect for surviving in the inner city for marginalized youth of color. Maintaining respect—being treated right—is part of the "code of the street," and slights to one's respect often result in retaliation and violence.[19] When I asked students what respect meant to them, several referred to this reciprocal notion of respect: "You have to give respect to get respect." This meant that when students did not feel respected by their teachers, they felt they needed to show disrespect back to maintain their reputations. For example, when I asked Black eighth grader Tyrone what he should do if a teacher gives him "attitude," he answered, "I think it should be sit there and take it, because there ain't no way, there ain't no way you're supposed to battle with a teacher because they're always going to win no matter what." He explained, however, that his mom taught him to not sit silently if someone disrespected him: "Because I wasn't raised like that—I'm not raised to sit there—if somebody says something to me and I don't say anything back. I was taught that if somebody disrespected me that you've got to give respect to get respect. So if they're not going to respect me, I'm not going to respect you. And they think that calling their parent—they call your parent that you're going to be in trouble. I act this way because I was taught this way. It's not like I'm going to get in trouble for acting this way." To prove his point, he told me how his mom came into school last year because one of his teachers was "laying her hands" on students. His mom cursed at his teacher, which resulted in the school calling the police to restrain her. According to Tyrone, his mom is still serving probation for that incident.

School leaders were aware that teachers' attitudes contributed to a negative school environment. During one staff meeting in January, Ms. Williams emphasized to the teachers how she wanted them to increase their positive interactions with students. She explained that saying "You weren't listening to what I said" is a negative interaction. She gave other examples of how teachers could be passive-aggressive. When asking a student to pick something up, a teacher might say, "Look on the floor, what do you see on the floor?" or when a student asks a question, a teacher might respond sarcastically, "What do you *think*?" instead of answering the question. She confessed that she was trying to be more positive herself: "I'm watching my tone and body language, I'm trying, it's hard." Ms. Lopez, a Latina teacher, felt that students' negative feelings toward the school resulted from these types of negative interactions with their teachers. "Sometimes [the kids are] so negative, and I feel like this hate from the kids about the place they're in, and that's not what school should be about, so that worries me a lot," she reflected. "And it's most often because they don't think a teacher's fair. They don't think the system is fair."

In a school where teachers are working tirelessly to close the achievement gap—what Ms. Anderson called the "civil rights issue of our time"— teachers do not see themselves as racist or as promoting racist practices. However, as teachers took on the role of disciplinarians, they became enmeshed in a racist system that perpetuated stereotypes of Black and Brown bodies as needing to be controlled rather than one that humanized students as individuals to be understood, cared for, and respected. It is unlikely that belittling and shouting at students, for example, would be acceptable at an affluent White school, yet these practices are common to no-excuses schools, which serve almost exclusively Black and Latino students.

Ms. Green, a Black mother of an eighth-grade son, explicitly made a connection between what she perceived as teachers' disrespectful actions and a history of slavery and oppression. Recounting an incident in which Mr. Bradley, who is White, yelled in her son's face for refusing to pick up an Oreo (which was not his) off the cafeteria floor, Ms. Green pushed back against what she saw as the principal's racist actions. "My child is not your slave," she commented. "[Mr. Bradley] just thinks—I always say he think he's the 'great White hope' to come save the Black folks, that's what I think he thinks about himself. It's just his arrogance that I don't like. . . . Don't feel like you doing me a favor, 'cause I appreciate what the school is doing, but it's not just you." Invoking metaphors of White do-gooders, she challenged the idea that the school was "saving" her child. While Ms. Green appreciated the school's efforts to teach her son, she asserted that she did not need the school to rescue her child or teach him how to behave—she saw this as her own job.

A Sense of Antagonism

"By coming in joking, talking, cracking on people. . . . The majority of us came in looking a hot mess," Ms. Evans lectured her class. She sent two students out of the classroom. "I had planned to put on sweatpants, relax, and grade some homework tonight. Instead, I'm going to have to call parents to tell them that their students don't know how to enter a classroom. That's ridiculous. Pathetic. Are you serious? I am serious. I've built in support." Ms. Evans told the students that she had put their writing drill on their desk. She had come to their prior classroom to pick them up and set up expectations for entering the classroom. She directed students to "turn and talk" to discuss what else she could do to help them be successful.

Ms. Evans, a Black teacher who had recently completed her two years with Teach for America, had the strongest classroom management of the teachers new to the school. It was early September, and I had already watched Ms. Evans marching many a class of students in and out of the classroom until they were compliant with her expectations for silence. Until now, I had not seen her engaging students in casual conversation or joking around; she rarely smiled. On this day, however, she opened the floor to a discussion about what might motivate the students to transition into the classroom silently. One student suggested an ice cream party; another said that it was on the students—Ms. Evans was not doing anything wrong. Midway through the conversation, Ms. Evans interrupted the conversation.

"This is not a playroom," she elevated her voice at a few students who were engaged in their own side conversation. "You won't want to be joining anyone in a fifth-grade classroom." She then delivered a warning to a student who was out of his seat and talking. When he tried to explain that he had just come in, she sent him out of the classroom to wait in the hallway. The girl seated in front of him spoke up to defend him, but Ms. Evans refused to listen. Her attention was now turned on Aniya, a girl who had been giving her trouble since the start of school. "Bye, I'll see you tomorrow," Ms. Evans turned to her, sending her out of the classroom. "I'm in charge here. This is not your show, it's the Ms. Evans show when you come in here. End of conversation."

On this day, Ms. Evans had tried to reason with her students and treat them more as equals by soliciting their opinions on how to improve their entry into the classroom. This kind of banter is a middle-class style of interaction between adults and children, where adults involve children in extended negotiations instead of issuing directives.[20] But what we see here is Ms. Evans quickly reverting to a more hierarchical relationship to maintain the level of control expected in a no-excuses school. Once some students started having side conversations, Ms. Evans took on an authoritarian role, shutting down the discussion and not providing students who had been accused with an opportunity to speak up and defend themselves. Although most teachers at Dream Academy themselves came from middle-class or upper-middle-class backgrounds, they often took on a more assertive role than they were accustomed to in order to adhere to the no-excuses script, as we will see in chapter 6. Students thus learned a singular script for how to interact with authority rather than a broad set of tools with which to navigate relationships.

Instead of developing a *sense of ease* with figures of authority, most of whom are White, these young Black and Latino kids developed a *sense of antagonism*, learning to be distant, suspicious, and resentful. A sense of antagonism impacts learning and classroom management, but also shapes how students learn to interact with authority more broadly. As sociologist Carla Shedd has argued, students' perceptions of the fairness of their teachers and schools have critical implications beyond the school doors, influencing how they perceive injustice and the legitimacy of social structures.[21]

Sociologist Pedro Noguera writes, "When children are presumed to be wild, uncontrollable, and potentially dangerous, it is not surprising that antagonistic relations with the adults who are assigned to control them develop."[22] Implicit in the rigid controls used by no-excuses schools is a narrative of Black and Brown bodies as "out of control." Such narratives shape the relationships that develop between students and teachers in spite of the positive regard teachers may have for their students. Goffman observed that in tightly controlled institutions like prisons, staff and inmates saw each other through "narrow hostile stereotypes, staff often seeing inmates as bitter, secretive, and untrustworthy, while inmates often see staff as condescending, high-handed, and mean."[23]

"In class, like the teachers always seem like the bad person and the criminal in our mind," said Sydney, a Black eighth grader. "It's not that easy to relate to the teachers or wanna talk to them at school." She went on to note that some teachers "are really cool after school," underscoring how students' views of their teachers were shaped by the strict school environment. It was not that their teachers were intrinsically people they could not relate to; it was that their teachers became seen as disciplinarians whom they did not want to relate to. Once students lost their trust in the legitimacy of their teachers, they could also give up trying to follow the school's expectations. The school's demands became overwhelming, especially for students who did not feel supported by their teachers. When I asked Sydney why some kids were always in trouble, she replied, "They probably feel like there's nobody out there, like, there's nobody that actually cares for them. Like every time a teacher says, 'We're here to help you,' the kids say, no, no, you're here to pressure me and make me feel terrible and you're just stressing me out throughout the day." Students who constantly were treated as bad kids ended up acting that way, creating a self-fulfilling prophecy.[24] For these students, consequences were no longer effective. "Now they're gonna do something about it, like, show I can be bad, I can really be bad . . . and they're going to be rebellious and they're going to say whatever," she continued. "They're gonna push their desk down, they're gonna say 'whoosh' and say, 'I'm out of here,' and just walk out of the class."

To be sure, not all teachers were viewed with distrust or antagonism. Ms. Wallace, the teacher who had led her first protest in second grade, earned the admiration of many students by establishing warmth, control, and high expectations. One technique that Ms. Wallace used, even in her first year of teaching when she was still working to establish her authority, was making sure that her students did not feel disrespected. She would squat down, talk to students when they misbehaved, and pull them outside of the classroom. She tried "really, really hard" not to talk down to students because they were younger and less experienced and tried to give them voice. "I'd talk to them like I would talk to my friend, not like a kid," she said. "I'd tell them, I'm not talking to you like you're a kid. Am I disrespecting you? Tell me if I'm disrespecting you because I want to know."

Over time, she has gotten better at talking with students: "So, it's either like, I can tell you're upset, you know, are you mad or sad? Help me figure this out about what's going on. Is there anything I can do?" If she knows why a student is upset, she will say something like, "Listen, you're frustrated and I'm not saying you're wrong to feel frustrated. I want to understand the frustration. You know, this is about you growing. This is about me growing to be a better teacher for you." Ms. Wallace used methods that are similar to those recommended by alternative disciplinary approaches like restorative justice, where a teacher will have the child explain his point of view, affirm it, and then share her own point of view, asking the child to step back and look at the situation from the teacher's perspective. Together they discuss what the student can do in the future and the consequence the student should receive for the behavior.

Building respect between students and teachers, however, is difficult when teachers are tasked with constantly monitoring student behavior and giving out consequences. This is compounded in no-excuses schools like Dream Academy by the lack of unstructured time when students and teachers can develop more positive relationships. With its *sense of urgency*, the school limited moments for informal banter and unscripted interaction.

A Sense of Urgency

The online stopwatch displayed on the overhead projector screen counted down. At zero, a raucous alarm broke the silence, followed by the sounds of pencils hitting desks, one after another.

"We forgot," Ms. Williams declared. "Pencils up."

Twenty-six little hands raised their pencils in the air.

"When you hear the sound, what should you do?" Ms. Williams asked her fifth graders.

Several hands shot up.

"Put your pencil down," one girl softly offered.

Ms. Williams nodded and reset the timer. It was early in the school year and Ms. Williams was rehearsing classroom routines with her reading class. Here, when the timer for independent work time ran out, students were to immediately stop their work and drop their pencils. The class practiced the drill until a single sound of pencils being slammed on desks was heard.

Continuing on to the next task, Ms. Williams asked students to clear their desks of everything except their worksheet. "When I say go, the only thing I want on your desk is your ELA [English language arts] drill," Ms. Williams directed. "5-4-3-2-1-0."

Ms. Williams scanned the room, dissatisfied. "Do it again, we still have stragglers. We don't have time to waste, we have learning to do. 5-4-3-2-1-0."

In *Teach Like a Champion*, a handbook the school used for teacher coaching, technique 48 is called "Engineer Efficiency." It is defined as, "Teach the simplest and fasted procedure for executing key classroom tasks, then practice so that executing the procedure becomes a routine."[25] It directs teachers to "plan for what they *and* their students will do at every step," and to "practice procedures against the clock, preferably with a stopwatch."[26] In having her students practice dropping pencils and taking out papers, Ms. Williams was working to engineer efficiency. To streamline procedures, teachers had students practice entering and exiting classrooms, walking up and down the stairs, and passing in papers.

Engineer Efficiency could be taken straight out of a scientific management handbook. In the early twentieth century, in response to labor unrest in factories, efficiency experts—many of whom were engineers—sought to find ways to make work more efficient. Replacing the former apprenticeship model by which workers passed down their craft, these experts proposed a new role for management that expanded its role from supervising workers to conceptualizing how work tasks were to be completed. Through the use of scientific study and new tools like the stopwatch, managers figured out the easiest, safest, and quickest way to complete a task, and then produced complete written instructions for how the task was to be completed. This was the birth of the assembly line.[27]

The goal of breaking down and planning out each step of a worker's task is to eliminate inefficiencies and increase productivity. School staff likewise saw mastering routines as leading to increased learning by maximizing instructional time. In an email sent to school staff reminding teachers to keep a tight rein on student behavior during transitions, Mr. Bradley made this point. Copying a section from *Teach Like a Champion*, he quoted, "If you were able to cut a minute apiece from ten transitions a day and sustained that improvement for two hundred school days, you would have created almost thirty-five hours of instructional time over the school year. Practically speaking you would have added a week to your school year."[28] This disciplinary logic seeks not only to avoid wasting time but also to extract more from time.[29] School leaders shared a "sense of urgency" that came from knowing that their students were already significantly behind and had a lot of catching up to do. To make up for lost time and learning, school leaders felt pressure to maximize instructional time. In an interview aired on PBS, Michael Feinberg, one of KIPP's founders, described their work as a "race" and "competition," with the prize being for students to acquire the knowledge, skills, and character to be successful in college and life. "And so there's a tremendous sense of urgency because we know by fifth grade the children we're working with in underserved communities are already behind where they need to be to win that competition and succeed in that race. And so we want to catch them up and get them where they need to be."[30]

School staff explained to students that "sweating the small stuff" eliminates minor distractions, which, in turn, increases time for learning. Dress code regulations, for example, keep students from getting distracted by jingling bracelets or logos on sweatshirts or sneakers. Forbidding items at the desk ensures that students will not be tempted to play with their backpacks or prod their neighbor with a water bottle. Requiring students to sit straight in a SLANT position with their hands folded on their desk keeps students focused on what the teacher is saying. As stated in Dream Academy's charter school application, "Through strong discipline systems, our students spend more time on task, more time paying attention to the teacher, and thus more time learning."

Dream Academy's rigid control of time and space, however, also created an environment characterized by urgency and efficiency where there was little time to slow down and get to know the students. Middle-class and upper-middle-class students learn to see themselves as "special," entitled to their teachers' time, attention, and interest.[31] Students at Dream Academy experienced otherwise. "So, that's the only downfall to sweating the small stuff," reflected Ms. Rivas. "It's like you have to move quickly, quickly, quickly, quickly. There's no time to waste and it's like, you know, sometimes I feel like, oh wait a second, I need a breather, like we're moving too fast. Like, slow down. Or [students] even need to feel like they're being heard, they're not being ignored." Although she saw the drawbacks of moving so quickly, she referred to the school's reasoning to justify its practices. "Like okay, the reason why we line up so quick is because this amount of time is wasted," she said. "When you add, you know, three minutes every single transition every single day, by the end of the year, like how much time did we lose on just how quick we walk into line."

In his seven years of teaching, including his first two in a struggling urban school, Mr. McCudden, a White teacher new to Dream Academy, felt that it had never taken so long to get students on his side. In his first teaching experience as part of a service corps program in a high-poverty urban school, one of the things he learned to do was to relate to kids different from himself. As a recent college graduate from a "pretty middle-class, pretty White, ethnocentric" background, he did not automatically win students' trust at the school, but he learned to relate to them "just by asking questions and talking to kids and living in their situation." Informal times with his students helped Mr. McCudden and his students build relationships with each other. "You know when you're a teacher in the classroom, you talk and you share life experiences and you do stuff together. I don't know, you just over time grow closer," he reflected. At Dream Academy, not until he went on a field trip to an ice skating rink with his students did he feel like he was able to make connections with them.

I also did not realize the extent to which the school's tight structures impacted my ability to get to know students until I visited a traditional public school. There, I noticed how easy it was to find time to chat with the students because they came to eat lunch with their teacher, hung out in the hallways, and had more down time during class. At Dream Academy, when I tried to engage students during class, I felt like I was interrupting them from their work or defying class expectations for silence. Lunch was brief, hallways were silent, and there was no recess. When the school day ended, students who were not participating in structured activities or sent to detention were marched out of the building and not permitted to hang around on the premises. The school did encourage teachers to develop close relationships with students through advising, a relatively less structured time when teachers met with the same group of students throughout the school year, and by urging them to take students out on weekends or after school. I joined one teacher and three girls on an outing to a movie and heard "shout-outs" during morning assemblies and staff meetings for teachers who took students to the mall and to the art museum. These outings, however, were additional to teachers' already filled work weeks, and not all teachers had the capacity to participate.

A sense of urgency is the opposite of "concerted cultivation," the strategy by which middle-class parents develop their children's potential. Middle-class parents engage with their children in constant dialogue and negotiation. They chauffeur them back and forth between organized activities to help nurture their skills and talents.[32] Concerted cultivation takes time and energy. It is an expensive strategy, a middle-class strategy. At Dream Academy, there was no time to deliberate with each student over every broken rule. There were insufficient resources to run an array of extracurricular activities; in fact, Dream Academy canceled its Friday afternoon clubs in order to give teachers additional time for lesson preparation. Unlike in elite boarding schools, there were no communal meals with teachers or shared living experiences. There was little time for students to interact informally with their teachers and develop a "sense of ease" with authority. There was no time for concerted cultivation. There was too much catching up to do.

If we think back to scientific management, we can see how these techniques made factories more efficient and productive, but also eliminated worker autonomy and creativity and deskilled workers so that they no longer developed the tools of their craft. Further, scientific management alienated workers from their work and from management. In adopting scientific management methods, no-excuses schools run the risk of dehumanizing students and distancing them from their teachers, producing "cogs in the machine." As education scholar Martin Haberman observed, "Before we can *make* workers, we must first *make* people. But people are not *made*—they are conserved and grown."[33] I also have previously argued that no-excuses schools create *worker-learners* rather than *lifelong learners*.[34]

In this book, we have seen the different ways in which Dream Academy's behavioral scripts impacted students' attitudes toward success, their skills and strategies, and their perceptions of and interactions with authority, limiting the middle-class cultural capital that these students developed. In the next chapters, we consider the broader implications of scripts for educational policy and practice by examining the expanding role of scripts in the charter school landscape and in teaching and teacher education.

CHAPTER FIVE

Copying a Script

STANDING AT THE FRONT of the room, Mr. Taylor, the Black director of the school, directed the two dozen or so new teachers' attention to the overhead projector. He explained how he had been principal of City Charter School, one of three charter schools that recently had closed in the city. "It looked like this," he said, starting to play a YouTube clip.

To the tune of "Welcome to the Jungle," the video showed a group of Black high school students pushing each other in the hallway, dealing drugs, and breaking windows. This was not City Charter School, he clarified, but the opening scene of *Lean on Me*, a 1980s movie about a failing inner-city school.

"When I was principal of City Charter School, that kind of chaos reigned in my building under my leadership," Mr. Taylor explained. "We had regular fights. We had students who tried to burn down the school, students who brought weapons, teachers who would quit in the middle of the school year, teachers who would work for a month, even teachers who worked for half a day." Halfway into his first year as a principal, Mr. Taylor tried to quit twice but had his resignation rescinded. His troubles were not new. In eleven years, City Charter School had cycled through thirteen principals.

In what he describes as an epiphany, Mr. Taylor was sitting at his desk one day and remembered visiting a successful urban school. "I was struggling with the question of what do I do, how do we fix this, how do we make this thing better? What, what can we do?" he recounted. "And I don't know why it occurred now. I don't know how it occurred to me. The thought occurred to me, 'Wait a second, I've been somewhere that it's working.'"

Mr. Taylor sent two of his staff to visit the school he had remembered and told them to write down every single thing they were doing. "Whatever they're doing, we're doing it," he insisted. One of his staff members cried when she saw the school because she was so impressed at seeing students silently filing down the hallways. By copying the school's practices, Mr. Taylor saw his own school transformed. He estimated that 80 percent of the changes his school made that pivotal year were cultural rather than academic—for example, having teachers escort students in straight lines through the hallway, greeting students at the door when they entered a classroom, and raising two fingers for silence. These cultural changes, however, translated into measurable academic success: double-digit increases in proficiency rates on the state test in every subject and at every grade level.

The school whose practices Mr. Taylor copied is regarded as one of the best urban charter schools in the nation. It is also a no-excuses school. The summer after his successful turnaround, Mr. Taylor drew up a 194-page proposal to found Dream Academy based on the no-excuses model. Despite the progress he had made at City Charter School, Mr. Taylor felt that the district superintendent was not fully supportive of the more structured direction he was taking the school. He therefore decided to leave City and start his own charter school. With him, he took a few other staff from the school, including Ms. Scott, who would later become Dream Academy's dean of student affairs.

When I asked Ms. Scott about her experiences putting together the charter application for Dream Academy, she replied, "We just didn't have any, you know, big egos or anything. And we saw this was working. And so it's not like we sat in a room and, you know—"

"And thought about what would be the best model," I offered.

"Yeah, [it wasn't] let's . . . kind of see what makes it [work]—no, it was like wow, this works? Let's do it."

Organizations tend to copy successful models when they face uncertainty about how to achieve goals and when there are fewer successful models in the field.[1] Schools fit this criterion well. Given the diversity of student needs, there is no standard formula that can be applied to improve schools. Decades of reform have not significantly improved the quality of urban schools, demonstrating the difficulty of the task.[2] Although schools have long copied structures and programs from each other, what may be distinctive here is the copying of a standardized and detailed set of practices—in essence, a script—not just a disciplinary approach or a stand-alone curriculum. Mr. Taylor found that other no-excuses schools were very willing to share their model and materials with him, down to their teaching evaluation rubrics, student assessments, chants, hand signals, rewards and consequences, and computerized disciplinary system. As Mr. Taylor put it, these successful schools sent the message, "If [other schools] wanted to then replicate it in their own typeface, go ahead."

In Dream Academy's charter school application, which details the school's plan for implementation, Mr. Taylor and his colleagues explain that they are copying the "no-excuses approach" used by high-achieving urban schools like KIPP, Amistad Academy in New Haven, and Boston Collegiate Charter School. They report consulting research on no-excuses schools, reviewing plans and practices of other schools, making site visits, and engaging in frequent communications with no-excuses school leaders. The application states, "Our mission and program draw on the program, plans and procedures used by a set of highly successful, high-poverty, random-selection urban middle schools from across the country." These key elements are a focus on urban adolescents, high and clearly articulated expectations, rewards and consequences, more time on task, and a focus on results. Included in the plan are also examples of the detailed behavioral scripts that no-excuses schools embrace. The application notes, for example, that students will focus on learning by "sitting up straight in class with both feet on the floor and all of the legs of the chair and desk on the floor" and respect adults by "standing up straight, facing and looking into the eyes of adults when being spoken to."[3]

In tracing the origins of Dream Academy's model, we will see how the copying of the no-excuses script has facilitated growth in the charter world. However, scripts—which are fixed—may not provide the flexibility organizations need to adjust their practices and priorities and respond to emerging needs and diverse goals. A *script* provides a one-size-fits-all solution that does not equip schools and teachers with the *tools* to navigate shifting expectations. As we will see, the copying of the no-excuses script, not only by Mr. Taylor but by an increasing number of charter schools, has profound implications for the larger promise of charter schools as diverse, innovative institutions that are responsive to community needs.

Educational Malpractice

Mr. Taylor came to embrace rigid behavioral scripts for urban schools after experiencing what he described as "educational malpractice" at City Charter School. Having worked in education for over a decade, Mr. Taylor, who is in his mid-forties, had imagined himself prepared to lead a school. The first in his family to attend college, he had completed a master's in public policy and worked with both charter and public school districts in different administrative capacities. Wanting to move into school leadership, his opportunity came when City Charter School needed a principal to fill in at the end of the school year. The experience turned out to be more difficult than he had anticipated. Recollecting his experiences, he told me how, every two to three days, someone pulled the fire alarm. He had a second grader come to school with bullets. Another student came to school with a razor blade hidden in his mouth. Once, sitting in front of him in his office, a student tried to knife another student.

Various efforts have been made to quell school violence. In the late 1980s and early 1990s, public concern over school violence and safety led to the advent of harsher zero-tolerance policies. Policies like the 1986 Drug-Free Schools Act and the 1994 Gun-Free Schools Act required schools to suspend or expel students who committed certain violent offenses or carried drugs and weapons to school. Although these policies were originally intended to target more dangerous behaviors, schools have applied zero-tolerance policies liberally, meting out suspensions for minor offenses like smoking, disruption, and verbal threats.[4] While suspension rates have soared, particularly for Black boys, these punitive reforms have not made schools substantially safer.[5] The American Psychological Association Zero Tolerance Task Force released a statement declaring that there is no systematic evidence that suspension maintains a safe learning environment or deters future misbehavior.[6] In fact, schools with high suspension rates tend to have low academic performance and poor school climate ratings.[7]

When I asked Mr. Taylor why City Charter School adopted the no-excuses model, he admitted that it was implemented as much for control reasons as for academic reasons. "It was just we could not manage student conduct," he explained. By copying the practices he saw at the no-excuses school, he was able to establish order in his school. Although academic achievement did rise significantly as a result of implementing these practices, at that time elevating test scores was not among his most immediate concerns.

From his experience at City Charter School, Mr. Taylor learned that urban schools needed to be much more hands-on to establish order than he had at first assumed. He found that college practices, where students take responsibility for their own learning, did not translate to an urban context. "College students just do what they're supposed to do far more frequently than in a setting of an urban public school," he asserted. He believes that in an urban context, school staff need to take a more proactive role in setting and enforcing precise expectations. "An important, I think, failure on my part . . . and on the part of many public schools is the failure to understand that the adult has to assert," Mr. Taylor commented. "If the adults want a certain outcome, the adults have to put in a whole series of structures that will lead to that particular outcome."

Ms. Johnson, a White teacher who eventually left City Charter School to work at Dream Academy, described how the school culture dramatically shifted after Mr. Taylor left. Instead of receiving a huge binder of rules and procedures at the start of the school year, she was met with school administrators asking, "So, how do we want to do things?" The school went from having three fights a year to several fights in the first week with police officers being brought in. "There was no discipline at all. And no consequences," she recalled. "It was like a very much, just love, give them more love. You know, we need some toughness here." Within the first couple of weeks, many of the staff left, including a few teachers who just walked out of their classrooms and never came back.

In Mr. Taylor's view, urban schools need to be more prescriptive to ensure that what the adults in the building think should be the norm becomes the norm. In a typical suburban classroom, one or two students may not follow school norms, but they are kept in check by the rest of their classmates. In an urban classroom, Mr. Taylor has observed that five, six, or seven of these norm breakers start shifting the classroom culture, producing a level of activity and disruption that is inconsistent with traditional learning practices. He commented, "That's just a function of everything that comes with an urban environment: poverty, lots of family changes, persons going off to prison or somebody, you know, a parent passing away or a parent in the life who disappears, or a job relocation, or a house relocation, or whatever." These types of traumatic events, which I heard students and teachers refer to in passing conversation, have been linked to behavioral problems among students in school.[8]

Mr. Taylor was not alone in discovering that what worked in urban education was rigid scripts for student behavior. Dream Academy's other school leaders had reached a similar conclusion through their own experiences in urban schools. Mr. Bradley, the school's principal, had his own epiphany as a teacher for Teach for America. He explained how, having grown up in a family of modest means, his first goal had been to make a lot of money. After studying finance in college, he worked in financial services for two years. Then, one day, as he recalled, "I just kind of woke up one morning and had a quarter-life crisis and said why am I doing this?"

He applied to Teach for America in part because he thought the experience would help make his application to a top business school stand out.

Teaching for two years in a struggling urban school in the South Bronx changed his perception about his future and how to teach. He described his Teach for America school as "a really, really bad institution of learning." Like City Charter School, leadership turnover was high. Four principals cycled through during his two-year commitment. The school lacked a common vision, and teachers largely were left to fend for themselves. To give people a sense of the environment, he liked to tell stories of the students running laps around the hallways after lunch until security guards pushed them into their classrooms, slamming the door behind them.

Of the twenty or so teachers in his school, Mr. Bradley found that only three had control over their classrooms—he was not one of them. Similar to Mr. Taylor, he found himself desperate for a solution and began to observe these successful teachers. One was a longtime teacher with over thirty years of experience, and the other two had military backgrounds. Mr. Bradley learned the most from the military teachers, one of whom was also a first-year Teach for America teacher, which impressed him. "[The teachers] were like, yeah, you got to build it, you know, break them down and then build them back up in what you expect and being very, very precise in what you're looking for," he recalled. Following their techniques, he was able to gain control over his classroom, turning it around his first year and having a successful second year. He learned to be very strict and precise, having students repeat procedures until they met his expectations.

Ms. Williams, the Black teacher who replaced Mr. Bradley, experienced a similar learning curve as a new Teach for America teacher in Newark, New Jersey. As a Black woman raised in an urban environment, she shared a background closer to her students but faced similar challenges in the classroom. "I think it was the hardest thing I've ever done in my life," she told me. She found that her school had few structures to support teachers, either behaviorally or instructionally. Because the school lacked any real consequences for students' actions, students did what they wanted. She recalled once teaching a writing lesson with a student who kept opening and slamming the door and calling her all sorts of names. "And I just did not know what to do," she recounted. "I had no support whatsoever. They basically put the basal reader on my desk, put the standards on my desk, and said, 'This is what you have to teach,' and like I tried to figure it out."

Without a role model, she started creating her own structures to help motivate students. She implemented a paycheck system, where students earned a paycheck each week based on homework, behavior, class work, and participation, a template she found "probably from TFA.net [Teach for America] or something." Every Friday, students could exchange their paycheck for fake dollars to spend at her school store, which she stocked with footballs, nail polish, lip gloss, and other items she had bought from Five Below—a store that primarily sells items priced at five dollars or less. Students also had the option of saving their paycheck, and she reminisced about how her students would save their money for something special. "They would save their money so that when holidays came around and, you know, they had events or their family member had a birthday, like they would get something for them out of the store with their money," she remembered. "Or they had little brothers and sisters and like after school on Fridays they would bring them upstairs and let them pick out what they wanted and give me the money for it."

Echoing the "no-excuses" mantra, she noticed that students always had excuses for not doing their homework. To address the problem, she had students who had not completed their homework stand up and recite a poem to the class: "Excuses are tools for the incompetent. They are used to fill monuments of nothingness. And those who specialize in their uses are seldom capable of anything else." By adding this embarrassing consequence, she found that missing homework dramatically declined.

Ms. Williams stayed at her school an additional two years after her Teach for America commitment. It was a difficult decision to leave, but she felt like she was in one of those "school-to-prison pipeline" schools. "This was a dropout factory; this was a school that was, by no means, helping kids to be successful," she said. Moreover, she wanted more support to become a better teacher. During those four years, she had basically taught herself everything she knew. When she saw the mission for Dream Academy, she felt, "it's just totally me." She had never heard of no-excuses schools before, though the KIPP schools had tried to recruit her when she had nearly completed her second year with Teach for America. Within six months of starting as an English teacher at Dream Academy, she was promoted to a team leader, and later instructional dean and principal, taking the place of Mr. Bradley so he could transition to a new position in the organization.

The similarities in what these three school leaders learned about establishing order are striking. To gain control of their classrooms and buildings, they all became convinced that rigid scripts for behavior were necessary. What we will see, though, is that embracing a scripted organizational model introduced new dilemmas for these school leaders. Adopting an organizational script that put strict limits on student and teacher behavior made it difficult to adjust to meet individual and collective goals.

Redefining Success

The no-excuses script worked for establishing order and also for academic achievement. Like the no-excuses school whose practices it had copied, Dream Academy has been recognized by the state as an academically successful school. Among schools serving a similar student demographic, Dream Academy's test scores placed it in the top quarter of its peer schools in the state. Over two-thirds of its students scored proficient on the state's math assessment, and over one-half did so on the state's literacy assessment. For these two important school goals, Dream Academy's organizational script seemed to work. But as school leaders began to question test scores as their primary metric of success, they were less certain that they would be able to adapt the no-excuses script to meet other school goals.

It was a warm April day, the temperature in the eighties. I sat in Mr. Bradley's office listening to him pass on advice to Ms. Williams, who had transitioned a few months earlier to becoming principal. The conversation meandered into a discussion about defining success for teachers. Ms. Williams asked Mr. Bradley how he defined success.

"How do I measure success?" he reflected. "I'm not sure. Getting those emails back from kids who move on and send back their report card."

"Success for me is seeing kids communicate effectively and constructively with adults," Ms. Williams countered. "I can witness a kid trying to have a constructive conversation with an adult and the adult is destructive."

Mr. Bradley noted that she had "hit on a piece of culture" and should share this during a professional development meeting.

"It will spill over into the academic portion," Ms. Williams continued. "Kids really talking, not just giving one word answers. That's what they do at home. They give one-word answers. Kids feel like they can just come and talk to me."

She noted that many teachers viewed success as kids' test scores. "I get it, I want kids to be successful in those things too," she said.

"The first three years, that was my definition of success," admitted Mr. Bradley. "This last year, when I got the [state] scores, I was like, eh. I need to look for a new venture; it wasn't completely fulfilling me."

Mr. Bradley had made student test scores his primary metric for success, which is not surprising given recent trends in education toward measuring a school's success by its students' performance on standardized tests. Passed in 2001, No Child Left Behind (NCLB) was sweeping federal legislation that required for the first time that all public school students in third grade through eighth grade be tested annually in reading and math and that schools report test results differentiated by students' race, ethnicity, low-income status, disability status, and limited English proficiency. The aim of standardized testing was to reveal achievement gaps between students and schools as a first and necessary step toward closing them. However, schools that failed to meet annual performance targets on standardized tests were subjected to sanctions, including student transfer to other schools, replacement of teachers and staff, and school closure. Although no states met NCLB's goal that all students achieve proficiency by 2014, NCLB's emphasis on standards, assessment, and accountability has continued through subsequent legislation at both the federal and state levels. Its impacts have been felt inside schools. Studies have found that as schools face greater pressures to meet benchmarks for student progress on standardized tests, they have narrowed their curriculum to focus on test preparation, adopted more formulaic instruction, and targeted bubble students on the cusp of proficiency.[9] Cheating has also been rampant.[10]

Critical scholars observe that when school and teacher effectiveness is reduced to a single metric—achievement on tests—other vital educational goals, like commitment to children, engagement with local communities, and culturally relevant teaching, are disregarded.[11] Informed by her own school experiences, where she felt she lacked a voice, Ms. Williams believes that there are other educational goals more important than improving student test scores. She wants students to learn to communicate effectively with adults so that they can make social changes. She envisions a school that is less hierarchical, a learning community of kids and adults. Mr. Bradley is also beginning to see test scores as a limited goal.

Teachers at Dream Academy also shared a broader vision of school success. At the first staff meeting Ms. Williams ran as principal two months earlier, she asked the teachers to brainstorm not only the "what" and "how" of their work, but also the "why." The reasons teachers gave for the "why" were lengthy and ambitious and reflected the many aims of education that are not fully captured by students' test scores: "to change the future for our children," "so they can learn from our mistakes," "because we love kids," "because we want our kids to impact the community," "most important civil rights issue of our generation," "some people want to change the stereotype that African American children can't learn," "close achievement gap," "the kids—they shape our future," "to give them opportunities to do things that we did/didn't have," "break cycle of stereotypes," "encourage their dreams," "instill discipline they need to be successful," "because they deserve it."

If the no-excuses script worked well in helping Dream Academy secure student compliance and meet its test score benchmarks, it presented roadblocks to achieving other goals. As we saw in chapter 3, the school's scripts did not provide students many opportunities to voice their opinions, demonstrate leadership, and enact social change. The problem with copying a rigid model was that it was difficult for school leaders to disentangle which practices and structures were necessary and which were auxiliary for meeting their needs. No-excuses practices were seen as a package deal, copied together, and only to be carefully tweaked. Having implemented a rigid script, school leaders found it difficult to adjust it without compromising the integrity of the system.

A Package Deal

When I asked Mr. Taylor to name the school's essential practices, he was reluctant to specify a particular practice or give examples of rules that could be eliminated. If the school were doing a hundred things, he argued, "we need to do ninety-two of them in order for the model to work." The analogy used by KIPP founder David Levin to describe this holistic approach is called one-twelfth. Mr. Bradley described it for me:

> So, they use this analogy—I don't know if you're a baseball fan of like Derek Jeter. So, Derek Jeter gets a hit once every three times he gets up to bat. And then [there is] some no-name baseball player who's been batting .250 for his entire career and nobody even knows who he is. And he gets a hit one every four times he goes to bat. And so, if you look at the difference between Derek Jeter, a sure thing Hall of Famer, all-star every year, the difference between one-third and one-fourth is one-twelfth. And so, you know, our philosophy is really, there's no one thing that we do that just revolutionizes education. It's, one hundred, like little tiny nuanced things that make the difference.

School leaders believe that what makes the no-excuses model work is its many detailed procedures and policies. If it takes a hundred little procedures to maintain order, it seems risky to eliminate even a single procedure. Any tinkering with the system can undermine it, a cost the school is unwilling to incur.

School leaders thus were not incognizant of the limitations of the school's scripts, but they faced a challenge in figuring out how to modify their practices. In the same meeting where Mr. Bradley and Ms. Williams were defining success for themselves, they also talked about modifying school behavioral policies. The lead-in to the conversation was a discussion of which books to send to the new hires for professional development. Mr. Bradley suggested *Smart Parenting*, a book he had been reading as a new father. It's about "making your children resourceful, from a parenting perspective but has a lot of applications to what we do as teachers," he noted. He explained how the book discussed different categories of parents, one type of which is overly critical. "I do tend to think we fall into that," he reflected. "We're very structured, don't let kids figure things out on their own. A lot of kids are already coming from environments where they have self-esteem issues."

Ms. Williams agreed and related an incident in which a teacher at the school confronted her for telling one of her students that she could bring a bottle of water to school on a hot day. This went against the school's "no water bottle" rule.

"I realize we're on the strict side of things, but we have to have that balance," Ms. Williams argued.

Mr. Bradley disagreed. "For years and years and years, we've said no because you're going to get—" He reached over to grab a plastic water bottle on his desk and scrunched it. "You're gonna have 250 kids doing—" He scrunched the bottle again.

"I get it, but as a teacher in my own class, if a student makes that sound, I will tell him, put it in your backpack," argued Ms. Williams.

"The tricky part is you can do that, it's really easy," said Mr. Bradley. "Can Ms. H. do it? Everyone can't handle the kids asking for water. Because your classroom management is so strong. It's why we ban little pencil sharpeners, not everyone can handle it; it's easier to make a rule." He reminded her that little things become big things. "Some of the things we do, it crushes kids' self-esteem. It does."

Although Mr. Bradley had earlier affirmed Ms. Williams's definition of success and questioned whether the school's rigid scripts were best preparing students to be resourceful and independent, he did not budge when Ms. Williams suggested modifying even a small rule. The worry that teachers would lose control if students were given greater freedoms was forefront on his mind. In fact, Ms. Williams had voiced similar concerns in a conversation we had about adjusting school disciplinary practices. While she wanted to extend the thirty-minute lunch period because it was the only time students had in the day to freely talk with each other, when the school had attempted this in the past, it did not work. "It was forty-five minutes and then the kids would kind of spiral out of control because it was too much time on their hands that they were idle after eating," she explained to me. "So, they would get in trouble." She also believes that older students should be able to earn the privilege of walking by themselves in the hallway, but she has never seen silent hallways in the school, not even for a week. To give students hallway privileges, she thinks the school would need to prepare kids to make this transition, and the teachers would also need to be on board. In past years, when Mr. Bradley suggested the idea of giving the older students the ability to walk freely in the hallways, the teachers said no. He explained that the school would need "superstar" teachers in order for a less structured environment to be successful. Dream Academy, however, had few experienced teachers because the school intentionally hired novice teachers who would be more willing to abide by the school's scripts. Without teachers who had the tools to effectively establish safe and engaging school environments, the school depended on a rigid behavioral script to establish control.

The no-excuses script enabled order and achievement. However, it proved difficult to modify to meet local needs (such as the desire to loosen rules) and diverse school goals (like giving students voice). In the last portion of this chapter, we will see how these tensions are reflected on a much broader scale. What we are finding in the charter field is a peculiar situation. The charter school movement, whose original intention was to give schools the flexibility to be more responsive to families and local communities, has narrowed around a group of charter networks operating under the no-excuses model. We will see how copying the no-excuses script has led urban charters to successfully expand, but has also made them less adaptive, reducing the diversity of choices available for families.

The First No-Excuses Schools

We have learned about the significance of copying practices in the story of Dream Academy's founding. Copying also takes center stage in the story of no-excuses schools and how they have spread through the urban charter landscape. Both the inception and the expansion of no-excuses schools relied heavily on copying practices, first from effective teachers of color, then between a group of charter school entrepreneurs, and finally through the support of corporate foundations.

In 1993, David Levin and Michael Feinberg, two young White Ivy League graduates, were in their second year teaching in Houston as part of the Teach for America program.[12] Teach for America, the result of a Princeton undergraduate's senior thesis, was in its early years. After a difficult first year struggling with classroom management, Levin and Feinberg were beginning to improve. They attributed their success to intensively studying and imitating the methods of effective teachers in their schools. Their most influential mentor was Harriett Ball, a charismatic and celebrated forty-six-year-old African American teacher who stood over six feet tall and who worked down the hallway from Levin. From Ball, Levin learned that what worked, in addition to songs and chants, was "instant and overwhelming response to any violation of the rules."[13]

Another model teacher was Rafe Esquith, the 1992 Disney teacher of the year and a fifth-grade teacher in South-Central Los Angeles. From Esquith, KIPP adopted its paycheck system, where students, based on their behavior, earned and lost "dollars" that could be used at a school store. Esquith tells this story of Levin's mimicry: Levin was so enamored of Esquith's example that Levin drove his students all the way from Houston to Arches National Park in Utah so that his students could attend the same field trip that Esquith's students had. Levin had not even come up with a plan for the trip. When he arrived at the park, he called Esquith, telling him he was there and asking what to do next.[14] Esquith was also the inspiration behind KIPP. After hearing Esquith speak at a Teach for America conference and exhorting the audience of new teachers that "there are no shortcuts," Levin and Feinberg spent the evening brainstorming an after-school program to help their fifth graders succeed. By four in the morning, they had outlined KIPP. This after-school program would transform into two successful schools, one in Houston and one in the South Bronx, and grow to become the first, and the largest, no-excuses network.

In reviewing KIPP's founding, we see striking similarities with the founding of Dream Academy. In both cases, novice educators were unable to maintain control over student behavior and ended up copying behavioral practices from other effective teachers and schools to reestablish control. In both cases, copying these practices resulted in high achievement for their students. In both cases, copying practices also introduced challenges.

Early on, KIPP's disciplinary practices were already controversial. In the first year of KIPP South Bronx, one new teacher left because she found

Levin's approach to discipline too harsh. Preferring to establish a more informal relationship with her students, she did not see a need to address a student immediately for every rule broken.[15] In codifying the behavioral practices they had copied from Harriet Ball and others, Levin and Feinberg may unintentionally have made these practices too rigid to be widely effective. Because no-excuses schools like KIPP are often staffed by young, inexperienced, middle-class, White educators, with similar backgrounds to those of Levin and Feinberg, these teachers often lack the years of teaching experience, relationships with their students and communities, and shared racial backgrounds that may have facilitated the use of strict disciplinary practices by Harriett Ball or Rafe Esquith.[16] Researchers have found that the most effective teachers of Black children balance warmth and strictness;[17] teachers not accustomed to delivering this balance might appear too harsh to students. A script, while providing a useful starting point, needs to be adjusted and adapted to individual teachers and schools. At KIPP, however, such disciplinary practices became mandatory. What's more, these practices did not remain only in KIPP; they soon became widely shared with other burgeoning charter schools.

Harriett Ball had given Levin and Feinberg a mandate to share everything she had shared with them with others. In good faith, Levin and Feinberg began sharing materials and practices with other newly developing charters, setting the example for other charter leaders to also openly share strategies. Soon, informal networks of charter founders were observing each other's schools, meeting together, and talking with each other about what was working and not working in their schools. In *The Founders*, Richard Whitmire argues that this open sharing and copying was unusual in the education field and pivotal to the eventual success of these charter schools. Reading through Whitmire's book gives a vivid sense of "who's who" in the no-excuses charter world and how interconnected they were.[18] Nearly all the founders of what we now consider no-excuses charters were part of this early network: Dacia Toll (Achievement First), Norman Atkins (Uncommon Schools), Don Shalvey (Aspire), Tom Torkelson (IDEA), Brett Peiser (Boston Harbor Academy, later renamed Boston Collegiate), John King and Evan Rudall (Roxbury Prep), Doug Lemov (Academy of the Pacific Rim), Chris Barbic (YES Prep), and Eva Moskowitz (Success Academy). It is not by happenstance that no-excuses schools can be characterized under a common name and model even though there is no specific model or philosophy from which they derive.

Although the no-excuses model was spreading, KIPP, like many charters before them, may have remained a small network of schools had Levin and Feinberg not connected with Scott Hamilton, who was working at the time for the education arm of the Fisher Foundation, the family foundation of the founders of the Gap clothing stores. In early 2000, Hamilton worked with Levin and Feinberg to propose to the Fishers a new program (with at least a fifteen-million-dollar budget) to offer business training for charter school founders as a way to expand KIPP. As *Washington Post* reporter Jay Mathews describes in his book, *Work Hard. Be Nice. How Two Inspired Teachers Created the Most Promising Schools in America*, to the surprise of Hamilton, Don Fisher reacted positively to the idea, as he had never before thought about running schools as businesses.[19] The Fisher Fellowship was launched and continues to train charter school leaders today.

The Fisher Foundation was among a group of influential corporate foundations, including the likes of the Walton, Gates, and Broad foundations, that in the early 2000s were developing a new set of philanthropic strategies for education centered around investing in entrepreneurial educational organizations.[20] Attracted by the idea of applying business strategies to education, an "education entrepreneur network" of mostly powerful White philanthropists, venture capitalists, and politicians began to take an interest in replicating and scaling high-performing charters.[21] Charter schools, which were intended to be spaces of innovation and experimentation, began to coalesce around a dominant model, which, paradoxically, would limit the diversity of school options that families in urban communities have for their children. We take a closer look at the nondemocratic power of foundations in shaping the charter school landscape next.

Charter Schools: From Innovation to Replication

The original idea behind the charter movement was to spur innovation and experimentation—to let a thousand flowers bloom. Charter schools come in many shapes and sizes: there are Afrocentric charters, arts charters, and Chinese language charters. There are charters that are exclusively online and those run by for-profit companies. To foster experimentation, charter schools are freed from many regulations governing traditional public schools. Charter school regulations, which vary by state, often exempt them of all state and local laws and regulations pertaining to traditional public schools with a few exceptions, such as those related to health and safety, civil rights, and assessments.[22] This gives charter schools the freedom, for example, to extend the school day and school year, hire teachers outside the teachers union, and develop their own curricula and evaluations. A wide range of actors typically can apply to start a charter—including teachers, parents, community members, nonprofit and for-profit organizations, school districts, and higher education institutions. To start a charter, one has to submit an application to a charter authorizer, which, depending on the state, can be a local school board, a government agency, a university, or a nonprofit organization. Charter schools, if approved, must operate under the terms of the contract set by the charter authorizer and must apply for reauthorization, usually after three to five years. This accountability is seen as the flip side to the greater freedoms granted to charters.

Charter schools, the first of which were opened in Minnesota in 1993, have mixed origins. In the 1980s, Albert Shanker, then president of the American Federation of Teachers, first proposed the concept of charter schools as a way to free teachers from the typical bureaucratic hurdles that restricted their abilities to teach effectively. Shanker believed that the key to effective education was a shift in the education paradigm from replicable, factory-style schools to unique, teacher-led schools that catered to individual communities.[23] In the early charter movement, charters tended to be small, stand-alone schools, initiated by educators or community members, and supported by progressives who wanted to give greater local control to schools.

Conservative support for school choice and charter schools has been tied to the idea of introducing free-market logics into public education. In the 1950s, economist Milton Friedman envisioned an educational marketplace where families, like consumers, had the buying power (in the form of what we now call vouchers) to choose which schools their children attended. He believed an educational marketplace would put pressure on schools to compete with each other for students, so that they would need to innovate and improve in order to survive.[24] This privileging of the free market, private control, and consumer choice reflects a broader global trend since the 1970s toward what has been called neoliberalism. The neoliberal perspective, to which many charter advocates subscribe, is a political economic theory that assumes that the private sector can provide services more efficiently and effectively than the public sector.[25] Public schools are seen as lacking in innovation because they are enmeshed in bureaucratic red tape and constrained by the interests of powerful teachers unions.

Despite the varied philosophies and intentions behind charter schools, a common thread among both progressive and conservative supporters has been the idea that charter schools can be spaces of innovation and experimentation. Both sides have argued that the bureaucratic constraints of public schools inhibit schools from meeting their educational aims and envision charter schools as an alternative space to germinate new practices and structures. The flexibility of charter schools has been a key tenet of their founding.

In the early 2000s, however, a group of powerful foundations and venture capitalists seeking to support market-based reforms in education began to invest in replicating effective charter school models.[26] They organized summits of no-excuses charter leaders and provided seed funding for these charters to develop business plans to grow into charter management organizations, or CMOs. The term "charter management organization," in fact, was first conceptualized in 1999 by Stanford MBA student Kim Smith, who started the NewSchools Venture Fund as a nonprofit to attract venture capital to support education entrepreneurship. Seeing how Silicon Valley had disrupted other industries, Smith saw an opportunity for venture capitalists to also disrupt education by supporting innovations in education.[27]

Between 1999 and 2009, major foundations spent approximately five hundred million dollars to support the development of CMOs to expand and replicate successful charter schools.[28] During that decade, CMOs increased by approximately 20 percent each year, growing at a much higher rate than independent charter schools.[29] By 2009, approximately 16 percent of all charters were under CMOs.[30] In 2015–16, 26 percent of charter schools were operated by CMOs, while 15 percent were run by education management organizations (EMOs), their for-profit equivalent.[31] CMOs are also concentrated in urban areas and serve students of color. A national study of CMOs found that almost 75 percent of CMOs were found in cities; in the average CMO, 91 percent of middle-school students were Black or Latino.[32]

Thus, while early charter schools were single schools run by individual parents, teachers, or community members, charter schools are increasingly dominated by a small network of CMO operators. CMOs oversee several schools, setting goals and standardizing practices, providing legal and financial support, and implementing expansion strategies.[33] They grant schools some autonomy but tend to be fairly prescriptive, making them potentially less flexible and open to innovation than stand-alone charters.[34] In a national study of CMOs, nearly all of the CMO principals reported that they had schoolwide behavioral standards enforced consistently across school, and nearly three-quarters of CMOs required

Table 5.1. No-Excuses Charter Schools

Network	No. of Schools	No. of Students	Locations	Founding Year
Achievement First	37	14,000	NY, CT, RI	1999
Aspire	38	15,500	CA	1998
Democracy Prep	21	6,500	NY, NJ, LA, NV, TX	2006
Green Dot	24	14,000	CA, TN	1999
IDEA	120	66,000	LA, TX	2000
KIPP	255	110,000	Nationwide	1994
Mastery	24	14,000	NJ, PA	2001
Match	3	1,250	MA	2000
Noble Network	18	12,000	IL	1999
Promise Academies	6	1,400	NY	2004
Rocketship	20	9,200	TN, DC, CA, WI	2007
Success Academy	47	20,000	NY	2006
Uncommon Schools	54	20,000	MA, NY, NJ	1997
YES Prep	21	15,400	TX	1998

Note: Data retrieved September 2020 from school websites. Founding year is that of the first school in the network, which in some cases predates the founding of the charter management organization.

students or parents to sign responsibility contracts like the one we saw in chapter 2.[35] CMOs also engaged in more intensive monitoring and coaching of teachers and were more likely to use test scores to evaluate teachers. While not all CMOs are no-excuses schools, many of the highest performing CMOs follow a no-excuses approach.[36] Thus, while charter schools were started as a way to diversify educational options, urban CMOs, in particular, seem to be converging around a similar set of no-excuses practices.

Although there is no official list of no-excuses schools, more than a dozen no-excuses CMOs nationwide serve over three hundred thousand students (see table 5.1).[37] In addition to CMOs, there are many unaffiliated charters that follow a no-excuses model. No-excuses charters thus serve a significant share of the over three million charter school students enrolled nationwide.[38] Moreover, because of their academic successes, no-excuses charters have become a rallying point for advocates of charter schools and school choice. While charters as a whole serve only about 6 percent of all public school students,[39] these schools have caught the imagination of school reformers and policy makers as a potential solution for addressing educational inequities.

If the original idea behind charters was to create a diversity of school choice options that reflected the preferences of families and local communities, the emergence of national charter chains seems to undermine this aim. A concern with the growth of CMOs is that these schools' practices will no longer reflect or be responsive to the needs of local communities. Under a market logic, the definition of the public narrows from society and the social good to the individual consumer, the educational "client" or "customer" who is maximizing her own benefits.[40] What may be beneficial for an individual or family may not be good for the community. While charters have historically received the support of Black communities,[41] CMOs have been criticized for taking a color-blind approach to education reform that neglects the significant role of race in shaping opportunities and characterizes racial groups and communities in need of "fixing" and "saving."[42]

New Orleans is a dramatic case of how charter takeover may not reflect local needs. In the aftermath of Hurricane Katrina, which destroyed or damaged the majority of public schools, the city became the grounds for an experiment in chartering an entire school district. In her critical analysis of the New Orleans case, based on ten years of qualitative research, educational scholar Kristen Buras describes the takeover as an assault on Black communities by White education entrepreneurs who replaced local knowledge in educating Black students with racialized management principles.[43] In chartering the district, approximately seven thousand predominantly Black teachers and staff were fired, many of whom were replaced by novice Teach for America teachers from outside the community. In 2015, one in five students in New Orleans was taught by a Teach for America teacher or alumnus, and thirty Teach for America alumni served as principals in the city schools.[44] Teach for America, in fact, is a key player in what has been called a "parallel education structure" within the public school system,[45] at the center of a web of connections among education entrepreneurs, no-excuses CMOs, charter advocacy groups, and foundations supporting charter schools.[46] Teach for America has intentionally recruited more diverse teachers over the years, and now just over half of its corps members identify as people of color.[47] However, with its model of placing inexperienced teachers in low-income communities of color for a two-year commitment, Teach for America, has been criticized as promoting a missionary or "White savior" orientation that is harmful to urban schools and communities.[48]

Traditionally, many Black community groups have supported charter schools as an opportunity to empower local communities and resist White dominance by restoring parental and community control to schools.[49] However, attempts in New Orleans by Black parents and educators to resist and start homegrown charters with strong ties to the local community were denied approval. Unlike the well-oiled CMOs that were seen as efficient and could demonstrate merit based on a record of improving student test scores, these "organic" charters were viewed by charter authorizers as disorganized and their relationships with children and their communities discounted.[50]

Unless parents can make informed decisions about their child's fit with a school, and have quality options from which to choose, there can be no incentive for charter schools to reflect a community's actual needs. What we then find in the urban charter field is that the market and its "consumers" are not driving the design of charter schools; rather, charter school models seem to be more driven by the needs of schools to maintain control and the desire of corporate foundations to extend market-based reform in education.

In this chapter, we've learned how Dream Academy became a no-excuses school and how no-excuses schools started and spread. It is important for us to recognize the origins of the no-excuses model because its scripts have come to be taken for granted as "what works" in urban education. Organizational theorists call this *institutionalization*. KIPP's paycheck system, its sweating-the-small-stuff approach, its chants, and its consequences have become "prefabricated formulae" that charters like Dream Academy have adopted.[51] Copying institutionalized practices, organizational theorists argue, lends legitimacy to an organization.[52] Had Mr. Taylor and his colleagues proposed an innovative new model, charter authorizers may have had more doubts over whether it would work. As in the case of New Orleans, single charter schools that reflected community values were denied authorization. As the executive director of education at the Gates Foundation explained as its reasoning for supporting CMOs, "We have a better chance of seeing a much higher quality of school when schools are part of a network. You get a proven model."[53]

Organizational theorists, however, argue that legitimacy can conflict with efficiency. In other words, organizations may model themselves on organizations that they perceive to be successful or legitimate, but the practices and structures they copy may not be effective at promoting organizational goals.[54] As a result, organizations can become stagnant not innovative, repeating the same practices instead of trying to figure out what works best for their students, teachers, and communities.[55] The no-excuses rules and systems were accumulated in an ad hoc way and may not serve the needs of each school, student, and teacher, as we have seen in the first half of this book. The system did not rise organically—like the system Ms. Williams developed for her students through trial and error—but was copied and imposed. As more charter schools come to replicate this same no-excuses model, they may become less responsive to local communities and families.

We conclude this chapter by turning to Dream Academy and its families to show how "school choice" can turn into constraint if the market does not provide a variety of desirable choice options.

Schools of Choice

The fact that Dream Academy is a charter school helped school leaders resolve personal conflicts between wanting to serve all children and not feeling able to because of the school's rigid behavioral scripts. As a school of choice, Dream Academy presents itself as one—but not the only—option for children. "We think that for the right families and for the right staff, for the right students . . . we believe that we are an excellent way to get a great education even if we're not for everybody," explained Mr. Taylor. In contrast to those who advocate for expanding no-excuses schools as a large-scale solution to closing racial achievement gaps,[56] Mr. Taylor did not see the no-excuses school model as fully scalable precisely because these schools would no longer be schools of choice.

What struck me most in my conversations with Dream Academy families, however, was how little they knew about the specifics of the school when they applied and enrolled. Besides hearing that it was a good school and that it was strict, they knew few details of the school's practices. Their choice was not an informed choice from many possibilities; it was the only choice they perceived that they had—and for that matter, their choice depended on a lucky spin of a wooden ball.

On a warm evening in March, hundreds of families gathered in the gym of Dream Academy's high school. Rows of metal chairs were filled with parents, grandparents, relatives, and children, each family holding a numbered ticket. The floors sparkled from having just been cleaned. It was lottery day. This year, three hundred families were competing for eighty spots. As Mr. Taylor, the school head, explained, "For these families, it's like winning the Mega Million, the Powerball."

I wandered around the room and entered into conversation with three Black mothers, each vying for a ninth-grade spot. They insisted that the local public high school was not an option for their children—"maybe in the fifties and sixties but it's deteriorating, it's not safe, my kid would not make it there," one mother asserted. The second mother agreed: "They would eat our kids up." The third mother said that if her son didn't get in to the school, she would sell her house and move to an apartment in an adjacent town so he could attend one of those high schools. "My child must have a good education," she insisted. "This is what our options are. We're sitting here with a ticket."

As I circulated around the room, I heard similar stories. One mother had been trying for two years to get her son into the school. In the meantime, she had homeschooled him. They were "getting desperate," she said. Another mother expressed her anger at having no other public options for her children. "I've lived here seventeen years. I pay taxes," she said. "They blame us parents," but her son's school had no music program, art program, or textbooks.

To understand the deterioration in public schools that these parents are describing, we need to recognize that many cities in the United States have become highly racially and economically segregated, and schools reflect these patterns. Beginning in the early twentieth century, discriminatory lending, redlining practices, and personal actions of violence against Black individuals led to the formation of Black ghettos in the inner cities. Segregation of cities was exacerbated after World War II, as many middle-class White families left cities and relocated to nearby suburbs in search of larger houses and more property to raise their children. This phenomenon, often called White flight, was supported by federal investment in highways and low-interest home mortgages for White families. As White families populated suburban areas, their tax dollars fueled strong suburban public schools while leaving urban schools underfunded. Throughout the 1970s and 1980s, public schools in urban areas continued to deteriorate as poor, minority populations became increasingly concentrated,[57] and efforts to desegregate schools through bussing were limited by legal action.[58] By the early part of the twenty-first century, urban revitalization efforts were attracting back wealthy and middle-class White families to inner cities. However, as these families returned, superior public schools began to populate the areas in which these families resided, while other urban areas maintained underperforming schools.[59] School quality thus maintained geographic divisions even within urban locations. Today, most cities have relatively few White children and many low-income Black and Latino children (and immigrants) in public schools.[60]

School choice, from an equity perspective, can be seen as breaking the link between neighborhood and schools, so that children can attend higher-quality schools. The families with whom I spoke indeed saw Dream Academy as an option to get their children out of traditional public schools, but they did not talk about an array of schooling options from which they could choose. With few other charter schools in the city, these families had few choices. Moreover, studies have found that low-income families face practical constraints, such as transportation and child care needs, as well as informational barriers, that prevent them from taking full advantage of school choice. In fact, it is middle-class parents who benefit most from school choice because they are able to engage in the "choice work" involved in researching schools, filling out applications, and following school procedures.[61]

If families were not actively choosing Dream Academy, then the school leaders' logic is flawed. Although no-excuses school leaders have publicly justified their rigid disciplinary practices on the basis that parents are "voting with their feet," many low-income parents are constrained in their choices.[62] Their "choice" is not an endorsement of a school's model per se but reflects the options available in the educational marketplace. While parents tended to be very satisfied with the academics at the school, they expressed more concerns over the school's disciplining students for minor student misbehaviors.[63] For example, Ms. Soto, a Latina mother of a sixth grader, grew frustrated at constantly receiving calls about her daughter's misbehavior. She recalled one phone conversation she had with the school: "I said, 'Wait, did she'—I said, 'did she curse?' No. I said, 'Did she disrespect another student?' No. I said, 'Did she disrespect you?' No. She was humming. I said, 'Okay, what did she do all day?' She was working all day. I said, 'She hummed. She was happy. Don't call me again.' I did not feel bad when I hung up." Like Ms. Soto, other parents also appreciated a strict school but felt that Dream Academy went overboard in their behavioral practices.

In a twist, however, families' purported "choice" of the school turned into an obligation to accept the school's practices, including its rigid disciplinary system. The summer before school began, each new family received a home visit in which one or two staff members came to their home and reviewed the school's five-page contract. As we saw in chapter 2, these families were told that the school was not for every family and that it was their choice to send their student there. Both parents and students had to sign a behavioral contract, with parents ensuring that their children would complete their homework each night, arrive to school on time, and accept school consequences.

Students also are told that it is their choice to be at the school, and if they do not like school rules, they can go elsewhere.[64] I once heard a teacher tell students about the school's long waiting list and how there were other students who would readily take their place. Yet, as was clear on lottery day, students did not always have a choice in the matter. At the lottery, I sat behind a Black girl who was selected from thirty applicants for the fourth and last seat in the eighth grade. When her name was called, her mom raised her arms and exclaimed, "God is good!" The girl, in contrast, tore up the slip of paper with her number. A local newscaster interviewed the pair. The daughter, visibly upset, spoke about how she was apprehensive about changing schools but her mom wanted her to go. "I'm ecstatic," her mom told the reporter. "There were only four spots." Her daughter mumbled, "I wish there were three."

This chapter has zoomed out from the classroom rules and student-teacher interactions we focused on earlier to situate Dream Academy and its rigid behavioral scripts in a broader policy context of no-excuses schools, school choice, and market-based reform. It has also shown how *scripts* can provide useful templates to meet imperative organizational needs, but do not necessarily equip school leaders with the *tools* to adapt these scripts to be more responsive to student and community needs. Scripts can achieve specific ends, like order and achievement, but may not be well suited for meeting the diverse goals schools have. One of the main impetuses for creating charter schools was to enable schools to be more responsive to teachers, families, and communities, yet the no-excuses model demands that families and students adhere to a rigid script that is imposed on them, not chosen by them. In the next chapter, we will see how this script is also imposed on teachers, limiting the tools they develop to manage their classrooms and respond to diverse student needs.

CHAPTER SIX

Teacher-Proof

"I AM FAILING MISERABLY," said Mr. Henig, matter-of-factly.

Mr. Henig, a White first-year Teach for America teacher at the school, was speaking with his supervisor, Ms. Costello, who was in her first year serving as a teacher-coach. It was mid-November and we were sitting in Ms. Costello's cubicle for Mr. Henig's weekly O3—a "one-on-one" conversation between teachers and supervisors intended to provide support and guidance to teachers.

Ms. Costello asked him why he thought he was failing.

"I think it's overwhelming," he replied. "Does that make sense?"

"No. No," she repeated. "Actually, can you give examples?"

He explained how the students would not follow his directions.

"The behaviors won't stop unless you implement the system," Ms. Costello insisted. "You have yet to deliver a consequence."

On her computer, she pulled up the video of his classroom, skipping to different segments. Coaches regularly videotaped newer teachers so they could review their classroom management and instruction with them. She paused the video to point out students calling out, students with their heads down, students with their legs propped up on desks.

"Did you notice that while you're teaching, do you see that there's seven kids' heads down or do you see that when you ask a question, nobody raised their hand and there were like three side conversations?" she asked. "Do you see it?"

I squinted. I could see them now, but I hadn't noticed the student behaviors in the first run-through of the video.

More insistent than she had been in previous meetings, Ms. Costello made clear his choices. "To be fair, I'm not giving you a choice, you must deliver a consequence."

"I'm scared to do it," Mr. Henig admitted. "I don't want to take away things from the kids."

"It's not being mean. You have to keep them accountable," Ms. Costello asserted. "Even if you don't want to be the bad guy, these behaviors are not getting them to college. Once you add the consequence, you're gonna get push back, then you're going to see results."

He still appeared reluctant.

Once more, Ms. Costello emphasized, "You gotta just do it, you're the boss." Again she told him to expect pushback when he started using more consequences like deducting students' weekly behavioral points for minor behaviors: "If all of a sudden calling out is points, they're gonna be pissed."

Every week, teacher leaders like Ms. Costello worked with more novice teachers on a "key lever"—a bite-sized instructional or classroom management technique. Key levers like "giving consequences" were typically taken from *Teach Like a Champion*, a handbook developed by no-excuses leader Doug Lemov. By observing and videotaping effective urban teachers, Lemov developed a common vocabulary for effective teaching, what he called a "taxonomy" of teaching practices.[1] He gave these strategies pithy names (e.g., "No Opt Out," "Do It Again," and "SLANT") and compiled them into *Teach Like a Champion*, a best seller that has become a core professional development guide for no-excuses schools.

Lemov argues that effective urban teachers need a set of specific, concrete techniques to establish control and increase engagement. This is seen as more important than any particular educational philosophy. "Mastering those techniques will be far more productive than being firm of convictions, committed to a strategy, and, in the end, beaten by the reality of what lies inside the classroom door in the toughest neighborhoods of our cities and towns," he writes.[2] Following in this mindset, in 2007 no-excuses leaders started their own graduate school of education, Teacher U (now renamed Relay Graduate School of Education), emphasizing practical, hands-on experience over theoretical knowledge. In contrast to traditional teacher-education programs that have long been criticized for being overly theoretical and disconnected from the realities of the classroom,[3] Relay has been criticized for being overly technical and relying on a highly scripted instructional and classroom management model.[4]

In this coaching session, we can see how Ms. Costello prescribed to Mr. Henig what he needed to do to manage his classroom. She dismissed his reluctance to give consequences and his assertion that he did not want to take things away from kids. Ms. Costello made clear that she was not merely suggesting that he follow school procedures and give out more consequences—he was being told to do so. Although part of the early impetus behind charter schools was to grant teachers greater autonomy and decision-making power, charter management organizations (CMOs) are fairly prescriptive and tend to enforce schoolwide disciplinary practices. Many high-performing, no-excuses CMOs follow a "coaching-intensive" model where they routinely observe teachers, provide feedback, and review lesson plans.[5] Some networks also use real-time coaching, where teachers wear earpieces through which their coaches give them the precise words to say to respond to student behavior in the moment.[6]

There are many benefits to being observed, given feedback, and taught techniques of classroom management. Teacher turnover rates are high, with nearly half of new teachers leaving teaching within five years,[7] and teachers more likely to leave high-poverty, high-minority schools where classroom management can be challenging for novice teachers.[8] Schools are now recognizing that new teachers need greater supports to overcome the initial obstacles they face, and the majority of new teachers now participate in some type of induction program that includes mentoring and professional development.[9] At the same time, greater controls over teachers' work can diminish their autonomy and sense of professionalism.[10] In the past two decades, as accountability pressures for schools have increased, teachers have experienced efforts to standardize curricula, script instruction, and allocate more time to test preparation, which have contributed to lower job satisfaction.[11]

Dream Academy aimed to create a *teacher-proof system*—a school structure that worked in spite of its teachers. That is, they designed a system that did not rely on teacher expertise or experience but depended on intensive and ongoing teacher coaching on school scripts. In this chapter, we will see how teachers at Dream Academy experienced and responded to these school scripts. Standardized scripts support novice teachers in managing their classrooms but limit teacher autonomy and discretion. Because *scripts* are fixed, they do not cultivate in teachers the *tools* to adapt practices to their own needs or to the needs of their students. A scripted approach to teacher training thus runs the risk of producing mechanical teachers who can follow protocol, rather than professional teachers who have the tools to diagnose problems and develop solutions.

Selecting Teachers

To understand how Dream Academy tried to create a teacher-proof system, it is important to first take a look at their process of teacher selection. Through their intensive recruitment efforts, Dream Academy sought teachers who would conform to the school's rigid scripts for teaching and behavioral management.

One morning in late March, I visited with Ms. Jansen and Ms. Thomas, the school's human resources team. Both women were relatively new to the organization. Ms. Jansen, with dark curly hair and glasses, had come to Dream Academy from a parallel position in the private sector. Ms. Thomas, sporting a short blond bob, had been hired as a temporary associate to help with recruiting. Their office was located at the high school; Ms. Jansen had a desk at the back of the room, and Ms. Thomas sat in a cubicle at the side.

I pulled a chair next to Ms. Thomas to watch her begin to review job applications. She began to file through the three new candidates who had appeared on her computer screen since her last login yesterday. Within minutes, Ms. Thomas had paper screened the candidates, reviewing their materials and checking off yes/no questions. I was impressed by her efficiency. She told me that she tries to review candidates within forty-eight hours of their application submission. To pass to the next round, she explained, candidates must have relevant experience, fewer than two grammatical mistakes on their application materials, a 3.0 GPA or greater, the possibility of making a significant contribution to the school, and a persuasive argument for working there.

This was the first step. A giant white board leaning against the cubicle listed out the remaining steps: paper screening, phone screening, reference check, school visit, teaching demonstration and interviews, capture call, supervisor call, and final approval. Since recruiting season began in January, they had received over one thousand applications. About one-fifth of them would make it to the phone interview. Only thirty-five would advance to the semifinalist round, where Ms. Thomas and Ms. Jansen would reach out to at least five recommenders via email or phone before deciding on which finalists to bring in for a school visit. Ultimately, only one of every one hundred applicants would be extended an offer. This highly selective teacher recruitment process was designed to find teachers who would be a good fit with the school's distinctive approach.

As I listened in on a phone interview Ms. Thomas had scheduled with a candidate applying for a middle school science position, I heard Ms.

Thomas ask the applicant why she was interested in teaching in a no-excuses urban school and whether she believed all students should go to college. To the first question, the woman replied that she had worked in the city before, had been referred by a current teacher, and specialized in urban education in college. To the second, she responded, "Absolutely." After about twenty-five minutes, the interview concluded. Despite the fact that the applicant had no prior teaching experience outside of student teaching, Ms. Thomas decided to move her forward. "She sounded open, coachable, and had knowledge of [the city]," Ms. Thomas explained to me.

The candidate had met the school's two most important criteria: *mission fit* and *coachability*. Coachable teachers who were committed to helping students in underresourced communities were sought over experienced teachers with the tools to independently manage their classrooms or build relationships with students. As we will see, these two criteria were prioritized because the school wanted teachers who would be amenable to the school's scripts. They were looking for raw material to mold.

MISSION FIT

In recruiting teachers, Dream Academy looked first for mission fit: teachers dedicated to urban education who wanted to make a difference in the lives of low-income Black and Latino children. To assess mission fit, Ms. Jansen and Ms. Thomas used the questions I had heard related to why candidates want to work here and whether they believe all students should go to college. The first question told them whether the applicant just wanted to be the best teacher, wanted to help kids generally, or was looking for any job out of college—not a mission fit. Instead they sought candidates who had taught in urban schools and recognized that this was different from teaching in suburban schools, had local knowledge about the city or prior experience in urban environments, or had majored in urban studies—like the candidate who was passed on to the next round. ("Urban," as scholars have noted, is often coded language for Black.)[12] They also favored candidates who were specifically looking for a no-excuses school and were determined to prepare all students for college. "Absolutely" was the right answer to Ms. Thomas's question of whether all students should go to college. When another candidate was brought in for a teaching demonstration, she was cut from consideration when she expressed doubts about the school's ambitious academic goals. After the principal had explained the school's goals for student proficiency rates on the statewide standardized tests, the candidate had sarcastically responded, "Good luck."

No-excuses schools in general attract young, energetic, mission-aligned teachers, not dissimilar from the population targeted by Teach for America.[13] Many teachers spoke about how they chose to work in an urban school over a suburban one because they wanted to do more meaningful work. Ms. Russo, a White music teacher who previously had taught in a suburban school, explained why she chose to work at Dream Academy. "Like I didn't need to teach these privileged kids who could get voice lessons and study with people," she told me. "I wanted to teach someone who needed me. I have a lot to give to kids and a lot of love and I wanted to love them and help them—help the kids who need music. And the rich kids didn't need music as much." As we can see from Ms. Russo's statement, mission fit can attract teachers who are committed to their students, but it can also attract teachers who may hold a "White savior" attitude, where predominantly White teachers see their work as saving Black and Brown kids from their negative environment and providing them with what they lack at home. Both Teach for America and charter school organizations have been criticized for displacing local teachers and depicting urban communities as needing to be "saved."[14]

From the school's perspective, the main reason for prioritizing mission fit was to get teachers who would persist through the difficult work. No-excuses schools are what one scholar has termed "greedy institutions,"[15] demanding the full commitment of their staff. From new teachers to seasoned veterans, educators at Dream Academy worked hard, up to sixty to seventy hours each week. Dream Academy's longer school year and school day translated into teachers working eleven months a year, from early August to late June. Teachers officially worked from seven fifteen to four thirty, with additional hours for weekly staff meetings and mandatory homework assistance where teachers were required to be available to students by cell phone until nine in the evening. At one school board meeting I attended, a board member suggested recruiting effective teachers from the local public schools. Mr. Taylor explained that, in seven recruitment seasons, they have not had more than twenty of these teachers apply. A parent in the audience who was also a teacher at a local public school explained why. She began work at eight forty in the morning and clocked out at three twenty-five; she knew people who clocked out at two forty-five each afternoon. Public school teachers wouldn't come here, she argued, because of the lower salary and the longer hours. Compared to the local public school district, Dream Academy's salaries for teachers with no experience started at forty-five thousand dollars, compared to approximately fifty thousand for a district teacher. Unlike the local district, Dream Academy also did not pay higher amounts for teachers with master's degrees.[16]

Ms. Harvey, the Teach for America teacher who had gotten upset when one of her student's parents questioned her qualifications, told me that she regularly sleeps four hours a night. On top of her school responsibilities, she was taking classes over the weekends to obtain a master's degree. Mr. McCudden, a seasoned teacher in his first year at Dream Academy, did not want to take work home, so he stayed at school late, often until nine o'clock. "I have eight years of teaching experience and my head is barely above water," I heard him tell a group of prospective teachers visiting one day. Teachers complained that teaching infringed on their personal lives, and many doubted whether they could continue teaching here once they had families. Ms. Wallace flat out told me that the job was not sustainable because it required so much of her time. "My husband is really resentful about this place and the time that I spend and the amount of energy it takes," she said. To explain the intense work culture, Ms. Jansen tells applicants that people here don't take much vacation. They get ten days but most take two. Teachers were also discouraged from taking sick days, a significant source of teacher stress because the school did not use substitute teachers as these teachers would not be familiar with the school's scripts. This meant that when teachers were absent, their colleagues had to cover for them.

Given the school's heavy workload expectations and lower compensation, it is unlikely that experienced teachers from the local community would seek out such an opportunity. Thus, mission fit was decidedly more aspirational than substantive. That is, the school ended up hiring teachers who were focused on the ends (helping kids in urban communities) but not necessarily equipped with the means to do so (experience and investment in the community). In emphasizing mission fit, the school sought teachers determined to help their students and thus willing to dedicate the long hours the school demanded of its staff. These teachers were also perceived as more willing to comply with the school's scripts. Ms. Williams, the Black teacher who later became principal, put it this way: "You have to see the big picture. You have to know that the goals that are set for you are to benefit you, and to help you grow and become better." In fact, as we will see next, the school intentionally sought out novice teachers over experienced teachers to ensure that they would be amenable to following the school's prescriptive approach.

COACHABILITY

The second quality Dream Academy sought in its teachers was coachability, that is, being open and responsive to feedback. Dream Academy was less interested in hiring professionals who had specialized skills, knowledge, and training, but instead recruited teachers who would benefit from, and be responsive to, the school's intensive coaching model. Coachability was considered an essential quality because school leaders dedicated an incredible amount of time and resources to coaching new teachers. One of the distinctive features of no-excuses schools, as earlier described, is their ongoing efforts to socialize teachers into schoolwide systems and procedures.

In a traditional school, teachers are given a fair amount of discretion over how they teach. At Dream Academy, school leaders wanted students to experience the same expectations no matter where they were in school. Because no-excuses schools have extensive rules and consequences, school leaders feared that a breach in the system would increase student resistance. If one teacher more loosely implemented school disciplinary practices, students might question the necessity or fairness of school rules. When procedures were consistent from day to day and from teacher to teacher, the school believed that students would internalize expectations.

To find teachers who were coachable and who would conform to school scripts, school leaders prioritized openness over experience. It is not that Dream Academy did not have the option of hiring more seasoned teachers; they deliberately chose not to do so, which may be surprising given that teachers significantly improve in effectiveness during their first years of teaching.[17]

This was made clear in the hiring of Ms. Monroe, a twenty-five-year-old, upper-class White teacher who previously had taught for one year in an urban school where she struggled with classroom management. During her interview at Dream Academy, she was told that the school was looking at another candidate who had ten years of experience. They asked her why they should hire her. She explained how she recognized that she was a novice. "Like I can't say that I know how to do everything perfectly, so the more feedback, I guess, the better I am because that's something I can implement," she recounted to me in an interview. "If I don't get feedback, then I'm going to keep making the same mistakes. So I'd rather just hear from people who know." In the end, she received the job offer. Her lack of experience was not a disqualifier. On the contrary, it counted in her favor. From the school's perspective, teachers with more experience might be less willing to change their techniques and less eager to cede their autonomy. A new teacher, by contrast, would likely welcome the additional support and direction, particularly if he or she had been hired with little teacher education training.[18]

Ms. Wasulik, the teacher who had won the Teacher of the Year award at an urban school in the same city, proved the school's point that experience did not necessarily provide an advantage to teachers at Dream Academy. As we saw earlier, Ms. Wasulik struggled with classroom management in her first and only year at Dream Academy, finding it hard to adjust to the new set of techniques for behavioral management that she was required to implement. On the instruction side, Ms. Wasulik also found the school's scripted approach to be "beyond exhausting." She said that she spent ten to twelve hours each Saturday writing and submitting detailed "twenty-page lesson plans" to her supervisor for review because teachers were expected to create their own materials. "I'm not the kind of person that can stand up and kind of look at her kids and read from a script, too," she told me. "I mean, you give a general sense of what you're doing, you know, you have the materials and you're not going to be reading from your lesson plan the whole time." She ended up leaving at the end of the year, discouraged and exhausted. "This is my twelfth year teaching, okay, and I have never had a professional year like the one at [Dream Academy]," she said. "It was the worst year of my life, professionally and personally."

Because Dream Academy's expectations were so specific, even experienced teachers had to relearn how to teach and manage their classrooms. As Mr. Bradley, the school principal, noted in one leadership meeting, "Ninety percent of our coaching is around technique and not content." To measure successful teaching at Dream Academy, the school used an elaborate teacher evaluation rubric that they had adapted from another no-excuses network. Teachers were rated from 1 to 5 points (unacceptable to outstanding) on twenty-three measures that fit into five broader categories, Ensure Measurable Student Learning (30 percent), Model the Core Values (15 percent), Sweat the Small Stuff (20 percent), Work Hard (20 percent), and Be a Good Teammate (15 percent). To be retained, first-year teachers had to score a minimum of 70 percent on their evaluations; returning teachers had to score 80 percent.

To illustrate the detail of the rubric, let's look at the Sweat the Small Stuff category (see table 6.1). To be rated outstanding, teachers had to demonstrate clear and efficient classroom policies and procedures; sweat the details "exceedingly well (no bags at desk, students track the teacher when speaking, etc.)"; assign students infractions on a consistent basis and at similar rates as other teachers; actively manage student behavior in the hallways, at lunch, during transitions, and at school assemblies; and keep an organized and clean classroom where student work is displayed and rotated every two weeks. To keep track of teachers' infraction rates, the school generated monthly performance metrics (MPMs) that they distributed to teachers, ranking teachers by name in terms of the number and percentage of total infractions assigned that month. These MPM reports also contained data ranking teachers based on their absences, student grade distributions (sorted by the percentage of As and Fs assigned), health office referral rates, and paper usage rates.

Implicit in the school's coaching model is the assumption that teachers can be coached—that is, they are able to conform to the school's expectations so long as they are committed and open to doing so. Yet while no-excuses schools provide teachers with a set of scripts, they ignore the fact that teachers, even coachable ones, bring with them their own toolkit of values and practices that may align with or diverge from the techniques they are being asked to implement. Sociologist Dan Lortie described the teacher socialization process as one of *self-socialization* where teachers filter school practices through the lens of their own experiences and values. "They portray the process as the acquisition of personally tested practices, not as the refinement and application of generally valid principles of instruction. They insist that influences from others are screened through personal conceptions and subjected to pragmatic trial."[19] As much as the school worked to standardize teacher practices, teachers demonstrated agency in using their own toolkits to modify school practices and go off script, developing what the sociologist Judson Everitt calls teachers' own "arsenals of practice."[20]

Teachers' Responses to School Scripts

Mr. McCudden, a thirty-year-old White teacher from the Midwest, began teaching as part of a service corps program run through his university. He taught Spanish, social studies, and gym and coached two sports teams in an underfunded, understaffed traditional urban school, while also being a full-time student. His mentor, the school's principal, tried to be supportive, but she was busy "fighting to keep the school open" and observed him only once during the semester. "It was really fending for myself," he said. "And I grew a lot in understanding kids and understanding how to relate to them. But I didn't grow a lot as a professional, and learning how to teach well." In his two years at the school, the only lesson

Table 6.1. "Sweating the Small Stuff" Section of Teacher Evaluation Rubric

Criteria	Rationale/Purpose of Category	1 (Unacceptable)
Teacher establishes and consistently reinforces smooth common and custom classroom policies and procedures (blackboard configuration, entry routine, materials distribution, transitions routine, etc.). As a result, the teacher accomplishes an overall calm, productive classroom environment that allows all our students to secure academic skills and knowledge, one in which "100%" of students naturally SLANT.	Outstanding teachers maximize the learning time in their classrooms by designing procedures and routines that are orderly and efficient.	There is little to no evidence that standard classroom policies and procedures are in place and enforced. As a result, learning time is often lost due to inefficient systems. Most policies and procedures such as BB (blackboard) configuration, entry routine, materials distribution, etc. are non-existent or inefficient, though a substantial amount of learning time is lost daily as a result of substandard implementation of policies and procedures.
Teacher handles minor misbehavior himself/herself by always addressing the "little things" in a positive way that does not embarrass students and maximizes in-class learning time. Teacher uses difficulties that arise as opportunities to teach core values. Teacher ensures that students remain in class unless the student is putting him/herself or others in physical danger.	Outstanding teachers notice and address the "little things," so that rules and policies are consistently reinforced throughout the school. Outstanding teachers use strategies and techniques to handle behavior difficulties that are not physically dangerous.	Teacher struggles with "sweating the details" (no bags at desk, students track the teacher when speaking, etc.); teacher consistently sends students to the main office, hallway, or to the Student Affairs Administrator (several times per week).

2 (Needs Improvement)	3 (Satisfactory)	4 (Good)	5 (Outstanding)
Some classroom policies and procedures are evident. As a result, learning time is sometimes lost due to inefficient systems. Some policies and procedures such as BB configuration, entry routine, materials distribution, etc. are organized and efficient, though a substantial amount of learning time is lost daily as a result of substandard implementation of policies and procedures.	Many classroom policies and procedures are evident and class runs systematically where learning time is maximized; students are aware of most policies and procedures but may not be able to articulate them; most policies and procedures such as BB configuration, entry routine, materials distribution, etc. are organized and efficient, though at times learning time is lost as a result of substandard policies and procedures.	Most classroom policies and procedures are clearly evident and class runs systematically where learning time is almost always maximized; students can articulate most policies and procedures; most policies and procedures such as BB configuration, entry routine, materials distribution, etc. are evident, organized and efficient.	Classroom policies and procedures are clearly evident and class runs systematically where learning time is maximized; students can articulate policies and procedures; all policies and procedures such as BB configuration, entry routine, materials distribution, etc. are evident, organized and efficient.
Teacher struggles with "sweating the details" (no bags at desk, students track the teacher when speaking, etc.); teacher frequently sends students to the main office, hallway, or to the Student Affairs Administrator (once per week or more).	Teacher "sweats the details" adequately (no bags at desk, students track the teacher when speaking, etc.); teacher addresses minor misbehavior and student misconduct on own and rarely sends students to the main office or to the Student Affairs Administrator (two to three times per month), but often sends students into the hallway.	Teacher "sweats the details" well (no bags at desk, students track the teacher when speaking, etc.); teacher addresses minor misbehavior and student misconduct on own and rarely (two to three times per year) sends students to the main office, hallway or to the Student Affairs Administrator unless persons are in physical danger.	Teacher "sweats the details" exceedingly well (no bags at desk, students track the teacher when speaking, etc.); teacher addresses minor misbehavior and student misconduct on own and never sends students to the main office, hallway or to the Student Affairs Administrator unless students are in physical danger.

Continued on next page

Table 6.1. (*continued*)

Criteria	Rationale/Purpose of Category	1 (Unacceptable)
Teacher consistently uses and reinforces the school-wide reward and consequence systems that are in place, such as merit point system (Level 1 infractions), detentions, bench referral rates, etc. both inside and outside of the classroom.	Outstanding teachers understand that great school cultures are largely a result of consistency. Thus, when examining the Monthly Performance Metrics (MPMs) each month, things like Level 1 infractions, homework assignment rates, bench referrals, and nurse referral rates are within a reasonable range and consistent from month to month.	MPMs show infractions and referrals (Level 1 infractions, bench referrals, nurse referrals, detentions assigned, and homework assignment rates) are > ±6% of colleagues and > ±6% difference from month to month, demonstrating strong consistency. For example, in Sept., teacher assigns 8% of schoolwide Level 1 infractions, teacher assigns less than 2% or greater than 14% of Level 1 infractions in October.
Teacher assists with student behavior outside of the classroom by seizing teachable moments whether the student is "yours" or not. Teacher ensures timely, silent transitions and orderly student behavior in hallways, Circle, lunch, awards ceremonies, etc.	Outstanding teachers realize that great school culture is also a result of enforcing school-wide policies and procedures outside of the classroom as well. Outstanding teachers proactively help manage student behavior outside of the classroom.	Teacher is almost never visible in the hallways during transitions, at lunch, during Circle, etc. managing student expectations, and often needs to be reminded to enforce school policies. When teacher is not teaching, teacher is rarely observed reminding students of schoolwide policies (tucking shirts, silent in hallways, etc.).

2 (Needs Improvement)	3 (Satisfactory)	4 (Good)	5 (Outstanding)
MPMs show infractions and referrals (Level 1 infractions, bench referrals, nurse referrals, detentions assigned, and homework assignment rates) are within ±5% of colleagues and no more than ±5% difference from month to month, demonstrating strong consistency. For example, in Sept., teacher assigns 8% of schoolwide Level 1 infractions, teacher assigns between 3% and 13% of Level 1 infractions in October.	MPMs show infractions and referrals (Level 1 infractions, bench referrals, nurse referrals, detentions assigned, and homework assignment rates) are within ±4% of colleagues and no more than ±4% difference from month to month, demonstrating strong consistency. For example, in Sept., teacher assigns 8% of schoolwide Level 1 infractions, teacher assigns between 4% and 12% of Level 1 infractions in October.	MPMs show infractions and referrals (Level 1 infractions, bench referrals, nurse referrals, detentions assigned, and homework assignment rates) are within ±3% of colleagues and no more than ±3% difference from month to month, demonstrating strong consistency. For example, in Sept., teacher assigns 8% of schoolwide Level 1 infractions, teacher assigns between 5% and 11% of Level 1 infractions in October.	MPMs show infractions and referrals (Level 1 infractions, bench referrals, nurse referrals, detentions assigned, and homework assignment rates) are within ±2% of colleagues and no more than ±2% difference from month to month, demonstrating strong consistency. For example, in Sept., teacher assigns 8% of schoolwide Level 1 infractions, teacher assigns between 6% and 10% of Level 1 infractions in October.
Teacher is rarely visible in the hallways during transitions, at lunch, during Circle, etc. managing student expectations, and often needs to be reminded to do so. When teacher is not teaching, teacher is rarely observed reminding students of schoolwide policies (tucking shirts, silent in hallways, etc.).	Teacher is often visible in the hallways during transitions, at lunch, during Circle, etc. managing student expectations, but may occasionally have to be reminded to do so or does so with repeated idle warnings. When teacher is not teaching, teacher is sometimes observed reminding students of schoolwide policies (tucking shirts, silent in hallways, etc.).	Teacher is often visible in the hallways during transitions, at lunch, during Circle, etc. actively managing student expectations. When teacher is not teaching, teacher is often observed reminding students of schoolwide policies (tucking shirts, silent in hallways, etc.).	Teacher is consistently visible in the hallways during transitions, at lunch, during Circle, etc. actively managing student expectations. When teacher is not teaching, teacher is consistently observed reminding students of schoolwide policies (tucking shirts, silent in hallways, etc.).

Continued on next page

Table 6.1. (*continued*)

Criteria	Rationale/Purpose of Category	1 (Unacceptable)
Teacher ensures a visually engaging, curriculum-relevant, comfortable, and clean classroom environment.	Outstanding teachers realize that "everything is everything" with regard to school culture, and that clean, organized, visually engaging classrooms have a positive impact on student achievement. As a result, outstanding teachers contribute to making classrooms comfortable and visually engaging.	Teacher's classroom regularly looks disorganized and messy throughout the school day but may become disorganized as the school day progresses; teacher rarely displays student work; classroom walls may be bare or rarely updated with new materials.

plans he wrote were for his graduate school portfolio to get certified. His was the typical "sink or swim" experience many new teachers experience where they are left to figure things out for themselves. In contrast, in his first year at Dream Academy, he found that he had less freedom but was growing as a teacher. "And now I feel more professional," he reflected. "And I'm really glad for a lot of the feedback and a lot of the time that is spent observing."

Ms. Larkin, a twenty-three-year-old White teacher from California, had a different experience at Dream Academy. Like Mr. McCudden, she felt that she had learned a lot during the school year and was grateful for the training. Yet she also felt constrained by the school's scripted practices. Prior to teaching at Dream Academy, she student taught in an urban school with a Montessori philosophy that emphasized exploration and individualized approaches to managing student behavior. As a teacher, she wanted to develop students' social and emotional skills, but she felt "this pushback of, well you don't know how it's done then." When she proposed alternative teaching or behavioral practices to her supervisor, she felt like her ideas were dismissed.

2 (Needs Improvement)	3 (Satisfactory)	4 (Good)	5 (Outstanding)
Teacher's classroom is sometimes organized and clean throughout the school day but may become disorganized as the school day progresses; teacher rarely displays student work without prompting; classroom walls may be lacking in visual posters and positive messages.	Teacher's classroom is sometimes organized and clean throughout the school day but may become disorganized as the school day progresses; teacher displays student work and changes it every month; teacher has visual posters and positive messages, some of which are relevant to current unit of study.	Teacher's classroom is consistently organized and clean throughout the school day (may have procedures in place for students to keep the classroom clean and organized); teacher displays student work and changes it every month; teacher has visual posters and positive messages, some of which are relevant to current unit of study.	Teacher's classroom is consistently organized and clean throughout the school day (may have procedures in place for students to keep the classroom clean and organized); teacher displays student work and changes it every two weeks; teacher has visual posters and positive messages that are relevant to current unit of study.

Teachers varied in their willingness and ability to implement the school's systems. While some teachers felt successful and treated like professionals, others felt micromanaged and treated like novices. In previous work, I classified teachers into four types: *conformers, imitators, adaptors*, and *rejecters*.[21] These four categories are what sociologist Max Weber calls "ideal types"—teachers don't perfectly conform to each category, but the categories provide an analytic lens to understand different teachers' strategies. In practice, teachers often used multiple strategies and also shifted strategies over time. *Conformers* are those teachers who feel at ease implementing school scripts because these practices align well with their own teaching tools. *Imitators* do not share this same natural ease but try to mold themselves to follow the school's scripts. *Adaptors*, rather than change to conform to an unfamiliar new script, modify school practices to better fit their own tools—that is, their attitudes, skills, and styles. Finally, *rejecters*, without the desire or tools to adhere to the school's practices, reject school practices. By looking more closely at these four teacher types, we can gain a better sense of the benefits and limitations of scripts for teachers and schools.

CONFORMERS: EMBODYING THE SCRIPT

Operating with a natural ease, conformers felt comfortable following the school's prescriptive disciplinary practices because these practices matched what they would do if left to their own devices. Conformers did not so much follow the school's scripts as simply speak and act in a way that felt natural to them. These teachers already possessed the tools to manage their classrooms without needing a script to follow.

Two of the most admired and academically successful teachers at the school fit this type. Ms. Anderson and Ms. Costello, both teacher leaders, shared a similar background. They were White women, just past thirty, raised in upper-middle-class families, who attended selective universities. Although they did not share their students' racial and social class background, they possessed an authoritative presence more characteristic of working-class parents.[22] Sociologists have noted how working-class parents take on more hierarchical roles, expecting deference from their children. By contrast, middle-class parents use more give-and-take, encouraging children to voice their opinions, negotiate, and bend rules.[23] "I'm very authoritarian by nature," Ms. Anderson told me. "Like, it's in my personality to be domineering, and . . . it works for me in that way." Ms. Costello, a former rugby player, described herself as "loud" and "stern." "As far as just, like, generally just having a demeanor that gets the kids' attention, I think that that's something I just have," she said. Both teachers attributed their assertiveness to "nature" or "something I just have," not a style they worked to acquire as teachers at Dream Academy.

Ms. Costello found her first year as a coach difficult. The toughest part was trying to change teachers' own styles. She found that the teachers she supervised, like Mr. Henig, had a different personality and teaching style from her, which made it harder for them to implement the school's scripts. "I think part of it is teachable but I think there's a part of it that kind of just comes a little bit naturally to some people," Ms. Costello observed. "It's really hard to teach management to teachers who don't naturally have the authoritative personality."

When she was a first-year teacher, she was told to observe another teacher to learn how to manage a classroom, but their management styles were completely different from each other. At the end of the day, she found a management style that she described as "100 percent my personality." When her friends and family have come to observe her, they are surprised to find that she interacts with her students the same way she interacts with them. "I never really thought about what I did, it just kind of fit," said Ms. Costello. "I don't talk to the kids differently than I talk in my life." With her authoritative personality, Ms. Costello found it easy to establish herself as an authority figure in the classroom; she did not follow a script, nor did she feel like she could have adjusted her own style to fit a different mold. This suggests that teachers may not be able to conform to a rigid script if it does not match their own personality and teaching styles.

Among the new cohort of teachers, Ms. Evans, the Black teacher who marched her students in and out of the classroom until they complied with her directions for silence, best fit the conformers category. Her success, however, resulted not only from her close adherence to the school's disciplinary practices, but also from her ease with commanding authority. She had what sociologist Willard Waller hails as the teacher's voice: through the voice, students gain a sense for "whether a teacher really means what he is saying and is quite sure that there will be no argument about it, whether he means it and thinks that there may arise some discussion, whether he is trying to convince himself, whether he is trying to bluff someone else, etc."[24] Unlike the other new teachers, she did not have to rework her body into new stances and deeper intonations to command authority. By contrast, Mr. McCudden tried to follow school procedures but had less success in getting students to comply. Frustrated, he asked a few of his students why they listened to Ms. Evans more than they listened to him. The students explained that both teachers disciplined and occasionally yelled, but "Ms. E, when she yells, she really means it. She throws down." By contrast, students often laughed at Mr. McCudden when he spoke more sternly.

Unlike Ms. Anderson, Ms. Costello, and Ms. Evans, many of the young, White, middle-class teachers at Dream Academy did not interact with students in a way that students found authoritative. Not sharing their students' racial and social class backgrounds, most teachers were less adept at knowing how to gain students' respect. Ms. Turner, a former teacher at Dream Academy, noted that many teachers at the school struggled with classroom management because they had no experience in urban classrooms. A Black woman in her mid-thirties, Ms. Turner had taught in a high-poverty urban school for five years before coming to Dream Academy. Having grown up in the suburbs, she struggled her first years, but by the end of her fifth year she was well seasoned. "Being able to stand in front of that room confidently and be able to look a child who's blatantly disrespectful and with just one look and one word put them in their place and know that you've done it respectfully and you haven't broken any laws or anything, that is very valuable," she observed. "And that is something that's hard to teach."

Because conformers command authority in their own right, they do not depend so heavily on consequences to get students to comply. They can thus more easily achieve a warm-strict balance. A teacher who is warm-strict is "caring, funny, warm, concerned, and nurturing—and also strict, by the book, relentless, and sometimes inflexible."[25] Teachers who use the warm-strict style have also been called "warm demanders" or "no-nonsense nurturers," and this teaching style has been found among effective teachers of Black children.[26] Both Ms. Anderson and Ms. Costello were considered to be among the school's strictest teachers, but they also lightened their classroom with humor, chants, and competitions. Ms. Wallace, another conformer, was enthusiastic in the classroom, occasionally standing on top of desks and organizing impromptu town hall sessions. She smiled, snapped her fingers when excited, and incorporated interactive activities into her teaching. I was surprised when she told me that she was aggressive in how she spoke with kids during her first year as a teacher. "I wanted it to be very clear that I'm not afraid of you," she explained. "Now, in hindsight, I would never talk to a child that way, but I have a very aggressive, assertive personality." Because she had already established her authority, she did not need to constantly pick on students and assign them consequences, which as we saw earlier, often incited student resistance and antagonism.

While school leaders believed that what worked for urban school students was a highly scripted approach, in practice what seemed to work best was teachers' ability to diminish the need for authoritarian structures by commanding their own authority. Teachers who fit the conformers category were considered highly effective by the school and tended to be well liked by students. By contrast, teachers who stuck too closely to school systems were perceived by students as unfair and out to get them.

IMITATORS: ADHERING TO THE SCRIPT

Imitators lacked the natural ease of the conformers but worked diligently to follow school scripts. These coachable and mission-driven teachers were the types of teachers the school sought, but they were not always the most liked by students. Teachers who adhered too closely to the school's scripts were seen by students and parents as "by the book" and overly mechanical, not professionals who used their own judgment and showed appropriate discretion.

Ms. Phelps is a White, middle-class woman in her late twenties who grew up in the suburbs and attended a state university where she studied psychology and education. Although she is more reserved, she was considered one of the toughest teachers at Dream Academy. She was not always so tough. During the years she taught in a suburban school, she described her management style as "very lax." When she took a job two years earlier in an urban charter school in the same city, she admitted to not having a clue as to what she was getting herself into. Luckily, she had a coteacher whom she described as very good at classroom management: "She was tough. Like it was like a tough love sort of thing. And [the students] like looked up to her a lot because she was young and African American and came from like a city. . . . So she was young and they saw somebody like them being successful. And they know how to talk to—like I don't know. I mean, I know I grew up in a White household, obviously. And I'll never forget when I tried to yell at them one time they laughed because I sounded like a mouse." Ms. Phelps recognized that she lacked culturally appropriate ways of speaking to and disciplining the students. As she put it, it was "a totally different way than what I grew up with." Her coteacher, by contrast, had an aligned cultural toolkit. Sharing a cultural background with her students, her coteacher displayed an African American "no nonsense" parenting style similar to that of the conformers.[27]

After her previous school was closed for restructuring, Ms. Phelps was hired at Dream Academy. She found that something snapped into place. She learned to adopt a sterner demeanor through observing "really good tough teachers" in her previous schools and being coached in classroom management techniques. She recognized that she had succeeded in not becoming a "roll-over teacher" when some former students of hers who had transferred to Dream Academy from her previous school accused her of having "become mean."

Because of her prior experiences in an urban school, Ms. Phelps was convinced that things would go haywire if she were not strict with her students. Ms. Phelps faced a problem, however, in acquiring the same ease as teachers like Ms. Anderson. Without an easy ability to wield authority, she became perceived as overly strict and inflexible. Ms. Phelps had the highest infraction count, assigning 1,619 infractions over the school year, or 8.5 infractions per day. She also received the lowest marks on student surveys evaluating how much they liked their teachers. Her coteacher noted that she "uses the discipline system almost to her detriment because—you know, I think now the kids see her, like they have this—she has this clipboard in there, and they're like petrified if she writes down their name on a clipboard."

Ms. Wasulik, the former teacher of the year who struggled during her one year at Dream Academy, faced a similar problem. While she had felt at ease developing relationships with students in her previous urban school, the more she tried to adhere to Dream Academy's scripts, the more she felt resistance and hatred from her students. "So I did exactly what they would ask me to," she told me. "Kids come in, they immediately sit down silently, you know, and get started on their Do Now or, you know, no questions within the first five minutes of the Do Now—I mean, exactly their policy, I would try to adhere to." She explained that her supervisor even told her that "you're doing everything I ask you to do." Try as she did to follow the school's scripts, she was unsuccessful in getting students to comply. Like Ms. Phelps, she was usually on the high end of assigning infractions to students.

Teachers who rigidly followed the school's scripts ran the risk of becoming authoritarian. "I've heard blanket statements, like teachers say this: 'Oh, well, this is culturally, you know, how kids are treated, like they respond to this kind of authority,'" said Ms. Lopez, a Latina teacher who described her own father as strict but kind. "Is it really the kind of authority that you're getting, or is it a different kind of authority? Is it a playful authority?" Psychologists have typically distinguished between *authoritarian* parenting (low in warm, firm control and high in negative, harsh control) and *authoritative* parenting (high in warm, firm control and low in negative, harsh control). Authoritarian parents expect children to follow strict rules, provide few choices for decision making, and rely on threats and punishments for compliance—a style familiar at Dream Academy. Authoritative parents allow for more dialogue with their children, setting high expectations but also providing support and nurture—a style often associated with middle-class White parenting.[28] However, there is also a third *tough love* parenting style (high in warm, firm control and high in negative, harsh control) that was first identified by Black graduate students—a style that mirrors that of the "warm demanders" or "no-nonsense nurturers."[29] In trying to follow the school's scripts, teachers like Ms. Phelps may switch from an authoritative style to an authoritarian style, not realizing that it is the tough love style that may be most familiar and effective with their students.

Parents, who generally supported a strict school culture, also reacted against teachers who seemed overly stringent. During one parent association meeting I attended, several parents raised concerns that the new teachers were too mechanical; in contrast, more experienced teachers did not jump on everything and assign detentions left and right. "I feel a lot of rules allow them to be robots," commented one parent. This problem was also recognized by school leaders. During one staff meeting, Ms. Scott, the student affairs dean, advised teachers, "We can't be so focused on the rules. I know it sounds like an oxymoron because we're supposed to be on the same page, but we are still dealing with children." These comments reveal a limitation of behavioral scripts for teachers: because scripts are fixed, they do not offer teachers the flexibility to respond to individual student needs, making teachers appear like "efficient technicians" who follow rote procedure rather than "educational experts" who have the tools to use their own discretion in making decisions.[30]

Had Dream Academy been successful in getting all its teachers to follow its scripts all the time, the types of resistance we saw in chapter 4 likely would have been magnified. Although the school tried to create a teacher-proof system—a scripted model that did not depend on teacher expertise—what made the school bearable to students were teachers who moderated the rigid systems, learning when to show discretion and how to balance strictness with warmth.

ADAPTORS: MODIFYING THE SCRIPT

Adaptors also lacked the ease of conformers, but they took a different strategy than imitators—they modified school practices to better fit their own style. Adaptors resemble what sociologist Robert Merton labeled "innovators"—lacking access to institutional means to achieve their goals, they instead find creative alternatives.[31] One teacher called it "trying to figure out how to make it work for myself and be like authentic"; another described it as "trying to really find what my groove is." Adaptors demonstrated flexibility in adjusting school scripts to better fit their personal toolkits.

Ms. Beckerman, a White, first-year special education teacher and recent college graduate, figured out how to "sweat the small stuff" in a way she felt was less authoritarian. By creating little chants or positively framing her corrections, she tried to make school rules less harsh. She found that this balance between being strict and being fun "really, really works" and produced less student pushback. She described her approach:

> I try to push my personality into each standard. . . . For 100 percent, I
> had a rhyme, "eyes on me, if you want to be . . . successful!" . . . I think
> I tried to push as much fun into applying the TLAC strategies so it was

less noticeable so that the students don't notice they're being asked to sit like this . . . it was just positive framing, "I know you want to reverse that and bring it around!" Make it sound like it was their choice when it really isn't. "I know you like things perfect so let's try it again." So to get eyes on me, I'd say, "Put your game faces on, put on your war paint and point at your target." The kids would look at me like I was crazy.

Unlike the imitators who can seem overly mechanical, Ms. Beckerman found a way to insert her personality into the school's disciplinary practices by creatively adapting them and couching them in a way that felt less controlling.

Mr. Purcell, a White teacher in his mid-twenties from an upper-middle-class family, can also be characterized as an adaptor. Prior to coming to Dream Academy, he had taught music for a year at an elite boarding school where he had few problems managing his classes. At Dream Academy, his proclivity for humming lines of music and dancing in class did not command authority. Watching his class the first month, I had a feeling he was not going to succeed. Although he tried to strictly follow the school's disciplinary practices, on many days he spent so much time on classroom management that he failed to even begin his lesson. Yet, returning to his class a few weeks later, I was surprised to see his students coming together to play music. When I asked him what happened, he told me that he found it impossible to end every class angry, upset, or stressed. "You can't do that every single hour, every single day," he commented. He had to find a way to make the system work for them.

"I remember one morning where I came in and was like, I'm not going to do this today," he recounted. "I can't do it. We're just gonna play music." Once the students started playing music, he found that many of the behavioral issues disappeared. The kids became less frustrated, and he became less angry. From then on, he decided he would not wait for absolute silence before starting to play as he had been instructed; he would just start counting down or playing and eventually the kids would catch on.

Here Mr. Purcell is referring to the "100 Percent" technique from *Teach Like a Champion*. The technique directs teachers to "expect 100 percent of students to do what you ask 100 percent of the time, 100 percent of the way."[32] This is impossible, of course, but Doug Lemov is not speaking in hyperbole when he insists on 100 percent. If all students do not comply with a direction, Lemov instructs teachers to give a consequence or redirect students (e.g., using a nonverbal intervention or a positive group correction). When Mr. Purcell tried to follow the school's 100 percent script by waiting until all students were silent and at attention before starting to play music, he did not feel at ease, nor did the students conform to his expectations. Instead, they resisted his authority.

Finding a style that better fit him made him more successful in the classroom. "At the beginning I was not, not as much there and like really strict. And it didn't work," he noted. "And so actually, when I came back to sort of being who I felt comfortable being—being *myself*, it worked out a lot better." Instead of adhering so tightly to the school's prescriptions, Mr. Purcell, like other adaptors, found a way to modify school practices to better align with his own skills, styles, and habits. In addition, he reinterpreted school practices to be consistent with his own practices. He felt not that he had compromised the school's goals, but rather that he misunderstood the nature of the goals. "I had too high of expectations on 100 percent," he said, referring to Lemov's technique. When he recognized that his classroom would not look like the classroom of the school's seasoned music teacher—"not this year, maybe in the future"—he felt free to adapt the school's practices to suit his needs.

Ms. Anderson, Mr. Purcell's supervisor, noted how she can be very prescriptive with other teachers, but she had to show Mr. Purcell how the school's scripts aligned with his own ideas: "[He] needs to see, like, the rationale behind everything. And, like, once he understands it, he figures out to do it and he implements it. It has to come almost from him though. You have to show him the explicit value in it in order for him to do it. And I think once he started seeing that, 'Okay, well, I can try to figure out how this works in my classroom without it compromising the integrity of what it is that I'm trying to do.' Or perhaps his mindset changed to, 'Well, this is perhaps the better way of doing things.'" Ms. Anderson recognized that Mr. Purcell needed to feel a sense of ownership over his classroom, even if his choices ultimately reinforced the school's prescribed model. Mr. Purcell's insistence on having a say in his own teaching practices reflects the process of self-socialization described by Lortie.

In a typical school setting where teachers learn by trial and error, adaptors are likely to be common. Adapting teaching practices to the needs of different students, to institutional demands, and to unexpected contingencies is a necessary skill for teachers.[33] At no-excuses schools, however, a priority on schoolwide consistency can limit teachers' ability to adapt. One reason why Mr. Purcell may have had more flexibility in implementing classroom policies is because music is seen as an extracurricular activity, not a subject tested on state exams. Similarly, Ms. Beckerman and two other special education teachers, who were also adaptors, worked in smaller group settings where they had more time to get to know students on an individual basis. For other teachers, the ability to adapt school practices was limited.

Ms. Johnson, the teacher who had started the mentoring program for Black boys, felt she deserved more freedom in her classroom because she had a track record of improving student test scores. Over time, she has learned different strategies for working with different types of students. "Their very hard shells are very easy to crack once you figure out like the code," she explained. "And it's not necessarily like a code for each individual student, but there's like common codes, I guess. Like you can start to see certain students that resembled other students' behaviors. And then like you realize what methods work for them." As the school placed more emphasis on consistency, however, she felt that her own creativity and enthusiasm for teaching waned. "But I feel like for me, the more I try to do 100 percent and the more I try to worry about certain things, like I lost the zest for the actual content," she commented.

When teacher practices are excessively scripted, teachers may not be able to adapt school policies to better fit and build on their own toolkit of knowledge and skills. As in the case of Ms. Johnson, this can potentially diminish teachers' commitment to their work.

REJECTERS: CHALLENGING THE SCRIPT

Instead of finding ways to adapt themselves to the school's scripts or adapt the scripts to themselves, the teachers of the last type rejected the scripts. Rejecters often came from elite colleges and schools of education and had formulated more specific ideals of teaching, such as fostering students' socioemotional skills or engaging students in hands-on learning. Unable to follow the school's strict disciplinary expectations and unwilling to put aside their ideological commitments, many of these teachers ended up leaving the school.

Ms. Armstrong, a White Ivy League graduate in her late twenties, decided she wanted to be a history teacher on September 11, 2001. As a sophomore in high school, she watched the news coverage of the event, her teachers devoting the entire day to letting students see "history as it was unfolding." She recalled watching the second plane crash into the World Trade Center tower. Ten years later, on September 11, she drove across the country to enroll in a teacher preparation program, listening to radio coverage commemorating the tragic day. She wanted to teach her students that history was not just learning random facts and figures but about understanding people and their motivations. She wanted her students to learn about the past to create a better future.

Although she began the school year with a bright smile, she grew increasingly disillusioned with her students' behaviors and her inability to deviate from the school's scripts for teaching and discipline. Her supervisor, Ms. Anderson, perceived the root of her problem as her commitment to the disciplinary model, as was apparent in their meeting at the end of November.

"Do you really believe you can sweat the details at a high level?" Ms. Anderson asked Ms. Armstrong.

A few seconds of silence elapsed. "I want to," Ms. Armstrong replied.

"Do you believe it's helpful?"

"I think it would be helpful," Ms. Armstrong reflected. "What's working now is not working—I need to really slow it down. . . . I was talking to my former teacher, and he says you just need to match their energy and enthusiasm. When I slow it down, I lose my enthusiasm, my energy."

"What do you mean by slowing it down?" Ms. Anderson asked.

"Slowing it down to make sure all the pencils are down."

"When things click in, you are a superstar teacher. Is it a mindset thing or is it, 'I don't know how to do it'?"

"I don't think I can't do it," Ms. Armstrong replied. "I'm not sure how to do it."

"I still want you to think really hard if this is something you really think you can do. This is not a question of whether you can do it. I know you can do it. Embrace your bitch. You have to be unrelenting. No, it's not okay to put your head down. You're not their friend. That may be the part you love."

"It's so hard." She took a deep breath. "It's so hard—knowing I have to do that every day." She leaned her head back against the cubicle wall.

"But that's every urban environment. But if you really want what some of the more experienced teachers have, they all did it. You have a mean teacher look, you need to use it more. I'm telling you, it's gonna set you up for more success."

In this exchange, Ms. Anderson focused on Ms. Armstrong's commitment to the school's disciplinary model, viewing this as the primary barrier to her success. Yet Ms. Armstrong was also trying to articulate that she was not sure if she could actually implement these practices. Sociologist Ann Swidler has argued that individuals can easily change their stated values, but they may be less able to change how they approach problems and situations, because "the cultural meanings and social skills necessary for playing [another] game well would require drastic and costly cultural retooling."[34] It was not only that some teachers disagreed with the school's scripts for discipline; they also did not feel like themselves implementing them.

In trying to become a disciplinarian, in having to wait until all the students put their pencils down before giving the next instruction, Ms. Armstrong did not feel like herself. She felt inauthentic when trying to be stern; her enthusiasm and energy for the material dissipated when she had to constantly attend to student behaviors. As much as Ms. Anderson wanted her to use her mean teacher look and be unrelenting, Ms. Armstrong did not find it easy to adapt her body to the demands of the job. "Being, like, unsmiling and authoritarian and stern stresses me out," she told me. "Like it makes me feel unhappy and it makes me feel inauthentic and so that was like the struggle that I was having because trying to come into every classroom, not smiling and like trying, you know, holding kids accountable for everything and like every little moment and motion and anything that they did, like just, it was very trying."

More than any other teacher, Ms. Armstrong most clearly articulated this feeling of being disconnected from herself in trying to adapt to an unfamiliar role. This sense of detachment became clear to her when she had a corrections officer who was considering a second career in teaching come observe her classes:

> She was observing me, observing seventh and eighth grade and when she had been observing me for like a few weeks, she was just, she told me that she could completely understand like and identify with the behavior the students were exhibiting in my class because that's the behavior she sees every day in prison inmates. And I remember that really hurt my feelings at the time. Like it really hurt my feelings and I was like, I'm not running a prison. I'm running a classroom. I want, I want my kids to be happy and to love it here and just the fact that like she could draw parallels based on thirty years of experience between prison inmates and seventh graders.

For Ms. Armstrong, this comparison between her students and prisoners was a very discouraging comment. "I feel like I'm watching myself standing there, frustrated," she said. "It's an out-of-body experience."

Having gone back to school to obtain a teaching certificate after working in the business field, Ms. Armstrong planned to pursue teaching as a career path. As such, she wanted to develop as a professional—someone who has the tools to make their own decisions. She contrasted herself with the Teach for America teachers who see their two-year assignment as more of an internship and thus do not mind following a script. From her previous experiences, she knew that students can learn in different types of structures. When she was working as a student teacher in an urban public school, her students did a three-day project on the French Revolution. The first day, the kids did not do anything for eighty-five minutes, and she told the teacher it was a waste of time. "You have to let them flop," he told her. "That's how they learn." By the third day, the students created great projects—they made books and performed skits. "Yes, it was loud, crazy, but they learned," she said. At Dream Academy, she lacked the freedom to spend three days on a project, let alone fifty minutes, because lesson plans were divided into short time segments. Her supervisor was resistant to the idea of group work because her management was still weak. Unlike Mr. Purcell, Ms. Armstrong found less room to adapt. Lacking the power to control how she instructed or disciplined students, Ms. Armstrong became increasingly detached from her work outcomes.[35]

If Ms. Armstrong could have adapted more easily to the school's scripts or adapted the scripts to fit her own style, she may have been more likely to accept the school's methods. In fact, she did show more buy-in at certain points in the year when she saw improvement in student behavior. However, when things were not improving, she questioned whether this was the right job for her.

Other teachers were fundamentally opposed to the school's scripts. Ms. Larkin had a different vision for her students and for herself as a teacher. When she first arrived at Dream Academy, Ms. Larkin envisioned creating a classroom where students felt safe and knew they would not be punished or yelled at. Growing up in a suburban school, she never remembered a teacher yelling at students. She described the "huge shock" in seeing Dream Academy students and teachers yelling down the hall. Her approach to teaching was reaffirmed in her student-teaching experience in an urban Montessori school where students were pulled out and spoken to when they caused problems. "It was never seen as you're doing something wrong," explained Ms. Larkin. "You're not going to go to college because you can't do this. It was, you need to go outside for a little bit and run around."

At Dream Academy, she felt forced to comply with the school's system. She was reprimanded by the school for not giving out enough detentions and judged by other teachers for not being strict. At the start of the year, she tried to explain her difficulties to her supervisor, but she always got pushback. She described one conversation she had with her supervisor:

> I think my numbers were low on the data, for not putting in enough infractions. And I said that's just not who I am as a teacher. And you told us to be who we are as teachers during the first week of orientation, but I feel like I'm—what I'm committed to as an educator isn't what's expected, you know? Is there a way that I can start doing that? And there was this pushback of, well you don't know how it's done then. Well, you just haven't had enough experience. You're a first-year teacher, you don't know what you're talking about kind of a thing.

In this exchange, Ms. Larkin drew from an earlier conversation where the school encouraged teachers to "be themselves" to challenge the school's demands for her to follow their disciplinary practices. Ms. Larkin believed her own values as an educator should be reflected in her teaching decisions, while her supervisor contended that new teachers should defer to school leaders' expertise.

Both Ms. Armstrong and Ms. Larkin left Dream Academy at the end of the school year. Like other rejecters, their personal toolkit did not align with the disciplinary methods promoted by the school, and they found the lack of fit too dissonant to sustain. As Ms. Larkin put it, "I've really come to the point where this is who I am as a teacher. This is it. I know who I am. It's just not really going to be compatible." After leaving Dream Academy, Ms. Larkin found a context in which she felt her own tools aligned with the school's expectations: she taught for two years in an affluent suburban school and then helped found a progressive urban school.

The successes and struggles of teachers at Dream Academy offer larger lessons for thinking about the use of scripts for teachers. One of the shortcomings of a heavily scripted approach is that it cannot take advantage of the expertise provided by experienced teachers, nor can it adapt to potential innovations that might come about as teachers apply their own existing tools to solve problems. It also runs the risk of producing teachers who are overly mechanical and lack the tools to exercise judgment and show discretion. Finally, a rigid script restricts the types of teachers a school can recruit and retain—not all teachers are willing or able to adhere to a particular script. As instructional and behavioral scripts extend into various forms of teaching and teacher education, we need to attend carefully to their impact on teachers' satisfaction and professional development as well as their consequences for the low-income students of color often at the receiving end of these scripts.[36]

Exit

Dream Academy's rallying cry for the year of my fieldwork was Making Dream Academy a Better Place to Work. The previous year, the school retained only 44 percent of its teachers, its lowest retention rate since the school started. Teacher turnover rates are often high in no-excuses schools and have raised concerns over the scalability of the model.[37] High levels of teacher turnover also pose significant problems for schools because of the time and energy invested into helping new teachers learn common school procedures. Further, a revolving door of teachers makes it difficult to develop school leaders, establish a positive school culture, and build trusting relationships with students. Teachers also significantly improve in effectiveness during their first years of teaching.[38]

Teachers at Dream Academy gave different reasons for their departure, including personal reasons unrelated to the school itself. No-excuses schools attract teachers who are at greater risk of leaving, such as younger teachers who have attended highly selective colleges and Teach for America teachers.[39] However, as Mr. Bradley pointed out, teachers also left because they did not feel successful, particularly around issues of classroom management. For many teachers, their first sense of failure is experienced in the classroom. Having excelled at school and in other endeavors, these high-achieving young men and women find themselves frustrated at not being able to control their classrooms. Mr. Bradley attributed the school's high teacher turnover in part to teachers' feelings of ineffectiveness: "You're standing up teaching a lesson and none of the kids are listening to you and you start to say, oh gosh, I've been successful at everything I've done in life. I'm really smart, you know, I was dean's list and this and that and so maybe this isn't for me. Maybe I'm just not cut out for this. The kids don't like me. You know, and you start to have just all these thoughts about—you start to question your effectiveness and how effective you can be and you really have to have a thick skin." Classroom management is a common struggle that new teachers face. But, as we've seen, the school's scripts for behavior, though intended to support teachers in this task, made it more difficult for certain teachers to feel successful. In fact, one study of a no-excuses network found that teachers' disagreement with the school's disciplinary system was one of the strongest predictors of teacher turnover.[40] In a study of the KIPP Bay Area schools, nearly all teachers agreed that consistently enforcing school rules was key to helping students succeed academically, yet one-third of teachers reported not feeling comfortable implementing school disciplinary policies.[41]

Dream Academy hired an outside consulting group to examine issues of teacher retention and morale during my fieldwork. From the perspective of the consulting group, schools should focus on retaining the top teachers in the school because they are much harder to replace than lower-performing teachers. The previous year, Dream Academy retained 75 percent of its top-rated teachers, 100 percent of A teachers, and 67 percent of B teachers. They retained less than a third of C teachers and none of their D teachers. In the eyes of the consulting group, these results were not bad. Yet the question remains whether the C and D teachers can become A and B teachers, or whether no-excuses scripts are too rigid to develop all teachers into effective teachers.

Ironically, the rigid scripts that the school believed were critical to its success made it difficult for teachers like Ms. Armstrong and Ms. Larkin to find success. "We don't really deviate from the norm at all," argued Ms. Johnson. "I think we achieved a lot of results but I think there are students and teachers that are limited because of this." She described the school's approach to teaching as "cookie-cutter" and partly attributed high teacher turnover to this lack of autonomy over decision making: "I think that's where a lot of people get frustrated because they went into teaching to be able to express themselves and be able to be creative and do their own thing and then everything is made to be one way." As sociologist Richard Ingersoll has argued, teachers desire autonomy, particularly over behavioral decisions: "My point is that decisions surrounding such issues as appearance, clothing, and demeanor lie at the heart of teachers' work and that teacher control—or lack of control—over the creation, content, and implementation of such rules is highly consequential."[42] Charter school teachers may be particularly desirous of autonomy as these schools emerged as a way to empower teachers and reduce the bureaucratic red tape of traditional school settings. Charter school teachers on average report higher satisfaction than public school teachers because of their greater decision-making power.[43]

The difficulty, of course, is how to navigate the line between uniformity and discretion. Teachers may not be able to fit themselves into scripts that are too rigid, but they also need guidance to develop tools to become effective teachers. The success of Lemov's teaching taxonomy demonstrates the demand for a more standardized set of teaching tools in education; at the same time, the high teacher turnover rates in no-excuses schools reveal the perils of overstandardization. Like the best doctors, the best teachers do not tie themselves to protocol but use their intuitive sense to diagnose problems and come up with solutions.[44] In the teaching profession, this flexibility is even more critical as the work of teaching is complex, the technology uncertain, and the goals diffuse, making it difficult to standardize.[45] Teachers cannot take a one-size-fits-all approach; they must recognize and adjust to the different needs of their students.

One recurring finding in studies of standardization in organizations is that flexible standards may actually work better than rigid standards.[46] If teachers are given less rigid models, they might be able to adapt them in a way congruent with their own values and practices. But flexible standards can be difficult to implement. Tightening controls helps schools ensure that teachers follow set methods to achieve set goals.[47] It is therefore not altogether surprising that charter schools whose reputation and success is predicated on achieving high test scores on standardized exams choose such methods. Yet the intense workload and prescriptive systems used by no-excuses schools are likely to present obstacles to recruiting teachers with more experience as well as retaining teachers as they advance. Studies have found that teacher turnover is lower when teachers have more discretion over how they teach and discipline.[48]

A question for no-excuses schools, then, is whether they are willing and able to transition from a rigid system tailored to novice teachers to more flexible standards designed to support experienced teachers. Nearly a century earlier, sociologist Willard Waller argued that the modern, more flexible classroom demands more of teachers: "It requires a greater imagination, a greater understanding, and a more fluid and adaptable technique. . . . But whereas a simple technique for defining the situation was sufficient for the highly regimented school, a complicated technique is required for a school that tries to maintain a more flexible life."[49]

CHAPTER SEVEN

Conclusion

SCHOOL REFORM HAS OFTEN been an area with great ambition but little progress. One urban school model that has attracted widespread attention for its progress in improving students' academic achievement is the no-excuses school model, adopted by high-performing charter schools like KIPP, Achievement First, Uncommon Schools, Success Academy, Mastery, Aspire, Democracy Prep, and YES Prep. These schools exemplify recent trends in education toward choice, competition, and accountability and, to supporters, provide proof that these reforms work. In this book, we have peered inside the black box of no-excuses schools to reevaluate their success. Instead of focusing on students' academic achievement, we have turned our attention to how the school's rigid scripts for student behavior shape students' expectations, skills, and styles of interacting with authority. Focusing on this "hidden curriculum" of schools has given us a more nuanced picture of no-excuses schools, one that highlights the trade-offs of the model for students, teachers, and schools.

This book has taken a close look at this important if understudied world of no-excuses schools, offering the reader a window into their history, their assumptions and practices, and their impact on students and teachers. Through an in-depth study of Dream Academy, we have heard a complex story of how well-intentioned educators, desperate to establish control, adopted a highly scripted approach to student behavior. These scripts became both a mechanism for control and a means of resocialization. As a means of resocialization, scripts for how to dress, when to speak, and how to show attention were understood by the school as a way to teach low-income students of color dominant norms that would enable upward mobility. In this book, I instead have argued that rigid scripts limit the opportunity for students to develop the types of tools that they need to thrive in college and other middle-class social institutions.

Detailed and standardized procedures for behavior—what I refer to as *scripts*—achieved short-term goals of order, but failed to prepare students with the *tools* critical to long-term success. The relentless mechanisms of control used by the school to socialize students into middle-class norms, I argue, paradoxically constrained students from developing middle-class attitudes, skills, and behaviors like entitlement, initiative, and ease. What college students, and middle-class professionals, use to get ahead are tools, not scripts. Middle-class students know when to follow rules but also when and how to deviate. They know when to defer to authority and when to negotiate advantages for themselves. They know how to interpret situations and choose among alternative actions—skills that are important for acquiring and maintaining a higher position in the social hierarchy.

This book has offered a new perspective on no-excuses schools and their success, suggesting that what has helped these schools get students to college may not help these same students *succeed* in college and beyond. We have seen how these scripts inform students' expectations about success, instilling in students a "no-excuses" mindset that places the burden on themselves to achieve and earn their way, opposite to the entitled attitude that middle-class and upper-class students develop that places the onus on others to help them get what they deserve. We have also seen how the school's fixed scripts shape the skills students develop, limiting opportunities for students to develop the flexibility to learn how and when to express an opinion, advocate a position, and make independent decisions—skills that middle-class students use to negotiate advantages in college and the workplace. Finally, we have observed how these scripts prompt students to develop a style of interaction with authority that leans toward antagonism, reinforcing the "sense of constraint" that working-class students are taught rather than the "sense of ease" that more affluent students acquire.[1] In each case, we have seen ways in which scripts fail to provide students with the full set of tools for social mobility despite the school's intention to cultivate in students the "cultural capital" needed for success.

In the second part of the book, we stepped back to see the ways in which scripts inform educational policy and practice, limiting the tools that schools and teachers have at their disposal to innovate and address local concerns. The no-excuses model subjects not only students but also teachers and schools to its unrelenting expectations. We saw how scripts constrained teacher practice, leading some teachers to become too mechanical in adhering to the school's model and others to become disillusioned and reject the whole enterprise of teaching. We also listened in as school leaders struggled to find a way to loosen structures, as they were hesitant to make adjustments to a system adopted wholesale and viewed as a package deal. Finally, in tracing the history of the no-excuses model, we considered how copying an organizational script has consequences for the diversity of the charter school field and the promises of school choice.

Lessons for Teaching Cultural Capital

Scholarly work on cultural capital has informed educational practice. College preparatory programs for first-generation and low-income students focus not only on preparing students for the academic rigor of college but also on teaching them dominant cultural capital. Programs like these can help students experience less culture shock once they arrive on campus, but, as we've seen in this book, institutional efforts to teach cultural capital can also have unintended and negative consequences.

Scripts for behavior codify the unspoken "rules of the game," and can make explicit the implicit cultural codes that are often difficult for students to perceive. Scripts, however, are also prescriptive, and leave little room for adaptation. Scripts thus do not give students the skills they need to interpret the current situation and then deploy strategies and behaviors advantageously. In addition, because scripts constrain individual autonomy, they do not help students develop the types of proactive skills characteristic of middle-class cultural capital. Cultural capital is not just knowing how to tuck in a shirt and give a firm handshake; it can be seen as a tool that helps individuals successfully navigate institutional demands. Middle-class and upper-class students are assertive, ask for attention, and know how to bend rules to their benefit; they feel comfortable making demands of authority figures.[2] These cultural tools help middle-class students negotiate opportunities for themselves, as sociologist Jessica Calarco has argued, which can result in stronger ties with teachers and professors, increased learning opportunities, and better job prospects.[3] College preparatory programs that attempt to transmit cultural capital need to be careful not to send students the message that success is based on compliance to behavioral norms when success is also a matter of actively seeking out resources and demanding accommodations.[4]

How do schools teach students the cultural capital they need to succeed academically without exerting a dominating control over them and divesting them of critical thought? For one, programs that aim to teach cultural capital to students can be more intentional in developing skills like assertiveness, initiative, and negotiation—empowering students with tools rather than controlling them through prescriptions. To do this, scholars like Lisa Delpit have argued for using culturally responsive approaches where teachers affirm and draw from students' own cultural knowledge to teach them dominant cultural norms.[5] Some educators go farther, recognizing that it is not enough for teachers to be sensitive to cultural differences; they must also help students understand and critique structures of power. In a study of effective teachers of Black children, Gloria Ladson-Billings showed how teachers encouraged students to reflect on structures of power by getting students to question why they had to use standard English in the classroom or why the texts they read left out certain perspectives.[6] Both these approaches recognize the importance of teaching students the culture of power without exerting undue power over them.

However, it is also important to acknowledge the limits to the returns on cultural capital, particularly for Black students. Because of stereotypes of Black girls as loud and assertive and Black boys as threatening and aggressive,[7] teachers and other authority figures may respond negatively to Black students' efforts to interrupt, assert their needs, and negotiate.[8] Given the history of institutionalized racism and police brutality in the United States, assertive behaviors can have severe consequences, especially for Black male youth. While studies suggest that Black students can benefit from activating middle-class cultural capital,[9] there is a need for more theorizing at the intersection of race and cultural capital.[10]

Recent work on "culturally sustaining pedagogies" takes a different approach to addressing the cultural mismatch that low-income students and students of color may face in schools. Instead of resocializing students to conform to dominant norms, advocates of culturally sustaining pedagogies like Django Paris and H. Samy Alim argue that schools should encourage a diversity of perspectives.[11] This viewpoint is consistent with that of scholars who call on teachers and schools to affirm and build upon students' own cultural wealth and "funds of knowledge."[12] The aim here is to revise the "culture of power" to incorporate other cultural practices and perspectives so that education is seen as sustaining local communities and cultures. As the United States becomes increasingly multicultural, with White students no longer in the majority in public schools, cultural dexterity is argued as being more valuable than assimilation into White, middle-class culture. In fact, more recent studies of cultural capital have found that "cosmopolitan capital" is increasingly valued among the higher social classes.[13] Cultural dexterity is a tool that these individuals use to disguise their privilege and be at ease with different kinds of people and cultures.

Given the challenges with explicitly teaching cultural capital, another alternative for schools is to focus less on resocializing students into dominant norms—which can easily reinforce deficit thinking—and more on meeting their present needs. In her study of parenting education programs for low-income mothers, sociologist Maia Cucchiara found that these programs focused on getting low-income parents to change their parenting attitudes, behaviors, and skills (e.g., by praising their children, letting children express their emotions, etc.) as a means of improving opportunity for their children.[14] This advice, however, was irrelevant to parents' immediate needs and stressors, like how to find a job or feed their children. By failing to address the structural challenges that these parents faced, these programs were not seen as useful by parents. Moreover, by reframing parents' concerns about food insecurity or violence to focus on parents' own actions, these programs reinforced a narrative of individual responsibility for success not dissimilar to the one students heard at Dream Academy about grit and earning your way. Schools and other education programs might benefit from worrying less about getting students to conform to "middle-class" behavioral norms and more on providing comprehensive supports to students so that students are physically, mentally, and emotionally ready to learn. Schools that build partnerships with local community organizations to offer wraparound services to students, like health and dental care, breakfast, mentoring, and counseling, are moving in this direction.[15]

Lessons for Schools

In January 2019, a White principal at Amistad High School, an Achievement First school and one of Connecticut's top charter schools, resigned after being caught on security camera shoving a Black student.[16] Shortly thereafter, a letter signed by sixty-eight staff members argued that this was not an isolated incident but one that "is representative of the systematic racial inequities that are observable throughout the network." In a series of communications that followed, the Achievement First leadership explained how practices "executed with power over purpose and without an *abundance of care and deep respect for the kids and families we serve*" are racist given the communities they serve. The school leadership described the moment as a "reckoning" around the nonacademic preparation and overall school experiences of their students, admitting to having had "too low of a bar for school culture for too long": "We've led from fear and lack of trust based on a time in our network when many of our schools were unsafe and unproductive for kids. Measuring time on task during the first six weeks of school is not the same as a vision for warm, affirming, joyful schools where we have high expectations and deep care for scholars and their performance. Our values should be rooted in love and the belief that every single AF kid deserves to have an exceptional student experience where they are known, loved, challenged, and excited to be at school."[17] Achievement First committed to reexamining their practices, including making organizational shifts toward promoting racial equity, creating an empowering student experience, increasing accountability for school leaders, and including students and families in decision making.

No-excuses schools are evolving. In the years since I began my fieldwork, more schools have revisited their disciplinary practices and distanced themselves from the no-excuses label.[18] They have had to address challenges, like reducing suspension rates, recruiting and retaining diverse teachers, and increasing support for special education students. The next reckoning for these schools, made urgent by the recent protests against racism and police brutality, is transforming school culture. High suspension rates, which in some no-excuses networks surpass those of traditional public schools, have fueled concerns that these schools are perpetuating racial disciplinary gaps.[19] Walkouts and protests have been organized.[20] Disgruntled teachers and staff have taken it upon themselves to expose harsh disciplinary practices at their schools, as happened in the case of Amistad High School. More and more, these schools are recognizing that overly rigid disciplinary practices may not be critical to their academic success (though some no-excuses leaders still vigorously defend these practices).[21] In fact, researchers have found that practices like data-driven instruction, extended instructional time, after-school tutoring, teacher coaching, and high expectations account for much of the academic success of no-excuses schools.[22] No-excuses schools would do well to build on these promising practices while softening their focus on rigid discipline.

We should not be too quick, however, to assume that school culture and discipline is an old story and that reckoning is easy or speedy. Symbolic gestures toward change are different from deep-rooted change, which can require new narratives, new practices, and new structures. As we've seen in this book, the no-excuses model relies on an organizational script that exerts high levels of control over students and staff. Because they have been so reliant on this script, students, teachers, and administrators may not have developed the tools to know how to effectively shift school culture. For schools, a first step to change is engaging in professional development and learning, mentoring, and modeling. This may include training staff in issues of race and racism; conducting a "listening tour" to learn how students, families, and teachers are experiencing the school; and visiting and learning from other schools and teachers who have been successful in promoting a positive and caring school culture. Schools can also invest in helping teachers learn about their school communities and families. A home visit, which in many no-excuses schools serves the function of securing parental commitment to school rules and expectations, could instead be turned into an opportunity to learn about students' daily lives and set the tone and structure for deeper respect and understanding between families and schools.[23] Having a teacher stop by in the summer to visit a child's room, play a game, and meet the family dog sets a foundation of trust, not of fear.

To equip students with the tools to be successful in college, schools need to examine their "hidden curriculum"—that is, the structures and social interactions through which students receive implicit messages about what's appropriate to say and do. First, schools must reconsider the narratives they tell themselves and students about success. The messages that children learn when they are told to "earn their way," "make no excuses," and "show grit" is that they must pull themselves up by their bootstraps and disregard out-of-school factors, a task both herculean and unsound. A different message that schools can send to students is that they are loved and that the complexity of their lives is appreciated and that schools will provide a safe space where children who have faced trauma can experience recovery and develop resilience.[24] Schools can also moderate a message of meritocracy by helping students understand (and challenge) the racist, classist, and gendered systems and practices that create and maintain social inequality in society. As education scholar Chezare Warren argues, "Justice involves being intentional about allowing young Black men and boys to conceive of a future for which they can be proud, instead of simply preparing them to talk, dress, and behave in ways palatable to a society that does not see them as fully human."[25]

Second, schools must give attention not only to the academic skills students acquire but also to the social and behavioral skills they learn. To teach students skills like assertiveness, initiative, and flexibility, schools will need to create pedagogical and disciplinary structures that allow students greater decision-making power and voice. Progressive school models like the Expeditionary Learning School I visited in Queens, New York, have students work together on interdisciplinary "expeditions" where they build case studies around central themes—these range from a unit on food where students surveyed the selection at local stores to a unit in which they worked with city buses to collect pollution samples and count the number of stops that buses made. These units culminate in a project or product: proposed engine designs for the city's buses that were presented to the city's transit authority and letters to elected officials regarding food deserts. In completing these projects, the students—70 percent of whom are economically disadvantaged—learn academic content but also develop tools like teamwork, advocacy, and problem-solving skills.[26] By learning about the social, economic, and political contexts of the issues they investigate, they also develop a critical lens for analyzing and addressing social problems, becoming "justice-oriented" citizens.[27] Reflecting its emphasis on developing students as leaders and agents of change, one of the school's mottos is, "We are crew . . . not passengers." On the disciplinary side, there are well-established disciplinary models like restorative justice and social and emotional learning (SEL) whose focus is not on behavioral compliance but on teaching students tools for expressing an opinion, solving problems effectively, managing emotions, showing self-control, and establishing positive relationships. Implementing these types of programs takes training and effort, but no-excuses schools have a cadre of young and dedicated teachers and administrators who can channel their energies in new directions.

Third, to prepare themselves for future interactions with professors at college and managers in the workplace, students need to develop tools to interact with authority. Schools can encourage a *sense of ease* with authority by creating opportunities for students to interact with their teachers in different ways, such as through advisories, extracurricular activities, civic engagement, and sports teams, practices that many of these schools already implement. More fundamentally, if they want to expand students' view of teachers beyond disciplinarians and create unstructured time where students and teachers can informally interact, no-excuses schools will need to rethink the extent to which they require teachers to use and enforce disciplinary scripts as well as the level of structure in the school and classroom (for example, silent hallways and silent entry into the classroom). This requires much greater flexibility and fluency, which can be difficult for novice teachers to manage, but also has the potential to help to foster more positive teacher-student relationships, which are known to aid classroom management. If no-excuses schools were to allow for greater teacher autonomy, they might also be able to revise their hiring models to recruit more experienced teachers as well as teachers who are more knowledgeable about the local community. Having a racially and ethnically diverse teaching staff is particularly important for schools that primarily serve students of color.[28]

These lessons, while directed at no-excuses schools, are also relevant to a much broader swath of educational institutions. What we find in Dream

Academy is an extreme version of the types of narratives, practices, and structures that seep throughout schools and society. In thinking about the complex goals of education, we need to ask ourselves what education is for and what are the best ways to prepare students to develop the skills they need, not only for work but for life.

Lessons for Policy

In a congressional hearing, U.S. Secretary of Education Betsy DeVos called for "more charter schools, not fewer," citing the more than one million students on charter school waiting lists.[29] Expanding school choice was a guiding principle of the Trump administration's education policy approach, and the 2020 federal education budget allocated half a billion dollars for charter schools.[30] Although charter schools serve only 6 percent of all public school students, market-based reforms like school choice are seen as one of the most promising tools in policy makers' toolkits, and charters have enjoyed bipartisan support as a way to equalize educational opportunity by providing low-income families with access to better schools. To counter the argument that charter school students as a whole perform no better on standardized assessments than traditional public school students, no-excuses charter schools have been singled out and hailed for their academic successes.[31] Recent charter school funding from foundations has largely been directed toward replicating successful charter schools, many of which are known to operate under no-excuses models.[32]

Before we rally around no-excuses charters as the solution to long-standing educational inequities, however, we need to pause and take stock of these schools and what is happening inside them. Measuring school success primarily by student test scores, as accountability reforms have pushed schools and states to do, obscures the many other metrics by which we should evaluate schools. In advocating for policies that support charter schools, policy makers need to recognize that the urban charter field is narrowing around the no-excuses model and that this model has very real costs to students and families. Students at Dream Academy on average received one infraction every three days for behaviors like putting a head down on a desk because of a headache or speaking during class in order to quiet another student. This is more than strict discipline—it is hyper-regulation of vulnerable students in the name of success. Such scripting of students' every move reinforces racialized systems of social control and punishment where Black and Brown bodies are contained so as to appear less threatening.

Sociologist Mary Haywood Metz has astutely observed, "We need to know what the schools do, why they do it, and with what consequences before we prescribe what they should do differently."[33] Too often policy makers have dictated an intervention or policy without any understanding of what schools do and need, without listening and learning from families and children. In the past two decades, we have seen the rise of a "parallel education structure" within the public school system represented by charter schools, alternative teacher certification programs, and Teach for America.[34] A new group of education reformers—many who are young White college graduates from elite universities—have pursued an alternative pathway to teaching and participating in urban education reform initiatives. Dismissing traditional schools as bureaucratic and hampered by ineffective teachers unions, these individuals have embraced market-based reform as a mechanism for improving schools. These solutions, however, do little to address the systemic issues that have long made education reform so difficult. They also have produced results that are consequential and in many cases counterproductive.[35] As the Achievement First network has begun to recognize, education inequities have deep structural and cultural roots. Without confronting the legacy of racism and engaging the communities they are trying to "fix," education reformers may inadvertently reproduce the very inequalities they set out to alleviate.

Tennessee's Achievement School District (ASD) offers an illustrative example of the costs of ignoring local contexts and the roots of educational inequality. Lacking a larger contextual understanding, the policies pursued in the ASD highlight the limitations of no-excuses schools in addressing deep-seated, systemic issues. In 2010, Tennessee created the ASD to take over and contract with charter management organizations (CMOs) to turn around the state's lowest-performing schools. By 2014–15, eighteen of the twenty-three ASD schools were managed by CMOs, many operating from a no-excuses framework. After five years of turnaround efforts, the ASD schools failed to show any significant gains in students' academic outcomes.[36] Unlike typical no-excuses charters, in which families must apply and agree to certain commitments, these charters had to accept all students from the zoned neighborhood, which resulted in low levels of commitment from families to the school's disciplinary practices, along with a student population that the school was unprepared to serve (e.g., students with special needs, students with high levels of residential mobility).[37] Moreover, Memphis's local history of White racism and paternalism made community members skeptical of the ASD's efforts and its predominantly White leadership.[38] By not engaging with or being responsive to local communities and their needs, these charter schools did not win their trust and support.

No-excuses schools can be viewed as a limited tool for addressing the problems of urban education. These schools have found a script for achieving academic success, as measured by test scores and college acceptance rates, but it is a solution that is limited in scale, scope, and outcomes, as this book has demonstrated. "Ultimately no-excuses charters schools are a failed solution to a much larger social problem," education scholar Maury Nation has argued. "How does a society address systemic marginalization and related economic inequalities? How do schools mitigate the effects of a system of White supremacy within which schools themselves are embedded?" Without attending to these problems, we will not solve the problem of educational inequality. "As with so many school reforms," Nation argues, "no-excuses discipline is an attempt to address the complexities of these problems, with a cheap, simplistic, mass-producible, 'market-based' solution."[39] This idea of solving educational—and societal—problems "on the cheap" resonates with education philosopher Barbara Stengel's arguments about the "naïve optimism" of today's education reformers.[40] To improve education for all children, we need to push against "naïve optimism" in favor of the long, hard road to reform.

I don't have the answer to what the long, hard road to reform looks like, but I would suggest that it involves a balance between standardization and flexibility, an ability to move between large-scale models and locally driven initiatives. What schools, teachers, and students may need instead of rigid *scripts* to follow is a diverse set of *tools* that they can tailor to different situations. For schools, this may mean using standardized tests and other assessments to measure student learning, but also providing schools (and students) with tools to build capacity and coherence rather than sanctions or prescriptions for what they need to do and how quickly they need to do it. Instead of external accountability imposed from above, schools may need more internal accountability measures and space to share, support, and sustain innovation.[41] For teachers, this may translate to helping teachers acquire a diverse set of pedagogical and classroom management techniques—a process that requires coaching, modeling, and practice—while also giving them the broader educational foundations and flexibility to be able to adapt these tools to their own needs and the needs of their students.[42] Finally, for students, what may work better than a rigid model that dictates student behavior is making explicit the "rules of the game" while giving students opportunities to navigate and negotiate these rules, and empowering them to, one day, write their own rules.

I WRITE THIS METHODOLOGICAL appendix with two aims in mind. The first is to assist future school ethnographers by reflecting on my own experiences with finding a school site, taking on a role in the school, and sharing results. Like many budding ethnographers, when I think back on the research for this book, I think about "what I would have done differently." I thus share my own steps and missteps as a way to inform the work of others. The second is to provide the reader with a better understanding of my methodological decisions and how they enabled or constrained my data collection and analysis. Understanding my positionality and approach can help the reader evaluate the arguments I make in the book and point to places where they may fall short.

Case Selection

I chose to study no-excuses schools as an extreme case of a school effort to explicitly teach students social and behavioral skills, as prior literature on these schools had found that they aimed to change students' behaviors and norms.[1] To choose a case study school, I used three criteria: (1) it followed the no-excuses model, particularly its behavioral approach; (2) it was a middle school; and (3) it had been in operation for at least two years and demonstrated evidence of effectiveness in increasing students' academic achievement. Because there is some variation between no-excuses schools and networks in their practices, I wanted to ensure that I chose a school that followed typical no-excuses behavioral practices, like establishing rewards and consequences for minor student behaviors. I decided to choose a middle school because I thought middle school students would be better able to articulate their feelings and perceptions than elementary school students and would be more responsive to learning new skills and behaviors than high school students.[2] In studying middle school students, I also saw an advantage in observing the same students with different subject teachers to examine whether the teaching and evaluation of social and behavioral skills varied by the teacher's experience or demographic characteristics or mode of instruction. Finally, I wanted to study a "successful" school to evaluate the model at its best. As a measure of academic achievement, I chose schools whose standardized test scores significantly exceeded those of the local school district, although I recognize this is an imprecise measure because of student selection and attrition.

I first emailed three no-excuses schools that met these criteria with my interest in conducting ethnographic research on how no-excuses schools taught "cultural capital" (or social and behavioral skills) in their schools. The first school declined my research request, explaining that it was hard to participate in projects like this because "our focus is laser-like on our kids and their progress." The other two schools eventually granted me permission, which was surprising to me given other researchers' struggles with access. For one school, I had to apply to conduct research through their charter management organization's central office and then obtain permission from the school itself. In the second school, which was not part of a large network, I met with the executive director and then obtained approval from the Board of Trustees. Ultimately, I decided to study the second school—which I call Dream Academy—because the school seemed very open to my fieldwork and was willing to share school behavioral data with me.

I suspect Dream Academy was open to research for a few reasons. First, the school director was familiar with research. Although I was the first researcher to conduct a long-term study of the school, the school had collaborated with other researchers before. Second, like other no-excuses schools, the school prided itself on being data-driven and focused on improvement. School leaders told me that they often did not have time themselves to reflect on their practices, but wanted to know what was working and what they could do better. Third, the school was transparent about its practices. The school had an open-door policy, in which parents could drop in at any time to observe in their children's classrooms. My request to observe thus did not appear terribly out of place. Finally, my research questions aligned with the school's own interests in teaching students the social and behavioral skills they needed to succeed in school.

In thinking about the generalizability of this research, my findings will not apply to all no-excuses schools, especially because there is variation among no-excuses schools in their practices. Some more established no-excuses networks, for example, have begun to experiment with modifying their disciplinary practices in response to negative reactions from students and staff.[3] There is also variation between elementary, middle, and high schools in their behavioral practices and expectations. No-excuses schools, however, do share common practices, and, as discussed in chapter 5, Dream Academy copied its practices directly from other no-excuses networks. The results from this study thus would likely apply to no-excuses schools that rely on sweating-the-small-stuff approaches, earning rewards and consequences, and rigidly structuring space and time. Supporting the wider relevance of these findings, there have been a number of subsequent studies of no-excuses schools that provide confirmatory support for my analysis.[4]

Case study research is also well-suited toward making theoretical generalizations. The concepts and ideas I develop in the book about scripts versus tools, the difficulty of teaching cultural capital, and teachers' responses to control of their work, for example, extend beyond the scope of no-excuses schools and can apply to understanding processes of socialization and social control in different educational and institutional settings.

Data Collection

Ethnography is a social science method that privileges "being there"—observing and participating in the everyday lives of the people one aims to study. The method is a tradition with roots in anthropology, and ethnographers have traditionally studied remote communities, spending years in the field to try to understand a people and its culture. Today, ethnographers study a wide range of people and places—from garbage collectors in the Big Apple to Minutemen patrolling the U.S.-Mexico border to the elite modeling industry.[5] By carefully observing people in a variety of situations, ethnographers collect rich data that allow them to make better inferences and fewer assumptions about what people say, do, and mean.

To understand what social and behavioral skills Dream Academy taught students and how they did this, I immersed myself in the school for the 2012–13 academic year. Prior to the academic year, I spent a few pilot months in the school, from March to June 2012, to begin to familiarize myself with the school, start establishing relationships with students and staff, and get my feet wet as an ethnographer. During the pilot period, I observed two to three days a week, typically four to five hours a day, rotating through different grades and classrooms to get a broader sense of the school.

Beginning in August 2012, I participated in a weeklong orientation for teachers and staff, three days of instruction in school culture and behaviors for the incoming fifth graders, and two weeks of summer school primarily focused on getting students to learn school skills and behaviors. During teacher orientation, I was formally introduced by the school director to the teachers as a graduate student conducting research on the school. I typically spent four to five hours per day at the school, four days per week. During the school day, I spent the majority of my time following individual classes, typically dividing my time between one fifth-grade and one eighth-grade class. I chose to focus on fifth graders to observe students' first exposure to the no-excuses school environment (the network did not have an elementary school) and eighth graders because I was initially interested in following these students to different high schools (this turned out not to be logistically feasible because the majority of students continued to Dream Academy's high school, and those who did not attended a wide array of schools). In addition to observing students in these two classes, I periodically visited the other fifth- and eighth-grade classes as well as the sixth- and seventh-grade classes to compare what I was finding to other groups of students and teachers. Individual teachers whose classes I observed sometimes introduced me to their students as a researcher. When I introduced myself to individual students, I told them that I was writing a book about their school. One common reaction I would get from students was, "Why do you want to write a book about *this* school?"

I began my research mostly as an observer, but over time I began to take a more active role. Because it was important to literally get closer to students to hear their conversations and see their classwork, I found the most natural role for me was to assist them with their work. Thus, I often circulated around the classroom and helped individual students. As I got to know students better, I would move from sitting in the back of the room to taking an absent student's seat. I also volunteered to tutor students after school and sat with them at lunch, though I felt a bit like a middle schooler approaching the lunch tables and awkwardly asking students if I could join them. I also observed and participated in a variety of other in-school and out-of-school activities, including homeroom, morning assemblies, mentoring meetings and outings, student ambassador meetings, field trips, school concerts, parent-teacher conferences, and parent association meetings. To better understand the teachers' perspectives, I also regularly observed teachers' one-on-one meetings with their supervisors, sat in weekly staff meetings, and hung out with teachers in their offices and after school.

On a daily basis, I felt conflicted over what to observe because I wanted to be everywhere at the same time. While I prioritized staying with the same two classes, I felt that it was hard to follow what was happening with the students if I missed even a few class periods or skipped a day of school. Moreover, I wanted to understand the perspectives of teachers and staff, which at times took me out of the classroom. In retrospect, I think it would have been useful, about halfway through my fieldwork, to be more systematic about sampling different settings, actors, events, and processes within my case.[6] For example, as the theme of "earning" emerged in my analysis, I could have mapped out a strategy to ensure that I observed the different forms of earning, the rewards and consequences for earning or failing to earn privileges, the students who succeeded or struggled to earn privileges, and so on.

During my school observations, I carried around a laptop or iPad to type notes. Students would sometimes peer over to see what I was writing or even type something themselves. They were surprised to see their words recorded verbatim. I felt awkward knowing that the students were watching me watch them, so I did not always type extensive field notes in school, sometimes jotting down key phrases or incidents to fill out after I returned home. I prioritized recording dialogue to preserve the voices of the students, teachers, and staff. I felt less awkward typing in staff meetings or teacher meetings because teachers had a better understanding of who I was and what I was doing. When I teach my students about writing ethnographic field notes, I suggest to them to take only limited jottings in the field because it can distract from participation and make others uncomfortable. Additionally, returning from the field to reflect on the day is an important step in developing one's ideas and focus. However, there is a trade-off, as ethnographers have acknowledged, between fully participating and participating in order to write, which is the ultimate task of the ethnographer.[7] In this book, I use quotation marks only for words I directly recorded during my fieldwork.

Ethnographers tend to favor situated listening over direct interviewing.[8] As William Whyte's informant told him in the research for his classic ethnography *Street Corner Society*, "Go easy on that who, what, why, when, where stuff. You ask those questions and people will clam up on you. If people accept you, you can just hang around, and you'll learn the answers in the long run without even having to ask the questions."[9] Though ethnographers do not rely on interviews, they often conduct interviews, typically later in fieldwork, to gather additional information and interpretations. In total, I interviewed 132 participants: 72 students, 33 teachers and staff, and 27 parents. Nearly all the interviews were audio-recorded and transcribed.

In the beginning of the 2012–13 academic year, I sent a research letter and consent form home with each of the 107 fifth-grade and eighth-grade students explaining who I was and what I was doing in the school and asking whether families would be interested in participating in student or parent interviews. I scheduled interviews with the students who completed these forms, typically by approaching them during class to meet with me during lunch, either individually or with a friend or two. From this group, I conducted interviews with thirty-seven eighth graders and twelve fifth graders. I later added two focus groups with nine seventh graders because I was interested in exploring the "seventh-grade slump" that teachers had mentioned when they encountered greater student resistance to school rules and practices. Of these fifty-eight middle school students, I interviewed thirty-eight girls and twenty boys; forty-two were Black, fourteen Latino, and two Asian. For all students, I gave the opportunity to choose their own pseudonyms and use those in the book when they were provided.

Because we were constrained by the lunch time, interviews typically lasted approximately thirty minutes, although I did complete some longer interviews after school. Topics included students' background, educational aspirations, perceptions of the school, perceptions of school discipline, relationships with teachers, and discipline and skills encouraged at home. I found that it was helpful to conduct interviews after getting to observe students for several months because most were already familiar with me and some even approached me to be interviewed. I also had the advantage of being able to ask students follow-up questions or provide them with examples that countered their remarks. Although some interviewers prefer to take a more neutral position during interviewing, I at times challenged their reports based on what I had seen or heard in other situations to elicit more information.[10] I also did this to prompt students who acted noticeably different in their interviews than they did in class, typically more deferential and less talkative.

From my fieldwork at the high school, I also interviewed two ninth graders and conducted three focus groups with ten eleventh graders; the sample was evenly divided by gender, with seven Black, three Latino, and two Asian students. In 2015, through snowball sampling, I tried to contact students from Dream Academy's first graduating high school class to learn about their first year of college. I was able to interview only two Black girls.

With the exception of two teachers, I interviewed all current teachers in the school in the 2012–13 school year. I also interviewed three teachers whom I had met in the 2011–12 school year who did not return the following year. In addition, I interviewed several staff members, including the school's director, the middle school and high school principals, the student affairs dean, the high school college advisor, and the development officer. Interviews followed a semistructured format and typically lasted one to two hours and were mainly conducted at school. Interviews covered teachers' and staff members' personal and professional backgrounds, school experiences and goals, perceptions of the disciplinary system, and overall reflections on the school year.

Finally, I interviewed parents to better understand their background, their decision to enroll their children in the school, their satisfaction with the school and its disciplinary practices, and their own disciplinary practices at home. In addition to the research letter sent home to participate in an interview, I also was given permission to recruit parents through in-person solicitations during parent-teacher conferences. I conducted parent interviews in their homes or in a public space, such as McDonald's, and interviews typically lasted an hour, though one lasted nearly three hours. All of the interviews, except for one, were with mothers; twenty-two participants were Black, three were Latina, and two were White.

Throughout my fieldwork, I also collected a number of school documents, including the school charter application and renewal application, the student and staff handbooks, annual reports, student worksheets, professional development presentations, newsletters, and monthly data reports to the staff. I also obtained anonymous student academic and behavioral records for all students for the 2012–2013 school year, which included every recorded behavioral infraction, by type, student identification number, assigning teacher, and consequence given, as well as students' grade point averages, free and reduced-price lunch status, race, and grade level.

Data Analysis: Revising and Returning

I initially wanted to study no-excuses schools as a case of an institutional effort to explicitly teach cultural capital to students from nondominant backgrounds. I titled my dissertation proposal "Learning How to Learn at a No-Excuses School," and I was primarily interested in how no-excuses schools were teaching students the social and behavioral skills they needed to be successful in school. My original research questions included the following:

1. What social and behavioral skills do no-excuses schools teach?
2. How do no-excuses schools teach students social and behavioral skills?
3. How do teachers evaluate and reward students' social and behavioral skills? Which behaviors do they reward and which do they sanction?

After a couple weeks at the school, however, I quickly began to rethink whether the school was trying to teach students cultural capital. There was certainly attention to behavior, but the school seemed less focused on transmitting particular skills (e.g., how to communicate effectively, how to organize one's work) and more focused on behavioral compliance. In one of my first analytic memos, I wrote reflections on school choice, accountability, and discipline: "For students, discipline is at the forefront of their school experience (or lack thereof, as a few students have lamented). School rules are typically the first thing that students talk about when I ask them whether they like the school." Through my research, I began to delve more deeply into the literatures on school discipline, charter schools, and neoliberal school reforms, none of which were on my radar when I began the project. My analysis moved away from cultural capital toward thinking more about social control.

To analyze my field notes and interview transcriptions, I used an inductive approach, generating hundreds of codes with the assistance of a qualitative analysis program. The process was iterative and messy, as I created, refined, added, deleted, and aggregated codes. This initial process helped me identify key concepts and ideas to explore further, which I developed through analytic memos. Memos included themes like clarity of expectations, consistency, earning privileges, expecting too much, grit, hard work, praise, relationships, respect, sense of urgency, and socialization of teachers. As I developed chapters and articles from my research, I subsequently returned to the interview data to recode the data with more focused questions in mind. I also returned to my field notes, selecting episodes that were related to the themes. Additionally, I organized and read through all the electronic and paper documents I collected, drawing from them for further examples or illustrations of themes. Finally, to analyze the school behavioral data, I ran descriptive statistics using a statistical analysis program.

Although this analytic process helped me identity themes and subthemes for the different chapters, I also spent a considerable amount of time developing the overarching argument for the book, trying on different theoretical framings. Through a process of reading, rewriting, and responding to feedback from colleagues, I began to see how my initial interest in cultural capital intersected with my emergent focus on social control. As a sociologist, I had interpreted the school's practices as not transmitting to students cultural capital, but I knew the school understood its strict disciplinary expectations as instilling in students the cultural capital they needed to be successful in college and a middle-class world. Rereading Ann Swidler's work on culture as toolkit, I found a hook: I saw how the school's efforts to rescript student behavior (through social control) did not provide students with the tools to navigate different situations (cultural capital).

Positionality

"I think these people are all the same people—each one of them is just motivated by a slightly different thing," reflected the school's director, as he commented on the school's teachers during one of our interviews. "They're all Type A personalities who want to accomplish a great deal. And they come from all the same schools. They look the same, they dress the same, they talk the same, right?" He paused. "Or not they, we. We talk the same, right?"

He was right. In appearance and background, I was most like the teachers and staff. I was young, well-educated, ambitious, and middle class. I could very well have been one of the teachers; like several of them, I had been accepted to Teach for America right after college, and I tutored Puerto Rican students at an after-school program throughout college. Not even five feet tall, I looked not much older than the students but dressed professionally, and typing field notes on an iPad, I was an outsider to the students. When students first met me, they often asked me whether I was training to be a teacher.

To help distinguish myself from the teachers, I came to an agreement with the school not to discipline students if I observed minor misbehaviors but to intervene only if children were at risk of harm. Because students were so accustomed to adults in the school monitoring their behavior, I found that positioning myself not as a disciplinarian allowed students to feel comfortable telling me how they felt about the school's practices. In time, the students recognized that I was not an authority figure but someone "writing a book" about the school. For example, at lunch a student would start to censor herself because I was there, and another would jump in, "It's okay, she doesn't do anything." I remember being surprised when a student accused me of switching sides when I told her not to talk in the hallway. Eventually, I began to align myself more with students, for example, by not standing apart from them in the hallway like a teacher but joining them in their silent, straight lines. Students referred to me by my first name as "Ms. Joanne."

Still, I never became a peer to the students as other school ethnographers have tried to do. As an Asian American raised in a middle-class suburban neighborhood who attended predominantly White public schools, I found myself struggling at lunch to follow the cultural references students used. I was not a part of their social circles, nor did I become a confidante. My position was closer to that of a teacher's assistant, or what I was—a graduate student writing a book on the school. At least once a week, a student would ask me how much I had written (very little was my usual reply) or whether I had thought of a title for my book (not yet). One of the school staff told me, "Students are telling me they like talking to you about their problems; you write them down." Had I gotten to know a few students well and taken a "key informant" approach like other ethnographers have, I think I would have gotten richer data on students' peer socialization processes and their individual development of skills and attitudes throughout the school year. My approach, however, had the advantage of allowing me to interact with a variety of students and to understand the perspectives of teachers and administrators.

My race and gender also shaped my interactions, especially with students. As one of a handful of Asian Americans in the school, I had students regularly ask me questions about my race and reference it in passing. For example, they teased a half-Asian boy that I was his sister and asked if I spoke Chinese. I felt that my race gave me an advantage in moving between both the predominantly White teaching staff and the Black and Latino students. As Asian Americans are often perceived as honorary Whites,[11] the mostly White teachers saw me as their peer and confidante. Yet by not being White, I suspect that students felt more open in telling me that a teacher was racist. I did not react, whereas I found that several White teachers became defensive or uncomfortable when students brought up issues of race.

My gender also significantly shaped my interactions. I became friendlier with female students, who tended to approach me and engage me in conversation. I almost always sat with a table of female students or at a mixed-gender table during lunch because I usually made my way to the tables by means of a student whom I knew better. Over time, I tended to sit at the same tables because I did not want to be an unwelcome presence at what was one of the few times of freedom for students. My role as a mother also helped build rapport with some girls. After revealing their shock that I was old enough to have a child, the girls liked looking at pictures of my toddler son on my iPad and asking me questions about him. As noted above, far more girls than boys participated in interviews with me, perhaps because of their greater rapport with me, which may have led me to not fully capture the meanings and experiences of boys in the school.

That said, I did get to know a few boys better at the school by sitting in a boys' mentoring group after school and by tagging along with them at mentoring activities organized by one of their teachers.

In addition to my social position and relationships with students, I think it is important to acknowledge my own tendencies toward flexibility. I think rules are negotiable. I am rarely on time. I once took a personality test that told me that I would be happiest working in an organization where I could make my own decisions. Although my parents are Chinese, they were very much the opposite of Tiger Mom and Dad. They gave my brother and me free rein to watch hours of Disney afternoon cartoons before dinner and to pursue what we wanted. Our Chinese piano teacher eventually refused to teach us because my mom would not make us practice. We were sent to take lessons from her French Canadian husband.

These preferences shaped what I observed, what I asked, and what I recorded. Although I tried to be attentive to these biases during my fieldwork (for example, I reflected in a field note, "I find their rules too harsh, too unbending, too impersonal. But I also recognize that maybe this is related to not holding high expectations. When you bend for students, are you saying it's okay that you can do less?"), I acknowledge that another observer might have interpreted my data differently. By immersing myself in the school for an extended period of time, I tried to understand the place and its people with greater nuance than a visitor passing through. The principal once remarked to me that people often thought they were crazy, but he trusted I would form my own opinion because I was there for so long. By rereading and rethinking my field notes and interviews, I stayed close to the data. Moreover, I sought to present the school through multiple perspectives, not only my own.

Sharing Results

During my fieldwork, I was asked casually from time to time what I was finding. I was open to sharing my emerging ideas and felt that it was instructive to hear teacher and staff responses to my interpretations. I did not ask, nor was I asked, to formally share my results with the school. On one occasion, I created a summary of student quotes for a teacher's presentation on student-teacher relationships.

After concluding my fieldwork and analysis, I reached back out to the school to share a draft of my first article, prior to submitting it to a journal. I sent the article to the school's director and the two principals with a note saying how this first article was critical but I hoped it would be useful. I received a brief thank-you, with no further comments, from the school's director and no reply from the principals. When I completed my dissertation, I sent them a copy of it along with a brief summary of my findings and recommendations. I also did not receive a reply. In drafting a second article on teachers, I reached out to two teachers highlighted in the article, particularly because I was concerned about protecting their confidentiality. They gave me the green light on the article, and one requested a small addition, which I included. For the book manuscript, I asked a former teacher in the school to review it and check for any factual errors, misinterpretations, or breaches of confidentiality.

When I give advice to graduate students who want to do school ethnography, I suggest that they talk with the school leaders to find out what the school is interested in studying. My experiences made me realize that an arrangement closer to a research-practice partnership might be beneficial in producing a study that is useful to both the researcher and the research participants. Although I have not had subsequent conversations with the school leaders, I worry that they may have been hurt or disappointed by my work. I think it is very different to see one's words in print and one's actions interpreted through theory and a critical lens, especially after having welcomed someone into your school for over a year.

That said, I also think it is important to develop a critical lens. I have been heartened by the many emails and conversations I've had with current and former teachers from other no-excuses schools, who have found my writing to reflect their experiences and to help them reflect on those experiences. One teacher wrote this to me: "I simply wanted to say thank you for your work. The level of detail you gave as a result of your ethnographic fieldwork honestly made me feel like I was reliving the past two years again. It was strikingly similar to the experiences I had and it very much helped me make more sense of those experiences."

A no-excuses school leader also cited my work as one of the reasons his school decided to shift from no-excuses disciplinary practices to a responsive classroom model. In a blog on the school website, Steven Wilson, the head of Ascend, a charter school network in New York City, discusses my article:[12]

> She ends by asking: "Can urban schools encourage assertiveness, initiative, and ease while also ensuring order and achievement? Is there an alternative to a no-excuses disciplinary model that still raises students' tests scores?"

Yes, we believe, emphatically yes. At Ascend, we are building one such model. To succeed in college, oft-cited "grit" is not enough. We must foster *agency*—our students' confidence that they are in control of their own lives and can act of their own free choices, their conviction that they can assert their voice and power in the world.

It has been very rewarding to be able to contribute to a dialogue around reforming the disciplinary practices in these schools and to see schools themselves commit to making changes.

It's one thing to write about school reform, however, and another to do it. The work of teaching is hard, and I want to end by reflecting on an experience I had during my fieldwork. I had arranged with a teacher to speak to her students about my research, but when I arrived I learned that she had swapped classes with another teacher who was not present. While waiting for her to arrive, I tried to get students to put their desks in a circle. There was little movement. I walked over and turned one student's desk, thinking she might be more receptive as I recently had been to her house to interview her mom. She turned her desk back. I started counting down from fifteen like I had seen other teachers do. Getting desperate, I asked one of the more popular girls in the class if she could help me get the students in a circle. She obliged, and the desks ended up in somewhat of a circle when the other teacher arrived. I was feeling proud of my small accomplishment when the teacher started scolding the students about how the desks were cluttered together and how some students sat at a seat but not a desk. In a matter of minutes, she got them in a U—one desk perfectly next to another, each student sitting at a desk.

Moving from the back of the room to the front was a very different experience, and I was caught off guard. It was intimidating to stand in front of a class, harder still when the students did not grant me their attention. I even used the techniques I had seen other teachers use. As a sociologist of education, I am always asked whether I have taught before. There is a feeling that you have to experience the classroom before you can judge what you see. This perspective has some merit. My aim in this book has been not to judge the educators and the school but to present the complicated reality of urban schooling, the difficulty of reform, and the possibilities for change.

Chapter One

1. To protect the confidentiality of the respondents, all names used in the book are pseudonyms.

2. I capitalize "Black" to recognize the identity of Black people as a racial group. I also capitalize "White." I use "Latino/a" instead of "Latinx," as these were the terms used by students and staff.

3. Sociologist Pierre Bourdieu coined the term "cultural capital." Cultural capital has been defined by scholars in numerous ways. For a helpful review, see Lamont and Lareau, "Cultural Capital"; Lareau and Weininger, "Cultural Capital in Educational Research."

4. This definition of cultural capital is taken from Jack, *Privileged Poor*, 19.

5. Bourdieu, "School as a Conservative Force"; Bernstein, *Class, Codes and Control*; Giroux, *Theory and Resistance in Education*.

6. Alexander, Entwisle, and Thompson, "School Performance, Status Relations, and the Structure of Sentiment"; Dee, "Teacher like Me"; Roscigno and Ainsworth-Darnell, "Race, Cultural Capital, and Educational Resources."

7. Farkas et al., "Cultural Resources and School Success"; Farkas, "Cognitive Skills and Noncognitive Traits"; Ferguson, *Bad Boys*; Tyson, "Notes from the Back of the Room"; Jennings and DiPrete, "Teacher Effects on Social and Behavioral Skills."

8. Streib, "Class Reproduction by Four Year Olds"; Willis, *Learning to Labour*.

9. Transcripts from Greg Duncan and Richard Murnane's Restoring Opportunity project were made publicly available via their website: http://restoringopportunity .com. This quotation is taken from one of the transcripts.

10. Education Commission of the States, "Charter Schools: Does the State Have a Charter Law?" (January 2020), http://ecs.force.com/mbdata/MBQuestNB2C?rep =CS2001"; National Alliance for Public Charter Schools, "Charter Law Database— States" (2020), https://www.publiccharters.org/our-work/charter-law-database.

11. Charter advocates argue that charter schools allow for greater innovation, choice, and competition. Critics argue that charters divert funding and "cream-skim" strong students from traditional public schools, fail to equitably serve all students such as those with special needs, and, with the growth of national charter networks like KIPP, have become less democratic and less responsive to local communities. For a review of key charter school issues, see Gross et al., "Hopes, Fears, and New Solutions."

12. Data are from 2017–18. See Hussar et al., "Condition of Education 2020."

13. KIPP, "KIPP Charter Schools History," https://www.kipp.org.

14. KIPP, "KIPP: Results," https://www.kipp.org/schools.

15. Ibid. KIPP reports that 88 percent of students qualified for federal free or reduced-price lunch.

16. U.S. Department of Education, "Successful Charter Schools" (June 2004), http://www2.ed.gov/admins/comm/choice/charter/report.pdf.

17. For KIPP's early media coverage, see Abrams, *Education and the Commercial Mindset*, 210–11.

18. Kretchmar, Sondel, and Ferrare, "Mapping the Terrain"; Scott, "Politics of Venture Philanthropy."

19. For a review of charter school outcomes, see Ferrare, "Charter School Outcomes."

20. In a meta-analysis of six experimental studies of no-excuses schools, Cheng et al., "'No Excuses' Charter Schools," found that attending a no-excuses school for one year improved student math scores by 0.25 of a standard deviation (SD) and reading scores by 0.16 SD. The authors note that it is unclear whether the achievement gains generalize to all no-excuses schools, or just those that are oversubscribed and part of these lottery studies. Other researchers have found, however, that outcomes for non-lottery no-excuses schools are comparable to those of lottery schools, although academic gains tend to be slightly lower (Abdulkadiroğlu et al., "Accountability and Flexibility in Public Schools"; Tuttle et al., "KIPP Middle Schools"). For high school graduation and college enrollment outcomes, see Coen, Nichols-Barrer, and Gleason, "Long-Term Impacts of KIPP Middle Schools."

21. Carter, *No Excuses*; Thernstrom and Thernstrom, *No Excuses*.

22. The Coleman Report, commissioned under the Civil Rights Act of 1964 as the first national study of schools, found that a student's family background was a much stronger determinant of student achievement than school quality (Coleman, "Equality of Educational Opportunity"). Research continues to show the power of family background in shaping children's future outcomes. See, for example, Duncan et al., "School Readiness and Later Achievement"; Lee and Burkam, "Inequality at the Starting Gate."

23. Milner, "But What Is Urban Education?"; Ladson-Billings and Tate, "Toward a Critical Race Theory of Education."

24. Mirón and St. John, *Reinterpreting Urban School Reform*; Payne, *So Much Reform, So Little Change*.

25. Milner, "Beyond a Test Score."

26. Cohodes, "Charter Schools and the Achievement Gap"; Wilson, "Success at Scale in Charter Schooling."

27. Hall and Lake, "$500 Million Question"; Scott, "Politics of Venture Philanthropy."

28. Angrist, Pathak, and Walters, "Explaining Charter School Effectiveness," identified 71 percent of schools in Boston as fully or somewhat "no excuses." Sondel, "'No Excuses' in New Orleans," reported that many charters in New Orleans self-identified as "no excuses."

29. Fryer, "Injecting Charter School Best Practices."

30. See also Brooks, *Education Reform in the Twenty-First Century*; Pondiscio, *How the Other Half Learns*; Carr, *Hope Against Hope*.

31. Dobbie and Fryer, "Getting beneath the Veil of Effective Schools"; Wilson, "Success at Scale in Charter Schooling."

32. Golann, "Paradox of Success"; Goodman, "Charter Management Organizations."

33. "2018–2019 KIPP Atlanta Collegiate High School Student & Parent Handbook," https://www.kippmetroatlanta.org.

34. Ibid., 50–51.

35. Prohibitions on personal grooming, facial expressions, and excessive volume codify racial and gender bias, playing into stereotypes of Black girls as loud, obnoxious, and hypersexualized and of Black boys as threatening and hostile. See Morris, "'Tuck in That Shirt!'"; White, "Charter Schools"; Sondel, Kretchmar, and Dunn, "'Who Do These People Want Teaching Their Children?'."

36. White, "Charter Schools"; Goodman, "Charter Management Organizations"; Ravitch, "How 'No Excuses' Schools Deepen Race, Class Divisions."

37. Whitman, *Sweating the Small Stuff*, 3.

38. Thernstrom and Thernstrom, *No Excuses*, 67.

39. Brooks, "Harlem Miracle."

40. Freire, *Pedagogy of the Oppressed*; Giroux, *Theory and Resistance in Education*.

41. Dreeben, *On What Is Learned in School*; Parsons, "School Class as a Social System."

42. Bowles and Gintis, *Schooling in Capitalist America*; Anyon, "Social Class and the Hidden Curriculum of Work"; Wilcox, "Differential Socialization in the Classroom."

43. Elsen-Rooney, "CEO's Response to George Floyd's Killing"; Barnum and Darville, "'Not a Proud Moment.'"

44. KIPP Foundation, "KIPP: National Results, 2017–18."

45. Coen, Nichols-Barrer, and Gleason, "Long-Term Impacts of KIPP Middle Schools."

46. Tuttle et al., "Understanding the Effect of KIPP."

47. Bourdieu, "School as a Conservative Force"; Bourdieu, *Distinction*; Bourdieu, "Forms of Capital."

48. In their review of cultural capital studies, Lamont and Lareau, "Cultural Capital," define cultural capital as "institutionalized, i.e., widely shared, high status cultural signals (attitudes, preferences, formal knowledge, behaviors, goods and credentials) used for social and cultural exclusion" (156).

49. For critiques of how cultural capital has been operationalized, see Kingston, "Unfulfilled Promise of Cultural Capital Theory"; Lareau and Weininger, "Cultural Capital in Educational Research"; and Golann and Darling-Aduana, "Toward a Multifaceted Understanding."

50. See, for example, Bodovski and Farkas, "'Concerted Cultivation' and Unequal Achievement"; Roksa and Potter, "Parenting and Academic Achievement"; Jæger, "Does Cultural Capital Really Affect Academic Achievement?"; Chin and Phillips, "Social Reproduction and Child-Rearing Practices."

51. Lareau and Weininger, "Cultural Capital in Educational Research," 569.

52. Bourdieu discusses how cultural capital is tied to a field. A field can be thought of as a social arena in which actors compete and cooperate to secure resources. Each field has its own "rules of the game" and legitimate action; different types of cultural capital are rewarded in different fields.

53. Bourdieu often discusses cultural capital and habitus together and at times defines habitus as embodied cultural capital. David Swartz, in *Culture and Power*, notes that Bourdieu, in coining habitus, drew from an idea of "habits" that was

broader than basic actions (such as brushing one's teeth). Habits of mind, interaction, and appreciation that shape the course of one's life are closer to what we call "dispositions." I prefer Swidler's tools to Bourdieu's habitus because one can deploy tools without a deeply ingrained disposition—as we see with code-switching. I also think "tools" is a more accessible concept for a general audience.

54. Lareau, *Unequal Childhoods*.

55. De Keere and Spruyt, "'Prophets in the Pay of State.'"

56. Jack, *Privileged Poor*; Collier and Morgan, "'Is That Paper Really Due Today?'"; Karp and Bork, "'They Never Told Me What to Expect.'"

57. Swidler, "Culture in Action," 273.

58. Lizardo and Strand, "Skills, Toolkits, Contexts and Institutions," 206.

59. The "feel of the game," for example, is what scholars often refer to as habitus. I acknowledge that other scholars might characterize tools of interaction as a "secondary habitus" rather than cultural capital.

60. Calarco, *Negotiating Opportunities*.

61. Khan, *Privilege*.

62. Bourdieu, "School as a Conservative Force."

63. For an exception, see Cox, "Mechanisms of Organizational Commitment."

64. Sleeter, "Confronting the Marginalization of Culturally Responsive Pedagogy."

65. Ferguson, *Bad Boys*; Morris, "'Tuck in That Shirt!'"; Tyson, "Notes from the Back of the Room"; Valenzuela, *Subtractive Schooling*.

66. On the intersections between race and cultural capital, see Richards, "When Class Is Colorblind."

67. Lewis-McCoy, *Inequality in the Promised Land*.

68. Yosso, "Whose Culture Has Capital?"

69. Carter, "'Black' Cultural Capital."

70. Delpit, "Silenced Dialogue."

71. Fernández-Kelly, *Hero's Fight*, 117–18.

72. See Garland, *Culture of Control*.

73. Wacquant, "Deadly Symbiosis."

74. In *Punished*, Rios defines a "youth control complex" as an "ubiquitous system of criminalization molded by the synchronized, systematic punishment meted out by socializing and social control institutions" (40).

75. Skiba and Peterson, "Dark Side of Zero Tolerance."

76. Losen et al., *Are We Closing the School Discipline Gap?*

77. Skiba et al., "Color of Discipline"; Welch and Payne, "Racial Threat and Punitive School Discipline"; Gregory, Skiba, and Noguera, "Achievement Gap and the Discipline Gap"; Lewis and Diamond, *Despite the Best Intentions*.

78. Morris, "'Tuck in that Shirt!'"; Ferguson, *Bad Boys*; Gregory and Weinstein, "Discipline Gap and African Americans."

79. Skiba et al., "Color of Discipline."

80. Noguera, *Trouble with Black Boys*. See also Saltman and Gabbard, *Education as Enforcement*.

81. Milner et al., *"These Kids Are Out of Control."*

82. No-excuses schools have less-defined instructional practices than they do behavioral ones. They do not subscribe to a specific curriculum or approach and

often develop their own materials. At the start of the year, teachers were instructed to "begin from the end," working with state standards to create a scope and sequence for the entire year, a common practice in no-excuses schools. Classes did not use textbooks to give teachers greater freedom to adapt their materials to meet students' needs.

83. In 2012–13, the sixth grade had three classes because the school had planned to expand.

84. These percentages are reported by Dream Academy, taking an average of proficiency and advanced proficiency rates from the state assessments in 2013. Data come from the state department of education.

85. *Federal Register* 77, no. 57 (March 23, 2012), https://www.govinfo.gov/content /pkg/FR-2012-03-23/pdf/2012-7036.pdf.

86. The school had only a handful of White, Asian, and Native American students.

87. Lake et al., "Learning from Charter School Management Organizations."

88. These numbers are for the middle school and high school combined. I did not have access to numbers for only the middle school.

89. Wilson, "Success at Scale in Charter Schooling"; Woodworth et al., "San Francisco Bay Area KIPP Schools."

90. Compared to the local public school district, Dream Academy's salaries for teachers with no experience were lower, starting at $45,000, compared to approximately $50,000 for a district teacher (with a bachelor's degree). Dream Academy also did not pay higher amounts for teachers with master's degrees.

Chapter Two

1. To disguise the city, these numbers are approximate.

2. Lareau, *Unequal Childhoods*; Calarco, *Negotiating Opportunities*.

3. Mehan, "Competent Student," 146.

4. Electronics and cell phones are confiscated if seen. On the first offense, the parent can come retrieve the device. On the second offense, the school keeps the device for thirty days. On the third offense, the school keeps the device for the entire school year.

5. Dream Academy Student Handbook 2012–13.

6. Foucault, *Discipline and Punish*.

7. Whitman, *Sweating the Small Stuff*, 21.

8. Kelling and Wilson, "Broken Windows."

9. In all, 15,042 out of 15,445 infractions were categorized by type. Tardy and minor disrespect were not assigned a category. I categorized tardy as category 2 because it resulted in detention and minor disrespect as category 1 because it is categorized as this in the Student Handbook.

10. The school also had category 4 offenses for "intolerable" behavior like fighting, stealing, and sexual harassment. These infractions were not recorded in the data I received from the school.

11. Jones, "Studying 'Success' at an 'Effective' School."

12. Lewis, "Culture of Poverty."

13. Ryan, *Blaming the Victim*.

14. Gorski, "Peddling Poverty for Profit"; Montano and Quintanar-Sarellana, "Undoing Ruby Payne"; Redeaux, "Framework for Maintaining White Privilege."

15. Delpit, "Silenced Dialogue."

16. See Paris and Alim, *Culturally Sustaining Pedagogies*.

17. Ferguson, *Bad Boys*.

18. Morris, "'Ladies' or 'Loudies'?"; Morris, *Pushout*.

19. Carter, *No Excuses*; Thernstrom and Thernstrom, *No Excuses*.

20. Milner and Ladson-Billings, *Start Where You Are*; Ferguson, "Teachers' Perceptions and Expectations."

21. Merton, "Self-Fulfilling Prophecy"; Ferguson, "Teachers' Perceptions and Expectations."

22. Weinstein, *Reaching Higher*.

23. Bonilla-Silva, *Racism without Racists*.

24. Pondiscio, *How the Other Half Learns*, 312–34.

25. Calarco, "Coached for the Classroom."

26. Valenzuela, *Subtractive Schooling*.

27. Yosso, "Whose Culture Has Capital?"

28. Ibid.

29. Lareau, *Unequal Childhoods*.

30. Streib, "Class Reproduction by Four Year Olds"; Calarco, "'I Need Help!'"

31. Lewis-McCoy, *Inequality in the Promised Land*. See also Cucchiara, *Marketing Schools, Marketing Cities*, on how professional White parents were regarded as highly sought-after consumers while working-class Black parents were framed as "guests."

32. See Milner and Ladson-Billings, *Start Where You Are*.

33. See Khan, *Privilege*.

34. Godfrey, Santos, and Burson, "For Better or Worse?"

35. On how Black boys are labeled and stigmatized in no-excuses schools, see Marsh and Noguera, "Beyond Stigma and Stereotypes."

36. See Noguera, *Trouble with Black Boys*.

37. Maynard et al., "Effects of Trauma-Informed Approaches in Schools."

38. Griffin, "Phenomenological Case Study of Four Black Males."

39. Ferguson, *Bad Boys*; Lewis and Diamond, *Despite the Best Intentions*; Losen, *Closing the School Discipline Gap*; Downey and Pribesh, "When Race Matters."

40. Morris, "'Ladies' or 'Loudies'?"; Morris, *Pushout*.

41. Seider et al., "Role of Moral and Performance Character Strengths," 34.

42. A study of nineteen KIPP schools found that Black males had the highest attrition rates of student subgroups (Nichols-Barrer et al., "Student Selection").

43. Miron, Urschel, and Saxton, "What Makes KIPP Work?" Nichols-Barrer et al., "Student Selection," found cumulative attrition rates of 34 percent by eighth grade but found that these rates were comparable to those for the local public school district.

44. Duckworth et al., "Grit," 1087–88.

45. Ibid.

46. KIPP Foundation, "Promise of College Completion."

47. This story is told in Tough, "What If the Secret to Success Is Failure?"

48. Ibid.

49. For a critique of grit, see Love, *We Want to Do More Than Survive*.

50. Giroux, *Against the Terror of Neoliberalism*, 70.

51. Nunn, *Defining Student Success*, argues that a "success identity" based on initiative and internal motivation matches the "sparkle" that elite colleges look for in applicants, whereas a success identity based on hard work and external motivation matches the expectations of lower tiers of higher education.

52. Mehta and Fine, *In Search of Deeper Learning*.

Chapter Three

1. Collier and Morgan, "'Is That Paper Really Due Today?'"; Karp and Bork, "'They Never Told Me What to Expect.'"

2. Studies have found that families and schools emphasize rule compliance and rote behavior with working-class and poor students, but they emphasize expression, independence, and negotiation with middle-class and upper-class students. See Anyon, "Social Class and the Hidden Curriculum of Work"; Lareau, *Unequal Childhoods*.

3. Collier and Morgan, "'Is That Paper Really Due Today?'"; Karp and Bork, "'They Never Told Me What to Expect'"; Jack, *Privileged Poor*; Lee, *Class and Campus Life*.

4. Giroux, *Theory and Resistance in Education*; Freire, *Pedagogy of the Oppressed*. Critical scholars argue that though schools are favored toward the dominant culture, they still remain sites of conflict and contestation.

5. There is a long debate over the benefits of direct instruction versus student-centered learning, for what kinds of students and for what types of outcomes. On the benefits of direct instruction, see Kirschner, Sweller, and Clark, "Why Minimal Guidance during Instruction Does Not Work."

6. Mehta and Fine, *In Search of Deeper Learning*.

7. Bowles and Gintis, *Schooling in Capitalist America*.

8. See Turco, *Conversational Firm*.

9. Lake et al., "Learning from Charter School Management Organizations."

10. Calarco, "'I Need Help!'"; Mehan, "Competent Student"; Streib, "Class Reproduction by Four Year Olds"; Kozlowski, "Socioeconomic Inequality in Decoding Instructions."

11. Calarco, "'I Need Help!'"; Calarco, *Negotiating Opportunities*; Streib, "Class Reproduction by Four Year Olds"; Kozlowski, "Socioeconomic Inequality in Decoding Instructions."

12. Ainsworth-Darnell and Downey, "Assessing the Oppositional Culture Explanation"; Lewis and Diamond, *Despite the Best Intentions*; Skiba et al., "Color of Discipline."

13. Kozlowski, "Doing School." On unequal returns to cultural capital by race, see also Roscigno and Ainsworth-Darnell, "Race, Cultural Capital, and Educational Resources."

14. Mehan, "Competent Student."

15. Ibid., 136.

16. Waters and Sroufe, "Social Competence as a Developmental Construct," 80.

17. Morris, "'Ladies' or 'Loudies'?"; Morris, *Pushout*; Carter Andrews et al., "Impossibility of Being 'Perfect and White.'"

18. Martin, "Becoming a Gendered Body."

19. Lareau, *Unequal Childhoods*; Calarco, *Negotiating Opportunities*; Rivera, *Pedigree*.

20. Western, *Punishment and Inequality in America*; Losen, *Closing the School Discipline Gap*; Parenti, *Lockdown America*.

21. Morris, "'Ladies' or 'Loudies'?"; Carter Andrews et al., "Impossibility of Being 'Perfect and White'"; Goff et al., "Essence of Innocence."

22. Thomas and Blackmon, "Influence of the Trayvon Martin Shooting."

23. Astramovich and Harris, "Promoting Self-Advocacy."

24. Scholars have expressed concern that the strict controls in no-excuses schools limit the civic skills students develop. See Ben-Porath, "Deferring Virtue"; Graham, "'In Real Life, You Have to Speak Up'"; Kerstetter, "Different Kind of Discipline"; Dishon and Goodman, "No-Excuses for Character."

25. Duckworth and Seligman, "Self-Discipline Outdoes IQ."

26. Duckworth, Gendler, and Gross, "Self-Control in School-Age Children," 200.

27. KIPP Foundation, "Promise of College Completion."

28. Ibid.

Chapter Four

1. Jack, *Privileged Poor*.

2. Khan, *Privilege*, 14.

3. Ibid.

4. Cookson and Persell, *Preparing for Power*, 26.

5. Goffman, *Asylums*, 304–5. Goffman argues that these minor behaviors, which he calls "secondary adjustments," do not challenge authority structures but provide individuals with a degree of autonomy.

6. See Giroux, *Theory and Resistance in Education*; MacLeod, *Ain't No Makin' It*; Willis, *Learning to Labour*. One of the more popular recent explanations is the "oppositional culture" theory developed by Ogbu, *Black American Students*. Given limited structural conditions for mobility, the argument goes, Black students are less committed to the American Dream and thus resist school. For a critique of this theory, see Harris, *Kids Don't Want to Fail*.

7. Erickson, "Transformation and School Success."

8. Way, "School Discipline and Disruptive Classroom Behavior."

9. Arum, *Judging School Discipline*, 33. Arum traces a decline in teacher authority to legal challenges to schools that occurred in the student rights contestation period of the 1960s and 1970s. Arum argues that as a result of changing legislation teachers became less likely to discipline students and students became less likely to accept discipline as legitimate.

10. Erving Goffman uses this description to characterize total institutions. See Goffman, *Asylums*, 41.

11. Merton, "Social Structure and Anomie," 673.

12. Ben-Porath, "Deferring Virtue"; Graham, "'In Real Life, You Have to Speak Up'"; Lamboy and Lu, "Pursuit of College for All"; Kerstetter, "Different Kind of Discipline."

13. Carter et al., "You Can't Fix What You Don't Look At."

NOTES TO CHAPTER 5 [197]

14. See Milner and Laughter, "But Good Intentions Are Not Enough"; Terrill and Mark, "Preservice Teachers' Expectations."

15. Warren, "Utility of Empathy"; Sondel, Kretchmar, and Dunn, "'Who Do These People Want Teaching Their Children?'"

16. Trujillo, Scott, and Rivera, "Follow the Yellow Brick Road."

17. Milner, *"These Kids Are Out of Control"*; Weinstein, Tomlinson-Clarke, and Curran, "Toward a Conception of Culturally Responsive Classroom Management."

18. Griffin, "Phenomenological Case Study of Four Black Males," 193.

19. Anderson, *Code of the Street*. Anderson refers to this reciprocal notion of respect as "a perversion of the Golden Rule, whose by-product in this case is respect and whose caveat is vengeance, or payment" (66). See also Lawrence-Lightfoot, *Respect*, and Rios, *Punished*. Respect becomes central in informal social exchanges because youth of color often do not gain respect and esteem through other social institutions.

20. Lareau, *Unequal Childhoods*.

21. Shedd, *Unequal City*.

22. Noguera, *Trouble with Black Boys*, 120.

23. Goffman, *Asylums*, 7.

24. Merton, "Self-Fulfilling Prophecy."

25. Lemov, *Teach Like a Champion 2.0*, 361.

26. Ibid., 363.

27. Taylor, "Principles of Scientific Management."

28. Lemov, *Teach Like a Champion*, 154.

29. Foucault, *Discipline and Punish*.

30. PBS, "School-by-School Reform: KIPP: Michael Feinberg Interview" (September 2005), http://www.pbs.org/makingschoolswork/sbs/kipp/feinberg.html.

31. Khan, *Privilege*; Calarco, *Negotiating Opportunities*; Lareau, *Unequal Childhoods*.

32. Lareau, *Unequal Childhoods*, Chin and Phillips, "Social Reproduction and Child-Rearing Practices."

33. Haberman, "Pedagogy of Poverty," 294.

34. Golann, "Paradox of Success."

Chapter Five

1. DiMaggio and Powell, "Iron Cage Revisited."

2. Payne, *So Much Reform, So Little Change*.

3. This is taken from the school's charter application, which is not cited for confidentiality.

4. Skiba and Peterson, "Dark Side of Zero Tolerance"; Nolan, *Police in the Hallways*.

5. Losen, *Closing the School Discipline Gap*.

6. American Psychological Association Zero Tolerance Task Force, "Are Zero Tolerance Policies Effective in the Schools?"

7. Christie, Nelson, and Jolivette, "School Characteristics Related to the Use of Suspension"; Skiba et al., "Where Should We Intervene?"; Sartain, Allensworth, and Porter, "Suspending Chicago's Students."

8. Perfect et al., "School-Related Outcomes."

9. Booher-Jennings, "Below the Bubble"; Darling-Hammond, "Race, Inequality and Educational Accountability"; Lipman, *High Stakes Education*.

10. Aronson, Murphy, and Saultz, "Under Pressure in Atlanta."

11. Lipman, "Neoliberal Education Restructuring Dangers and Opportunities."

12. For KIPP's history, I draw from Mathews, *Work Hard* and Jones, "Studying 'Success' at an 'Effective' School."

13. Mathews, *Work Hard*, 172.

14. Jones, "Studying 'Success' at an 'Effective' School," 27.

15. Mathews, *Work Hard*, 173–74.

16. On staffing of no-excuses schools, see Wilson, "Success at Scale in Charter Schooling."

17. Ladson-Billings, *Dreamkeepers*.

18. Whitmire, *Founders*.

19. Mathews, *Work Hard*, 266.

20. See Ravitch, *Reign of Error*; Scott, "Politics of Venture Philanthropy."

21. Kretchmar, Sondel, and Ferrare, "Mapping the Terrain."

22. Charter school regulations vary by state. See Education Commission of the States, "Charter Schools: What Rules Are Waived for Charter Schools?" (January 2020), http://ecs.force.com/mbdata/MBQuestNB2C?rep=CS2014.

23. Kahlenberg, *Tough Liberal*; Kahlenberg and Potter, *Smarter Charter*; Stulberg, "What History Offers Progressive Choice Scholarship."

24. Friedman, "Public Schools." See also Chubb and Moe, *Politics, Markets, and America's Schools*.

25. Neoliberal supporters view the government as bureaucratic, inefficient, and self-interested, and see markets as generating competition, spurring innovation, and holding organizations accountable to their clients and customers. In the 1970s and 1980s, Britain prime minister Margaret Thatcher and U.S. president Ronald Reagan set into motion a number of neoliberal policies favoring deregulation, privatization, and the expansion of free markets.

26. Kretchmar, Sondel, and Ferrare, "Mapping the Terrain"; Scott, "Politics of Venture Philanthropy."

27. Whitmire, *Founders*.

28. Lake et al., "National Study of Charter Management Organization (CMO) Effectiveness," 1. See also Farrell, Wohlstetter, and Smith, "Charter Management Organizations"; Scott, "Politics of Venture Philanthropy."

29. Furgeson et al., "Charter-School Management Organizations," xxii.

30. Ibid.

31. National Alliance for Public Charter Schools, "Closer Look at the Charter School Movement."

32. Furgeson et al., "Charter-School Management Organizations," xxiii. This is compared to 76 percent of students in the host districts.

33. Lake et al., "National Study of Charter Management Organization (CMO) Effectiveness."

34. Ibid.

35. Lake et al., "Learning from Charter School Management Organizations."

36. Furgeson et al., "Charter-School Management Organizations."

37. For a similar list, see Abrams, *Education and the Commercial Mindset*, 192.

38. Total charter school student enrollment was estimated at 3.1 million in fall 2017. See Hussar et al., "Condition of Education 2020."

39. Ibid.

40. Wilson, "Negotiating Public and Private"; Wells et al., "Charter Schools as Postmodern Paradox."

41. Stulberg, *Race, Schools, and Hope*; Pattillo, "Everyday Politics of School Choice in the Black Community."

42. Hernández, "Race and Racelessness in CMO Marketing."

43. Buras, *Charter Schools, Race, and Urban Space*, 47.

44. Sondel, "Raising Citizens or Raising Test Scores?"

45. Mungal, "Teach for America."

46. Kretchmar, Sondel, and Ferrare, "Mapping the Terrain."

47. Teach for America, "Who We Are" (2020), https://www.teachforamerica.org/what-we-do/who-we-are.

48. Darling-Hammond, "Who Will Speak for the Children?"; Milner and Howard, "Counter-Narrative as Method"; and White, "Teach for America's Paradoxical Diversity Initiative."

49. Pattillo, "Everyday Politics of School Choice."

50. Henry and Dixson, "'Locking the Door before We Got the Keys.'"

51. Meyer and Rowan, "Institutionalized Organizations," 344.

52. DiMaggio and Powell, "Iron Cage Revisited."

53. See Lake et al., "National Study of Charter Management Organization (CMO) Effectiveness," 3.

54. Meyer and Rowan, "Institutionalized Organizations"; DiMaggio and Powell, "Iron Cage Revisited."

55. In a comprehensive review of innovations in charter schools, Lubienski ("Innovation in Education Markets") found that charters tended to copy curricular and instructional practices from other successful schools rather than develop their own.

56. Cohodes, "Charter Schools and the Achievement Gap."

57. Cucchiara, *Marketing Schools, Marketing Cities*; Massey and Denton, *American Apartheid*.

58. The legality of bussing was upheld in *Swann v. Charlotte-Mecklenburg Board of Education* in 1971. However, in 1974, the Supreme Court ruled in *Milliken v. Bradley* that schools did not need to bus between districts. This ruling reduced the ability of school districts to desegregate because many regions were both racially and socioeconomically segregated by school districts.

59. See Cucchiara, *Marketing Schools, Marketing Cities*.

60. In 2019–20, New York City public schools were 15 percent White (New York City Department of Education, "DOE Data at a Glance" [2020], https://www.schools.nyc.gov/about-us/reports/doe-data-at-a-glance), Chicago public schools were 11 percent White (Chicago Public Schools, "Stats and Facts" [2020], https://cps.edu/About_CPS/At-a-glance/Pages/Stats_and_facts.aspx), and Philadelphia public schools were 14 percent White (School District of Philadelphia, "Fast Facts" [2020], https://www.philasd.org/fast-facts/).

61. André-Bechely, *Could It Be Otherwise?*; Pattillo, "Everyday Politics of School Choice"; Rhodes and DeLuca, "Residential Mobility and School Choice"; Corcoran et al., "Leveling the Playing Field."

62. Moskowitz, "Why Students Need to Sit Up."

63. See Golann, Debs, and Weiss, "'To Be Strict on Your Own.'"

64. For a discussion of choice, see Goodman, "Charter Management Organizations."

Chapter Six

1. This history is discussed in Green, *Building a Better Teacher.*

2. Lemov, *Teach Like a Champion,* 4.

3. Lortie, *Schoolteacher*; Ball and Cohen, "Developing Practice, Developing Practitioners."

4. Mungal, "Teach for America."

5. Lake et al., "Learning from Charter School Management Organizations."

6. Ibid.

7. Ingersoll, "Teacher Shortage."

8. Borman and Dowling, "Teacher Attrition and Retention."

9. Ingersoll, "Beginning Teacher Induction."

10. Mehta, *Allure of Order.*

11. Dee et al., "Impact of No Child Left Behind"; Jennings and Sohn, "Measure for Measure"; Ingersoll, *Who Controls Teachers' Work?*

12. Milner, "But What Is Urban Education?"; Ladson-Billings and Tate, "Toward a Critical Race Theory of Education."

13. Wilson, "Success at Scale in Charter Schooling."

14. Hernández, "Race and Racelessness in CMO Marketing"; White, "Teach for America's Paradoxical Diversity Initiative."

15. Coser, *Greedy Institutions.*

16. During the year, Dream Academy hired a consulting agency and developed a new, performance-based compensation system to be more competitive with the local district and with other charter networks. Novice teacher salaries were changed to begin at approximately $50,000, with promotions based on tenure and performance. After five years at the school with demonstrated exemplary performance, a teacher could earn between $79,000 and $98,000.

17. Henry, Fortner, and Bastian, "Effects of Experience and Attrition"; Kane, Rockoff, and Staiger, "What Does Certification Tell Us about Teacher Effectiveness?"

18. Weiner and Torres, "Different Location or Different Map?"

19. Lortie, *Schoolteacher,* 79–80.

20. Everitt, "Teacher Careers."

21. Golann, "Conformers, Adaptors, Imitators, and Rejecters."

22. Bernstein, *Class, Codes and Control.*

23. Lareau, *Unequal Childhoods*; Calarco, *Negotiating Opportunities.*

24. Waller, *Sociology of Teaching,* 227.

25. Lemov, *Teach Like a Champion,* 213.

26. Ladson-Billings, *Dreamkeepers.*

27. Brody and Flor, "Maternal Resources, Parenting Practices, and Child Competence."

28. Brody and Flor, "Maternal Resources, Parenting Practices, and Child Competence."

29. Brooks-Gunn and Markman "Contribution of Parenting to Ethnic and Racial Gaps," 148. Parents who used the "tough love" approach had higher IQs and vocabulary scores than parents who used the classic authoritarian approach, suggesting that this parenting style might also be beneficial for children.

30. Stitzlein and West, "New Forms of Teacher Education."

31. Merton, "Social Structure and Anomie."

32. Lemov, *Teach Like a Champion Field Guide*, 300.

33. Everitt, *Lesson Plans*.

34. Swidler, "Culture in Action," 277.

35. See Gecas and Schwalbe, "Beyond the Looking-Glass Self."

36. Datnow and Castellano, "Teachers' Responses to Success for All"; Mittenfelner Carl, "Reacting to the Script"; Milner, "Scripted and Narrowed Curriculum Reform."

37. Yeh, "Re-analysis of the Effects of KIPP"; Wilson, "Success at Scale in Charter Schooling"; Abrams, *Education and the Commercial Mindset*.

38. Henry, Fortner, and Bastian, "Effects of Experience and Attrition"; Kane, Rockoff, and Staiger, "What Does Certification Tell Us about Teacher Effectiveness?"

39. Donaldson and Johnson, "Price of Misassignment."

40. Torres, "Is This Work Sustainable?" See also Torres, "Teacher Efficacy."

41. Woodworth et al., "San Francisco Bay Area KIPP Schools."

42. Ingersoll, *Who Controls Teachers' Work?*, 215–16.

43. Renzulli, Parrott, and Beattie, "Racial Mismatch and School Type."

44. Timmermans and Berg, *Gold Standard*.

45. Metz, *Classrooms and Corridors*.

46. Timmermans and Epstein, "World of Standards."

47. Rowan, "Commitment and Control."

48. Ingersoll, *Who Controls Teachers' Work?*; Rosenholtz and Simpson, "Workplace Conditions."

49. Waller, *Sociology of Teaching*, 308–9.

Chapter Seven

1. Lareau, *Unequal Childhoods*; Khan, *Privilege*.

2. Lareau, *Unequal Childhoods*; Jack, *Privileged Poor*; Khan, *Privilege*; Calarco, *Negotiating Opportunities*.

3. Calarco, *Negotiating Opportunities*.

4. See Cox, "Engineered Struggle and 'Earned' Success."

5. Delpit, "Silenced Dialogue."

6. Ladson-Billings, *Dreamkeepers*.

7. Milner et al., *"These Kids Are Out of Control"*; Morris, "'Tuck in That Shirt!'"

8. Kozlowski, "Doing School"; Roscigno and Ainsworth-Darnell, "Race, Cultural Capital, and Educational Resources."

9. Lareau, *Unequal Childhoods*; Jack, *Privileged Poor*.

10. Wallace, "Reading 'Race' in Bourdieu?"; Richards, "When Class Is Colorblind."

11. Paris and Alim, *Culturally Sustaining Pedagogies*.

12. Yosso, "Whose Culture Has Capital?"; Moll et al., "Funds of Knowledge for Teaching."

13. Prieur and Savage, "Emerging Forms of Cultural Capital"; Weenink, "Cosmopolitanism as a Form of Capital."

14. Cucchiara, Cassar, and Clark, "'I Just Need a Job!'"

15. Chang, "Maximizing the Promise of Community Schools."

16. Peak, "Student-Shoving Principal Leaves Post."

17. Barnum and Darville, "'Not a Proud Moment.'" The emails and statements from AF are linked at the end of the article.

18. Disare, "'No Excuses' No More?"; Strauss, "Some 'No-Excuses' Charter Schools Say They Are Changing."

19. Decker, Snyder, and Darville, "Suspensions at City Charter Schools."

20. Shapiro, "Student Protests at Success Academy's High School"; Elsen-Rooney, "CEO's Response to George Floyd's Killing."

21. Disare, "'No Excuses' No More?"; Wilson, "Beyond No Excuses"; Zappa, "How We're Shifting School Culture." For a defense of these practices, see Moskowitz, "Why Students Need to Sit Up."

22. Dobbie and Fryer, "Getting beneath the Veil of Effective Schools"; Chabrier, Cohodes, and Oreopoulos, "What Can We Learn from Charter School Lotteries?" For a review of studies on no-excuses disciplinary practices, see Golann and Torres, "Do No-Excuses Disciplinary Practices Promote Success?"

23. Smrekar, *Impact of School Choice and Community*; Smrekar, "Missing Link in School-Linked Social Service Programs."

24. See Maynard et al., "Effects of Trauma-Informed Approaches in Schools."

25. Warren, *Urban Preparation*, 19.

26. Metropolitan Expeditionary Learning Enrollment (2018–19), https://data .nysed.gov/enrollment.php?year=2019&instid=800000069162.

27. Westheimer and Kahne, "What Kind of Citizen?," describe similar types of social justice modules that help to develop what they term "justice-oriented" citizens. Drawing on their framework, Sondel, "Raising Citizens or Raising Test Scores?," found that teachers in a no-excuses school did not develop "justice-oriented" citizens, only "personally responsible" citizens who obey laws and take responsibility for their own actions.

28. Redding, "Teacher Like Me."

29. Strauss, "Single Most Telling Sentence."

30. U.S. Department of Education, "President's Budget Expands Education Freedom, Supports Teachers, Protects Vulnerable Students" (March 11, 2019), https:// www.ed.gov/news/press-releases/presidents-budget-expands-education-freedom -supports-teachers-protects-vulnerable-students.

31. See Cohodes, "Charter Schools and the Achievement Gap."

32. Farrell, Wohlstetter, and Smith, "Charter Management Organizations."

33. Metz, *Classrooms and Corridors*, ix.

34. Mungal, "Teach for America."

35. For a review of market-based reform in education, see Scott and Holme, "Political Economy of Market-Based Educational Policies."

36. Zimmer, Henry, and Kho, "Effects of School Turnaround."

37. Massell, Glazer, and Malone, "'This Is the Big Leagues'"; Glazer and Egan, "Ties That Bind."

38. Glazer and Egan, "Ties That Bind."

39. Nation, "Point/Counterpoint," 10.

40. Stengel, "From the Editor."

41. On external versus internal accountability, see Mehta, *Allure of Order*. On scaling up innovation, see Bryk et al., *Learning to Improve*; Redding, Cannata, and Haynes, "With Scale in Mind."

42. See Stitzlein and West, "New Forms of Teacher Education."

Methodological Appendix

1. Whitman, *Sweating the Small Stuff*; Thernstrom and Thernstrom, *No Excuses*.

2. Studies suggest that children's noncognitive skills are particularly sensitive to investments between the ages of eight and thirteen. See Cunha and Heckman, "Formulating, Identifying and Estimating the Technology of Cognitive and Noncognitive Skill Formation."

3. See Whitmire, *Founders*, for a discussion of the evolution of no-excuses practices.

4. Graham, "'In Real Life, You Have to Speak Up'"; Kerstetter, "Different Kind of Discipline"; Sondel, "Raising Citizens or Raising Test Scores?"; Torres, "'Are We Architects or Construction Workers?'"

5. Nagle, *Picking Up*; Shapira, *Waiting for José*; Mears, *Pricing Beauty*.

6. For a helpful discussion of within-case sampling, see Miles, Huberman, and Saldana, *Qualitative Data Analysis*.

7. For a discussion on ethnographic marginality and jottings, see Emerson, Fretz, and Shaw, *Writing Ethnographic Fieldnotes*.

8. Sanjek, *Fieldnotes*.

9. Whyte, *Street Corner Society*.

10. See Weiss, *Learning from Strangers*, 66.

11. Tuan, *Forever Foreigners or Honorary Whites?*

12. Wilson, "Beyond No Excuses."

BIBLIOGRAPHY

Abdulkadiroğlu, Atila, Joshua D. Angrist, Susan M. Dynarski, Thomas J. Kane, and Parag A. Pathak. "Accountability and Flexibility in Public Schools: Evidence from Boston's Charters and Pilots." *Quarterly Journal of Economics* 126, no. 2 (2011): 699–748.

Abrams, Samuel E. *Education and the Commercial Mindset.* Harvard University Press, 2016.

Ainsworth-Darnell, James W., and Douglas B. Downey. "Assessing the Oppositional Culture Explanation for Racial/Ethnic Differences in School Performance." *American Sociological Review* 63, no. 4 (1998): 536–53.

Alexander, Karl L., Doris R. Entwisle, and Maxine S. Thompson. "School Performance, Status Relations, and the Structure of Sentiment: Bringing the Teacher Back In." *American Sociological Review* 52, no. 5 (1987): 665–82.

American Psychological Association Zero Tolerance Task Force. "Are Zero Tolerance Policies Effective in the Schools? An Evidentiary Review and Recommendations." *American Psychologist* 63, no. 9 (2008): 852–62.

Anderson, Elijah. *Code of the Street: Decency, Violence, and the Moral Life of the Inner City.* Norton, 2000.

André-Bechely, Lois. *Could It Be Otherwise? Parents and the Inequalities of Public School Choice.* Routledge, 2005.

Angrist, Joshua D., Parag A. Pathak, and Christopher R. Walters. "Explaining Charter School Effectiveness." NBER Working Paper 17332, National Bureau of Economic Research, August 2011. http://www.nber.org/papers/w17332.

Anyon, Jean. "Social Class and the Hidden Curriculum of Work." *Journal of Education* 162, no. 1 (1980): 67–92.

Aronson, Brittany, Kristin M. Murphy, and Andrew Saultz. "Under Pressure in Atlanta: School Accountability and Special Education Practices during the Cheating Scandal." *Teachers College Record* 118, no. 14 (2016): 1–26.

Arum, Richard. *Judging School Discipline: The Crisis of Moral Authority.* Harvard University Press, 2003.

Astramovich, Randall L., and Katrina R. Harris. "Promoting Self-Advocacy among Minority Students in School Counseling." *Journal of Counseling & Development* 85, no. 3 (2007): 269–76.

Ball, Deborah Loewenberg, and David K. Cohen. "Developing Practice, Developing Practitioners: Toward a Practice-Based Theory of Professional Education." In *Teaching as the Learning Profession: Handbook of Policy and Practice*, edited by Linda Darling-Hammond and Gary Sykes, 3–22. Jossey-Bass, 1999.

Barnum, Matt, and Sarah Darville. "'Not a Proud Moment': How Turmoil at One School Could Shake Up the Achievement First Charter Network." *Chalkbeat*, February 28, 2019. www.chalkbeat.org/2019/2/28/21107034/not-a-proud-moment-how -turmoil-at-one-school-could-shake-up-the-achievement-first-charter-network.

Baumrind, Diana. "An Exploratory Study of Socialization Effects on Black Children: Some Black-White Comparisons." *Child Development* 43 (1972): 261–67.

Ben-Porath, Sigal. "Deferring Virtue: The New Management of Students and the Civic Role of Schools." *Theory and Research in Education* 11, no. 2 (2013): 111–28.

Bernstein, Basil B. *Class, Codes and Control.* Routledge and Kegan Paul, 1971.

Bodovski, Katerina, and George Farkas. "'Concerted Cultivation' and Unequal Achievement in Elementary School." *Social Science Research* 37, no. 3 (2008): 903–19.

Bonilla-Silva, Eduardo. *Racism without Racists: Color-Blind Racism and the Persistence of Racial Inequality in the United States.* 3rd ed. Rowman & Littlefield, 2010.

Booher-Jennings, Jennifer. "Below the Bubble: 'Educational Triage' and the Texas Accountability System." *American Educational Research Journal* 42, no. 2 (2005): 231–68.

Borman, Geoffrey D., and N. Maritza Dowling. "Teacher Attrition and Retention: A Meta-Analytic and Narrative Review of the Research." *Review of Educational Research* 78, no. 3 (2008): 367–409.

Bourdieu, Pierre. *Distinction: A Social Critique of the Judgment of Taste.* Harvard University Press, 1984.

——. "The Forms of Capital." In *Handbook of Theory and Research for the Sociology of Education,* edited by John Richardson, 241–58. Greenwood, 1986.

——. *The Logic of Practice.* Stanford University Press, 1990.

——. "The School as a Conservative Force: Scholastic and Cultural Inequalities." In *Contemporary Research in the Sociology of Education,* edited by John Eggleston, 32–46. Methuen, 1974.

Bowles, Samuel, and Herbert Gintis. *Schooling in Capitalist America: Educational Reform and the Contradictions of Economic Life.* Basic Books, 1976.

Brody, Gene H., and Douglas L. Flor. "Maternal Resources, Parenting Practices, and Child Competence in Rural, Single-Parent African American Families." *Child Development* 69, no. 3 (1998): 803–16.

Brooks, David. "The Harlem Miracle." *New York Times,* May 8, 2009. http://www.nytimes.com/2009/05/08/opinion/08brooks.html.

Brooks, Erinn. *Education Reform in the Twenty-First Century: The Marketization of Teaching and Learning at a No-Excuses Charter School.* Palgrave, 2020.

Brooks-Gunn, Jeanne, and Lisa B. Markman. "The Contribution of Parenting to Ethnic and Racial Gaps in School Readiness." *Future of Children* 15, no. 1 (2005): 139–68.

Buras, Kristen L. *Charter Schools, Race, and Urban Space: Where the Market Meets Grassroots Resistance.* Routledge, 2014.

Bryk, Anthony S., Louis M. Gomez, Alicia Grunow, and Paul G. LeMahieu. *Learning to Improve: How America's Schools Can Get Better at Getting Better.* Harvard Education Press, 2015.

Calarco, Jessica. "Coached for the Classroom: Parents' Cultural Transmission and Children's Reproduction of Educational Inequalities." *American Sociological Review* 79, no. 5 (2014): 1015–37.

——. "'I Need Help!' Social Class and Children's Help-Seeking in Elementary School." *American Sociological Review* 76, no. 6 (2011): 862–82.

——. *Negotiating Opportunities: How the Middle Class Secures Advantages in School.* Oxford University Press, 2018.

Carr, Sarah. *Hope Against Hope: Three Schools, One City, and the Struggle to Educate America's Children.* Bloomsbury, 2013.

Carter, Prudence L. "'Black' Cultural Capital, Status Positioning, and Schooling Conflicts for Low-Income African American Youth." *Social Problems* 50, no. 1 (2003): 136–55.

Carter, Prudence L., Russell Skiba, Mariella I. Arredondo, and Mica Pollock. "You Can't Fix What You Don't Look At: Acknowledging Race in Addressing Racial Discipline Disparities." *Urban Education* 52, no. 2 (2017): 207–35.

Carter, Samuel Casey. *No Excuses: Lessons from 21 High-Performing, High-Poverty Schools.* Heritage Foundation, 2000.

Carter Andrews, Dorinda J., Tashal Brown, Eliana Castro, and Effat Id-Deen. "The Impossibility of Being 'Perfect and White': Black Girls' Racialized and Gendered Schooling Experiences." *American Educational Research Journal* 56, no. 6 (2019): 2531–72.

Chabrier, Julia, Sarah Cohodes, and Philip Oreopoulos. "What Can We Learn from Charter School Lotteries?" *Journal of Economic Perspectives* 30, no. 3 (2016): 57–84.

Chang, Theodora. "Maximizing the Promise of Community Schools: Streamlining Wraparound Services for ESEA." Center for American Progress, 2011. https://eric.ed.gov/?id=ED536077.

Cheng, Albert, Collin Hitt, Brian Kisida, and Jonathan N. Mills. "'No Excuses' Charter Schools: A Meta-Analysis of the Experimental Evidence on Student Achievement." *Journal of School Choice* 11, no. 2 (2017): 209–38.

Chin, Tiffani, and Meredith Phillips. "Social Reproduction and Child-Rearing Practices: Social Class, Children's Agency, and the Summer Activity Gap." *Sociology of Education* 77, no. 3 (2004): 185–210.

Christie, Christine A., C. Michael Nelson, and Kristine Jolivette. "School Characteristics Related to the Use of Suspension." *Education and Treatment of Children* 27, no. 4 (2004): 509–26.

Chubb, John E., and Terry M. Moe. *Politics, Markets, and America's Schools.* Brookings Institution, 1990.

Coen, Thomas, Ira Nichols-Barrer, and Philip Gleason. "Long-Term Impacts of KIPP Middle Schools on College Enrollment and Early College Persistence." Mathematica, September 26, 2019. https://www.mathematica.org/our-publications-and-findings/publications/long-term-impacts-of-kipp-middle-schools-on-college-enrollment-and-early-college-persistence.

Cohodes, Sarah. "Charter Schools and the Achievement Gap." *Future of Children,* Winter 2018, 1–20.

Coleman, James S. "Equality of Educational Opportunity." National Center for Educational Statistics, 1966. https://eric.ed.gov/?id=ED012275.

Collier, Peter J., and David L. Morgan. "'Is That Paper Really Due Today?' Differences in First-Generation and Traditional College Students' Understandings of Faculty Expectations." *Higher Education* 55, no. 4 (2008): 425–46.

Cookson, Peter W., and Caroline Hodges Persell. *Preparing for Power: America's Elite Boarding Schools.* Basic Books, 1985.

Corcoran, Sean P., Jennifer L. Jennings, Sarah R. Cohodes, and Carolyn Sattin-Bajaj. "Leveling the Playing Field for High School Choice: Results from a Field Experiment of Informational Interventions." NBER Working Paper 24471, National Bureau of Economic Research, 2018. https://www.nber.org/papers/w24471.

Coser, Lewis A. *Greedy Institutions: Patterns of Undivided Commitment.* Free Press, 1974.

Cox, Amanda Barrett. "Engineered Struggle and 'Earned' Success." *Du Bois Review* 15, no. 2 (2018): 467–88.

———. "Mechanisms of Organizational Commitment: Adding Frames to Greedy Institution Theory." *Sociological Forum* 31, no. 3 (2016): 685–708.

Cucchiara, Maia Bloomfield. *Marketing Schools, Marketing Cities: Who Wins and Who Loses When Schools Become Urban Amenities.* University of Chicago Press, 2013.

Cucchiara, Maia Bloomfield, Erin Cassar, and Monica Clark. "'I Just Need a Job!' Behavioral Solutions, Structural Problems, and the Hidden Curriculum of Parenting Education." *Sociology of Education* 92, no. 4 (2019): 326–45.

Cunha, Flavio, and James J. Heckman. "Formulating, Identifying and Estimating the Technology of Cognitive and Noncognitive Skill Formation." *Journal of Human Resources* 43, no. 4 (2008): 738–82.

Darling-Hammond, Linda. "Race, Inequality and Educational Accountability: The Irony of 'No Child Left Behind.'" *Race Ethnicity and Education* 10, no. 3 (2007): 245–60.

———. "Who Will Speak for the Children? How 'Teach for America' Hurts Urban Schools and Students." *Phi Delta Kappan* 76, no. 1 (1994): 21–34.

Datnow, Amanda, and Marisa Castellano. "Teachers' Responses to Success for All: How Beliefs, Experiences, and Adaptations Shape Implementation." *American Educational Research Journal* 37, no. 3 (2000): 775–99.

Decker, Geoff, Stephanie Snyder, and Sarah Darville. "Suspensions at City Charter Schools Far Outpace Those at District Schools, Data Show." *Chalkbeat*, February 23, 2015. http://ny.chalkbeat.org/2015/02/23/suspensions-at-city-charter -schools-far-outpace-those-at-district-schools-data-show/.

Dee, Thomas S. "A Teacher like Me: Does Race, Ethnicity, or Gender Matter?" *American Economic Review* 95, no. 2 (2005): 158–65.

Dee, Thomas S., Brian A. Jacob, Caroline M. Hoxby, and Helen F. Ladd. "The Impact of No Child Left Behind on Students, Teachers, and Schools [with Comments and Discussion]." *Brookings Papers on Economic Activity*, Fall 2010, 149–207.

De Keere, Kobe, and Bram Spruyt. "'Prophets in the Pay of State': The Institutionalization of the Middle-Class Habitus in Schooling between 1880 and 2010." *Sociological Review* 67, no. 5 (2010): 1066–85.

Delpit, Lisa D. "The Silenced Dialogue: Power and Pedagogy in Educating Other People's Children." *Harvard Educational Review* 58, no. 3 (August 1988): 280–98.

DiMaggio, Paul J., and Walter W. Powell. "The Iron Cage Revisited: Institutional Isomorphism and Collective Rationality in Organizational Fields." *American Sociological Review* 48, no. 2 (1983): 147–60.

Disare, Monica. "'No Excuses' No More? Charter Schools Rethink Discipline after Focus on Tough Consequences." *Chalkbeat*, March 7, 2016. http://ny.chalkbeat.org /2016/03/07/no-excuses-no-more-charter-schools-rethink-discipline-after-focus -on-tough-consequences/.

Dishon, Gideon, and Joan F. Goodman. "No-Excuses for Character: A Critique of Character Education in No-Excuses Charter Schools." *Theory and Research in Education* 15, no. 2 (2017): 182–201.

Dobbie, Will, and Roland G. Fryer. "Are High-Quality Schools Enough to Increase Achievement among the Poor? Evidence from the Harlem Children's Zone." *American Economic Journal: Applied Economics* 3, no. 3 (2011): 158–87.

———. "Getting beneath the Veil of Effective Schools: Evidence from New York City." *American Economic Journal: Applied Economics* 5, no. 4 (2013): 28–60.

Donaldson, Morgaen L., and Susan Moore Johnson. "The Price of Misassignment: The Role of Teaching Assignments in Teach for America Teachers' Exit from Low-Income Schools and the Teaching Profession." *Educational Evaluation and Policy Analysis* 32, no. 2 (2010): 299–323.

Downey, Douglas B., and Shana Pribesh. "When Race Matters: Teachers' Evaluations of Students' Classroom Behavior." *Sociology of Education* 77, no. 4 (2004): 267–82.

Dreeben, Robert. *On What Is Learned in School*. Addison-Wesley, 1968.

Duckworth, Angela L. *Grit: The Power of Passion and Perseverance*. Scribner, 2016.

Duckworth, Angela L., Tamar Szabó Gendler, and James J. Gross. "Self-Control in School-Age Children." *Educational Psychologist* 49, no. 3 (2014): 199–217.

Duckworth, Angela L., Christopher Peterson, Michael D. Matthews, and Dennis R. Kelly. "Grit: Perseverance and Passion for Long-Term Goals." *Journal of Personality and Social Psychology* 92, no. 6 (2007): 1087–1101.

Duckworth, Angela L., and Martin E. P. Seligman. "Self-Discipline Outdoes IQ in Predicting Academic Performance of Adolescents." *Psychological Science* 16, no. 12 (2005): 939–44.

Duncan, Greg J., Chantelle J. Dowsett, Amy Claessens, Katherine Magnuson, Aletha C. Huston, Pamela Klebanov, Linda S. Pagani, Leon Feinstein, Mimi Engel, and Jeanne Brooks-Gunn. "School Readiness and Later Achievement." *Developmental Psychology* 43, no. 6 (2007): 1428–46.

Elsen-Rooney, Michael. "CEO's Response to George Floyd's Killing Spurs a Racial Reckoning at Success Academy." *Daily News*, June 17, 2020. https://www.nydailynews.com/new-york/education/ny-success-charter-school-racism-20200617-cdj4zuuiwva6zkvk63a7cfqfce-story.html.

Emerson, Robert M., Rachel I. Fretz, and Linda L. Shaw. *Writing Ethnographic Fieldnotes*. University of Chicago Press, 2011.

Erickson, Frederick. "Transformation and School Success: The Politics and Culture of Educational Achievement." *Anthropology & Education Quarterly* 18, no. 4 (1987): 335–56.

Everitt, Judson G. *Lesson Plans: The Institutional Demands of Becoming a Teacher*. Rutgers University Press, 2018.

———. "Teacher Careers and Inhabited Institutions: Sense-Making and Arsenals of Teaching Practice in Educational Institutions." *Symbolic Interaction* 35, no. 2 (2012): 203–20.

Farkas, George. "The Black-White Test Score Gap." *Contexts* 3, no. 2 (2004): 12–19.

———. "Cognitive Skills and Noncognitive Traits and Behaviors in Stratification Processes." *Annual Review of Sociology* 29 (2003): 541–62.

Farkas, George, Robert P. Grobe, Daniel Sheehan, and Yuan Shuan. "Cultural Resources and School Success: Gender, Ethnicity, and Poverty Groups within an Urban School District." *American Sociological Review* 55, no. 1 (1990): 127–42.

Farrell, Caitlin, Priscilla Wohlstetter, and Joanna Smith. "Charter Management Organizations: An Emerging Approach to Scaling Up What Works." *Educational Policy* 26, no. 4 (2012): 499–532.

Ferguson, Ann. *Bad Boys: Public Schools in the Making of Black Masculinity.* University of Michigan Press, 2001.

Ferguson, Ronald F. "Teachers' Perceptions and Expectations and the Black-White Test Score Gap." *Urban Education* 38, no. 4 (2003): 460–507.

Fernández-Kelly, Patricia. *The Hero's Fight: African Americans in West Baltimore and the Shadow of the State.* Princeton University Press, 2015.

Ferrare, Joseph. "Charter School Outcomes." In *Handbook of Research on School Choice*, edited by Mark Berends, Ann Primus, and Matthew G. Springer, 160–73. Routledge, 2019.

Foucault, Michel. *Discipline and Punish: The Birth of the Prison.* Translated by Alan Sheridan. Pantheon Books, 1977.

Freire, Paulo. *Pedagogy of the Oppressed.* New York: Herder and Herder, 1970.

Friedman, Milton. "Public Schools: Make Them Private." *Education Economics* 5, no. 3 (1997): 341–44.

Fryer, Roland G. "Injecting Charter School Best Practices into Traditional Public Schools: Evidence from Field Experiments." *Quarterly Journal of Economics* 129, no. 3 (2014): 1355–407.

Furgeson, Joshua, Brian Gill, Joshua Haimson, Alexandra Killewald, Moira McCullough, Ira Nichols-Barrer, Natalya Verbitsky-Savitz, et al. "Charter-School Management Organizations: Diverse Strategies and Diverse Student Impacts." Mathematica Policy Research, 2012. http://eric.ed.gov/?id=ED528536.

Garland, David. *The Culture of Control: Crime and Social Order in Contemporary Society.* University of Chicago Press, 2012.

Gecas, Viktor, and Michael L. Schwalbe. "Beyond the Looking-Glass Self: Social Structure and Efficacy-Based Self-Esteem." *Social Psychology Quarterly* 46, no. 2 (1983): 77–88.

Giroux, Henry A. *Against the Terror of Neoliberalism: Politics Beyond the Age of Greed.* Routledge, 2015.

———. *Theory and Resistance in Education: A Pedagogy for the Opposition.* Critical Perspectives in Social Theory. Bergin & Garvey, 1983.

Glazer, Joshua L., and Cori Egan. "The Ties That Bind: Building Civic Capacity for the Tennessee Achievement School District." *American Educational Research Journal* 55, no. 5 (2018): 928–64.

Godfrey, Erin B., Carlos E. Santos, and Esther Burson. "For Better or Worse? System-Justifying Beliefs in Sixth-Grade Predict Trajectories of Self-Esteem and Behavior across Early Adolescence." *Child Development* 90, no. 1 (2019): 180–95.

Goff, Phillip Atiba, Matthew Christian Jackson, Brooke Allison Lewis Di Leone, Carmen Marie Culotta, and Natalie Ann DiTomasso. "The Essence of Innocence: Consequences of Dehumanizing Black Children." *Journal of Personality and Social Psychology* 106, no. 4 (2014): 526–45.

Goffman, Erving. *Asylums: Essays on the Social Situation of Mental Patients and Other Inmates.* Anchor Books, 1961.

Golann, Joanne W. "Conformers, Adaptors, Imitators, and Rejecters: How No-Excuses Teachers' Cultural Toolkits Shape Their Responses to Control." *Sociology of Education* 91, no. 1 (2017): 28–45.

———. "The Paradox of Success at a No-Excuses School." *Sociology of Education* 88, no. 2 (2015): 103–19.

Golann, Joanne W., and Jennifer Darling-Aduana. "Toward a Multifaceted Understanding of Lareau's 'Sense of Entitlement': Bridging Sociological and Psychological Constructs." *Sociology Compass* 14, no. 7 (2020): e12798.

Golann, Joanne W., Mira Debs, and Anna Lisa Weiss. "'To Be Strict on Your Own': Black and Latinx Parents Evaluate Discipline in Urban Choice Schools." *American Educational Research Journal* 26, no. 5 (2019): 1896–929.

Golann, Joanne W., and A. Chris Torres. "Do No-Excuses Disciplinary Practices Promote Success?" *Journal of Urban Affairs* 42, no. 4 (2020): 617–33.

Goodman, Joan F. "Charter Management Organizations and the Regulated Environment: Is It Worth the Price?" *Educational Researcher* 42, no. 2 (2013): 89–96.

Gorski, Paul C. "Peddling Poverty for Profit: Elements of Oppression in Ruby Payne's Framework." *Equity & Excellence in Education* 41, no. 1 (2008): 130–48.

Graham, Eliot J. "'In Real Life, You Have to Speak Up': Civic Implications of No-Excuses Classroom Management Practices." *American Educational Research Journal* 57, no. 2 (2020): 653–93.

Green, Elizabeth. *Building a Better Teacher: How Teaching Works (and How to Teach It to Everyone)*. Norton, 2014.

Gregory, Anne, Russell J. Skiba, and Pedro A. Noguera. "The Achievement Gap and the Discipline Gap: Two Sides of the Same Coin?" *Educational Researcher* 39, no. 1 (2010): 59–68.

Gregory, Anne, and Rhona S. Weinstein. "The Discipline Gap and African Americans: Defiance or Cooperation in the High School Classroom." *Journal of School Psychology* 46, no. 4 (2008): 455–75.

Griffin, Ramon. "A Phenomenological Case Study of Four Black Males Exposed to Cumulative Trauma That Attended a 'No Excuses' Charter School." Doctoral dissertation, Michigan State University, 2018.

Gross, Betheny, Christine Campbell, Sivan Tuchman, and Roohi Sharma. "Hopes, Fears, and New Solutions: Charter Schools in 2018." In *Handbook of Research on School Choice*, edited by Mark Berends, Ann Primus, and Matthew G. Springer, 103–17. Routledge, 2019.

Haberman, Martin. "The Pedagogy of Poverty versus Good Teaching." *Phi Delta Kappan* 73, no. 4 (1991): 290–94.

Hall, Kevin, and Robin Lake. "The $500 Million Question." *Education Next*, October 20, 2010. http://educationnext.org/the-500-million-question/.

Harris, Angel L. *Kids Don't Want to Fail: Oppositional Culture and the Black-White Achievement Gap*. Harvard University Press, 2011

Henry, Gary T., C. Kevin Fortner, and Kevin C. Bastian. "The Effects of Experience and Attrition for Novice High-School Science and Mathematics Teachers." *Science* 335, no. 6072 (2012): 1118–21.

Henry, Kevin Lawrence, and Adrienne D. Dixson. "'Locking the Door before We Got the Keys': Racial Realities of the Charter School Authorization Process in Post-Katrina New Orleans." *Educational Policy* 30, no. 1 (2016): 218–40.

Hernández, Laura E. "Race and Racelessness in CMO Marketing: Exploring Charter Management Organizations' Racial Construction and Its Implications." *Peabody Journal of Education* 91, no. 1 (2016): 47–63.

Horn, Jim. "Corporatism, KIPP, and Cultural Eugenics." In *The Gates Foundation and the Future of US "Public Schools,"* edited by Philip E. Kovacs, 80–103. Routledge, 2011.

Hussar, Bill, Jijun Zhang, Sarah Hein, Ke Wang, Ashley Roberts, Jiashan Cui, Mary Smith, Farrah Bullock Mann, Amy Barmer, and Rita Dilig. "The Condition of Education 2020" (NCES 2020-144). U.S. Department of Education, National Center for Education Statistics, 2020. https://nces.ed.gov/pubsearch/pubsinfo.asp?pubid =2020144.

Ingersoll, Richard M. "Beginning Teacher Induction: What the Data Tell Us." *Phi Delta Kappan* 93, no. 8 (2012): 47–51.

——. "The Teacher Shortage: Myth or Reality?" *Educational Horizons* 81, no. 3 (2003): 146–52.

——. *Who Controls Teachers' Work? Power and Accountability in America's Schools.* Harvard University Press, 2006.

Jack, Anthony Abraham. *The Privileged Poor: How Elite Colleges Are Failing Disadvantaged Students.* Harvard University Press, 2019.

Jæger, Mads Meier. "Does Cultural Capital Really Affect Academic Achievement? New Evidence from Combined Sibling and Panel Data." *Sociology of Education* 84, no. 4 (2011): 281–98.

Jennings, Jennifer L., and Thomas A. DiPrete. "Teacher Effects on Social and Behavioral Skills in Early Elementary School." *Sociology of Education* 83, no. 2 (2010): 135–59.

Jennings, Jennifer L., and Heeju Sohn. "Measure for Measure: How Proficiency-Based Accountability Systems Affect Inequality in Academic Achievement." *Sociology of Education* 87, no. 2 (2014): 125–41.

Jones, Sarah E. "Studying 'Success' at an 'Effective' School: How a Nationally Recognized Public School Overcomes Racial, Ethnic and Social Boundaries and Creates a Culture of Success." Doctoral dissertation, University of California, Santa Barbara, 2004.

Kahlenberg, Richard D. *Tough Liberal: Albert Shanker and the Battles over Schools, Unions, Race, and Democracy.* Columbia University Press, 2007.

Kahlenberg, Richard D., and Halley Potter. *A Smarter Charter: Finding What Works for Charter Schools and Public Education.* Teachers College Press, 2014.

Kane, Thomas J., Jonah E. Rockoff, and Douglas O. Staiger. "What Does Certification Tell Us about Teacher Effectiveness? Evidence from New York City." *Economics of Education Review* 27, no. 6 (2008): 615–31.

Karp, Melinda Jane Mechur, and Rachel Julia Hare Bork. "'They Never Told Me What to Expect, so I Didn't Know What to Do': Defining and Clarifying the Role of a Community College Student." *Teachers College Record* 116, no. 5 (2012): 1–40.

Kelling, George L., and James Q. Wilson. "Broken Windows: The Police and Neighborhood Safety." *Atlantic*, March 1982. https://www.theatlantic.com/magazine/archive /1982/03/broken-windows/304465/.

Kerstetter, Katie. "A Different Kind of Discipline: Social Reproduction and the Transmission of Non-cognitive Skills at an Urban Charter School." *Sociological Inquiry* 86, no. 4 (2016): 512–39.

Khan, Shamus Rahman. *Privilege: The Making of an Adolescent Elite at St. Paul's School.* Princeton University Press, 2011.

Kingston, Paul W. "The Unfulfilled Promise of Cultural Capital Theory." *Sociology of Education* 74 (2001): 88–99.

KIPP Foundation. "KIPP: National Results, 2017–18." 2019. https://www.kipp.org/wp-content/uploads/2019/07/KIPP-2017-18-National-Results-and-Appendix.pdf.

———. "The Promise of College Completion: KIPP's Early Successes and Challenges." 2011. https://www.kipp.org/wp-content/uploads/2016/09/CollegeCompletionReport.pdf.

Kirschner, Paul A., John Sweller, and Richard E. Clark. "Why Minimal Guidance during Instruction Does Not Work: An Analysis of the Failure of Constructivist, Discovery, Problem-Based, Experiential, and Inquiry-Based Teaching." *Educational Psychologist* 41, no. 2 (2006): 75–86.

Kozlowski, Karen. "Doing School: Learning Behavior, Classroom Interactions, and the Racial Achievement Gap." Doctoral dissertation, University of North Carolina, 2016.

———. "Socioeconomic Inequality in Decoding Instructions and Demonstrating Knowledge." *Qualitative Sociology* 43 (2020): 43–66.

Kretchmar, Kerry, Beth Sondel, and Joseph J. Ferrare. "Mapping the Terrain: Teach for America, Charter School Reform, and Corporate Sponsorship." *Journal of Education Policy* 29, no. 6 (2014): 742–59.

Ladson-Billings, Gloria. *The Dreamkeepers: Successful Teachers of African American Children*. Jossey-Bass, 1994.

Ladson-Billings, Gloria, and William F. Tate. "Toward a Critical Race Theory of Education." *Teachers College Record* 97, no. 1 (1995): 47–68.

Lake, Robin, Melissa Bowen, Allison Demeritt, Moira McCullough, Joshua Haimson, and Brian Gill. "Learning from Charter School Management Organizations: Strategies for Student Behavior and Teacher Coaching." Mathematica Policy Research, 2012. http://eric.ed.gov/?id=ED530801.

Lake, Robin, Brianna Dusseault, Melissa Bowen, Allison Demeritt, and Paul Hill. "The National Study of Charter Management Organization (CMO) Effectiveness: Report on Interim Findings." Center on Reinventing Public Education, Mathematica Policy Research, 2010. http://eric.ed.gov/?id=ED516865.

Lamboy, Lily, and Amanda Lu. "The Pursuit of College for All: Ends and Means in 'No Excuses' Charter Schools." *Theory and Research in Education* 15, no. 2 (2017): 202–29.

Lamont, Michele, and Annette Lareau. "Cultural Capital: Allusions, Gaps and Glissandos in Recent Theoretical Developments." *Sociological Theory* 6, no. 2 (1988): 153–68.

Lareau, Annette. "Invisible Inequality: Social Class and Childrearing in Black Families and White Families." *American Sociological Review* 67, no. 5 (2002): 747–76.

———. *Unequal Childhoods: Class, Race, and Family Life*. University of California Press, 2003.

Lareau, Annette, and Elliot B. Weininger. "Cultural Capital in Educational Research: A Critical Assessment." *Theory and Society* 32, nos. 5–6 (2003): 567–606.

Lawrence-Lightfoot, Sara. *Respect: An Exploration*. Perseus, 2000.

Lee, Elizabeth M. *Class and Campus Life: Managing and Experiencing Inequality at an Elite College*. Ithaca, NY: Cornell University Press, 2016.

Lee, Valerie E., and David T. Burkam. "Dropping Out of High School: The Role of School Organization and Structure." *American Educational Research Journal* 40, no. 2 (2003): 353–93.

———. "Inequality at the Starting Gate: Social Background Differences in Achievement as Children Begin School." Economic Policy Institute, 2002.

Lemov, Doug. *Teach Like a Champion: 49 Techniques That Put Students on the Path to College.* Jossey-Bass, 2010.

———. *Teach Like a Champion Field Guide: A Practical Resource to Make the 49 Techniques Your Own.* Jossey-Bass, 2012.

———. *Teach Like a Champion 2.0: 62 Techniques That Put Students on the Path to College.* 2nd ed. John Wiley, 2015.

Lewis, Amanda E., and John B. Diamond. *Despite the Best Intentions: How Racial Inequality Thrives in Good Schools.* Oxford University Press, 2015.

Lewis, Oscar. "The Culture of Poverty." *Scientific American* 215, no. 4 (1966): 19–25.

Lewis-McCoy, R. L'Heureux. *Inequality in the Promised Land: Race, Resources, and Suburban Schooling.* Stanford University Press, 2014.

Lipman, Pauline. *High Stakes Education: Inequality, Globalization, and Urban School Reform.* Routledge, 2003.

———. "Neoliberal Education Restructuring Dangers and Opportunities of the Present Crisis." *Monthly Review* 63, no. 3 (2011): 114–27.

Lizardo, Omar, and Michael Strand. "Skills, Toolkits, Contexts and Institutions: Clarifying the Relationship between Different Approaches to Cognition in Cultural Sociology." *Poetics* 38 (2010): 205–28.

Lortie, Dan. *Schoolteacher: A Sociological Study.* University of Chicago Press, 1975.

Losen, Daniel J. *Closing the School Discipline Gap: Equitable Remedies for Excessive Exclusion.* Teachers College Press, 2014.

Losen, Daniel J., Cheri Hodson, Michael A. Keith II, Katrina Morrison, and Shakti Belway. *Are We Closing the School Discipline Gap?* Center for Civil Rights Remedies, 2015.

Love, Bettina L. *We Want to Do More Than Survive: Abolitionist Teaching and the Pursuit of Educational Freedom.* Beacon, 2019.

Lubienski, Christopher. "Innovation in Education Markets: Theory and Evidence on the Impact of Competition and Choice in Charter Schools." *American Educational Research Journal* 40, no. 2 (2003): 395–443.

MacLeod, Jay. *Ain't No Makin' It: Leveled Aspirations in a Low-Income Neighborhood.* Westview, 1987.

Marsh, L. Trenton S., and Pedro A. Noguera. "Beyond Stigma and Stereotypes: An Ethnographic Study on the Effects of School-Imposed Labeling on Black Males in an Urban Charter School." *Urban Review* 50, no. 3 (2018): 447–77.

Martin, Karin A. "Becoming a Gendered Body: Practices of Preschools." *American Sociological Review* 63, no. 4 (1998): 494–511.

Massell, Diane, Joshua Glazer, and Matthew Malone. "'This Is the Big Leagues': Charter-Led Turnaround in a Non-charter World." Tennessee Consortium on Research, Evaluation, & Development, 2016.

Massey, Douglas S., and Nancy A. Denton. *American Apartheid.* Harvard University Press, 1993.

Mathews, Jay. *Work Hard. Be Nice. How Two Inspired Teachers Created the Most Promising Schools in America*. Algonquin Books of Chapel Hill, 2009.

Maynard, Brandy R., Anne Farina, Nathaniel A. Dell, and Michael S. Kelly. "Effects of Trauma-Informed Approaches in Schools: A Systematic Review." *Campbell Systematic Reviews* 15, nos. 1–2 (2019): 1–18.

Mears, Ashley. *Pricing Beauty: The Making of a Fashion Model*. University of California Press, 2011.

Mehan, Hugh. "The Competent Student." *Anthropology & Education Quarterly* 11, no. 3 (1980): 131–52.

Mehta, Jal. *The Allure of Order: High Hopes, Dashed Expectations, and the Troubled Quest to Remake American Schooling*. Oxford University Press, 2013.

Mehta, Jal, and Sarah Fine. *In Search of Deeper Learning: The Quest to Remake the American High School*. Harvard University Press, 2019.

Merton, Robert K. "The Self-Fulfilling Prophecy." *Antioch Review* 8, no. 2 (1948): 193–210.

———. "Social Structure and Anomie." *American Sociological Review* 3, no. 5 (1938): 672–82.

Metz, Mary Haywood. *Classrooms and Corridors: The Crisis of Authority in Desegregated Secondary Schools*. University of California Press, 1979.

———. "Order in the Secondary School: Strategies for Control and Their Consequences." *Sociological Inquiry* 48, no. 1 (1978): 59–69.

Meyer, John W., and Brian Rowan. "Institutionalized Organizations: Formal Structure as Myth and Ceremony." *American Journal of Sociology* 83, no. 2 (1977): 340–63.

———. "The Structure of Educational Organizations." In *Environments and Organizations*, edited by Marshall W. Meyer, 78–109. Jossey-Bass, 1978.

Miles, Matthew B., A. Michael Huberman, and Johnny Saldana. *Qualitative Data Analysis: A Methods Sourcebook*. Sage, 2014.

Milner, H. Richard, IV. "Beyond a Test Score: Explaining Opportunity Gaps in Educational Practice." *Journal of Black Studies* 43, no. 6 (2012): 693–718.

———. "But What Is Urban Education?" *Urban Education* 47, no. 3 (2012): 556–61.

———. "Scripted and Narrowed Curriculum Reform in Urban Schools." *Urban Education* 48, no. 2 (2013): 163–70.

Milner, H. Richard, IV, Heather B. Cunningham, Lori Delale-O'Connor, and Erika Gold Kestenberg. *"These Kids Are Out of Control": Why We Must Reimagine "Classroom Management" for Equity*. Corwin Press, 2018.

Milner, H. Richard, IV, and Tyrone C. Howard. "Counter-narrative as Method: Race, Policy and Research for Teacher Education." *Race Ethnicity and Education* 16, no. 4 (2013): 536–61.

Milner, H. Richard, IV, and Gloria Ladson-Billings. *Start Where You Are, but Don't Stay There: Understanding Diversity, Opportunity Gaps, and Teaching in Today's Classrooms*. Harvard Education Press, 2010.

Milner, H. Richard, IV, and Judson C. Laughter. "But Good Intentions Are Not Enough: Preparing Teachers to Center Race and Poverty." *Urban Review* 47, no. 2 (2015): 341–63.

Miron, Gary, Jessica Urschel, and Nicholas Saxton. "What Makes KIPP Work? A Study of Student Characteristics, Attrition, and School Finance." National Center for the

Study of Privatization in Education, Teachers College, Columbia University and the Study Group on Educational Management Organizations, Western Michigan University, 2011. https://ncspe.tc.columbia.edu/working-papers/OP195_3.pdf.

Mirón, Louis F., and Edward P. St. John. *Reinterpreting Urban School Reform: Have Urban Schools Failed, or Has the Reform Movement Failed Urban Schools?* State University of New York Press, 2003.

Mittenfelner Carl, Nicole. "Reacting to the Script: Teach for America Teachers' Experiences with Scripted Curricula." *Teacher Education Quarterly* 41, no. 2 (2014): 29–50.

Moll, Luis C., Cathy Amanti, Deborah Neff, and Norma Gonzalez. "Funds of Knowledge for Teaching: Using a Qualitative Approach to Connect Homes and Classrooms." *Theory into Practice* 31, no. 2 (1992): 132–41.

Montano, Theresa, and Rosalinda Quintanar-Sarellana. "Undoing Ruby Payne and Other Deficit Views of English Language Learners." *Counterpoints* 402 (2011): 199–213.

Morris, Edward W. "'Ladies' or 'Loudies'? Perceptions and Experiences of Black Girls in Classrooms." *Youth & Society* 38, no. 4 (2007): 490–515.

———. "'Tuck in That Shirt!' Race, Class, Gender, and Discipline in an Urban School." *Sociological Perspectives* 48, no. 1 (2005): 25–48.

Morris, Monique. *Pushout: The Criminalization of Black Girls in Schools*. New Press, 2018.

Moskowitz, Eva. "Why Students Need to Sit Up and Pay Attention." *Wall Street Journal*, November 13, 2015. https://www.wsj.com/articles/why-students-need-to-sit-up-and-pay-attention-1447373122.

Mungal, Angus Shiva. "Teach for America, Relay Graduate School, and Charter School Networks: The Making of a Parallel Education Structure." *Education Policy Analysis Archives* 24, no. 17 (2016): 1–25.

Nagle, Robin. *Picking Up: On the Streets and Behind the Trucks with the Sanitation Workers of New York City*. Farrar, Straus and Giroux, 2014.

Nation, Maury. "Point/Counterpoint: No-Excuses Discipline." *UCEA Review*, Fall 2017, 9–10.

National Alliance for Public Charter Schools. "A Closer Look at the Charter School Movement: Schools, Students, and Management Organizations, 2015–16." February 3, 2016. https://www.publiccharters.org/publications/charter-school-movement-2015-16.

Nichols-Barrer, Ira, Philip Gleason, Brian Gill, and Christina Clark Tuttle. "Student Selection, Attrition, and Replacement in KIPP Middle Schools." *Educational Evaluation and Policy Analysis* 38, no. 1 (2016): 5–20.

Noguera, Pedro A. *The Trouble with Black Boys: . . . And Other Reflections on Race, Equity, and the Future of Public Education*. John Wiley, 2009.

Nolan, Kathleen. *Police in the Hallways: Discipline in an Urban High School*. University of Minnesota Press, 2011.

Nunn, Lisa M. *Defining Student Success: The Role of School and Culture*. Rutgers University Press, 2014.

Ogbu, John U. *Black American Students in an Affluent Suburb: A Study of Academic Disengagement*. Lawrence Erlbaum, 2003.

Parenti, Christian. *Lockdown America: Police and Prisons in the Age of Crisis*. Verso, 1999.

Paris, Django, and H. Samy Alim. *Culturally Sustaining Pedagogies: Teaching and Learning for Justice in a Changing World*. Teachers College Press, 2017.

Parsons, Talcott. "The School Class as a Social System: Some of Its Functions in American Society." *Harvard Educational Review* 29, no. 4 (1959): 297–318.

Pattillo, Mary. "Everyday Politics of School Choice in the Black Community." *Du Bois Review* 12, no. 1 (2015): 41–71.

Payne, Charles M. *So Much Reform, So Little Change: The Persistence of Failure in Urban Schools*. Harvard Education Press, 2008.

Peak, Christopher. "Student-Shoving Principal Leaves Post." *New Haven Independent*, January 17, 2019. https://www.newhavenindependent.org/index.php/archives /entry/discipline_amistad_/.

Perfect, Michelle M., Matt R. Turley, John S. Carlson, Justina Yohanna, and Marla Pfenninger Saint Gilles. "School-Related Outcomes of Traumatic Event Exposure and Traumatic Stress Symptoms in Students: A Systematic Review of Research from 1990 to 2015." *School Mental Health* 8, no. 1 (2016): 7–43.

Pondiscio, Robert. *How the Other Half Learns: Equality, Excellence, and the Battle over School Choice*. Avery, 2019.

Prieur, Annick, and Mike Savage. "Emerging Forms of Cultural Capital." *European Societies* 15, no. 2 (2013): 246–67.

Ravitch, Diane. "How 'No Excuses' Schools Deepen Race, Class Divisions." *Diane Ravitch's Blog*, June 15, 2013. http://dianeravitch.net/2013/06/15/how-no-excuses -schools-deepen-race-class-divisions/.

———. *Reign of Error: The Hoax of the Privatization Movement and the Danger to America's Public Schools*. Knopf, 2013.

Redding, Christopher. "A Teacher Like Me: A Review of the Effect of Student–Teacher Racial/Ethnic Matching on Teacher Perceptions of Students and Student Academic and Behavioral Outcomes." *Review of Educational Research* 89, no. 4 (2019): 499–535.

Redding, Christopher, Marisa Cannata, and Katherine Taylor Haynes. "With Scale in Mind: A Continuous Improvement Model for Implementation." *Peabody Journal of Education* 92, no. 5 (2017): 589–608.

Redeaux, Monique. "A Framework for Maintaining White Privilege: A Critique of Ruby Payne." *Counterpoints* 402 (2011): 177–98.

Renzulli, Linda A., Heather Macpherson Parrott, and Irenee R. Beattie. "Racial Mismatch and School Type: Teacher Satisfaction and Retention in Charter and Traditional Public Schools." *Sociology of Education* 84, no. 1 (2011): 23–48.

Rhodes, Anna, and Stefanie DeLuca. "Residential Mobility and School Choice among Poor Families." In *Choosing Homes, Choosing Schools*, edited by Annette Lareau and Kimberly Goyette, 137–66. Russell Sage Foundation, 2014.

Richards, Bedelia Nicola. "When Class Is Colorblind: A Race-Conscious Model for Cultural Capital Research in Education." *Sociology Compass* 14, no. 7 (2020): 1–14. https://doi.org/10.1111/soc4.12786.

Rios, Victor M. *Punished: Policing the Lives of Black and Latino Boys*. New York University Press, 2011.

Rivera, Lauren A. *Pedigree: How Elite Students Get Elite Jobs.* Princeton University Press, 2016.

Roksa, Josipa, and Daniel Potter. "Parenting and Academic Achievement: Intergenerational Transmission of Educational Advantage." *Sociology of Education* 84, no. 4 (2011): 299–321.

Roscigno, Vincent J., and James W. Ainsworth-Darnell. "Race, Cultural Capital, and Educational Resources: Persistent Inequalities and Achievement Returns." *Sociology of Education* 72, no. 3 (1999): 158–78.

Rosenholtz, Susan J., and Carl Simpson. "Workplace Conditions and the Rise and Fall of Teachers' Commitment." *Sociology of Education* 63, no. 4 (1990): 241–57.

Rowan, Brian. "Commitment and Control: Alternative Strategies for the Organizational Design of Schools." *Review of Research in Education* 16 (1990): 353–89.

Ryan, William. *Blaming the Victim.* Vintage, 1976.

Saltman, Kenneth, and David Gabbard, eds. *Education as Enforcement: The Militarization and Corporatization of Schools.* 2nd ed. Routledge, 2011.

Sanjek, Roger, ed. *Fieldnotes: The Makings of Anthropology.* Cornell University Press, 1990.

Sartain, Lauren, Elaine M. Allensworth, and Shanette Porter. "Suspending Chicago's Students." University of Chicago Consortium on Chicago School Research, 2015.

Scott, Janelle. "The Politics of Venture Philanthropy in Charter School Policy and Advocacy." *Educational Policy* 23, no. 1 (2009): 106–36.

Scott, Janelle, and Jennifer Jellison Holme. "The Political Economy of Market-Based Educational Policies: Race and Reform in Urban School Districts, 1915 to 2016." *Review of Research in Education* 40, no. 1 (2016): 250–97.

Seider, Scott, Jennifer K. Gilbert, Sarah Novick, and Jessica Gomez. "The Role of Moral and Performance Character Strengths in Predicting Achievement and Conduct among Urban Middle School Students." *Teachers College Record* 115, no. 8 (2013): 1–34.

Shapira, Harel. *Waiting for José: The Minutemen's Pursuit of America.* Princeton University Press, 2013.

Shapiro, Eliza. "Student Protests at Success Academy's High School Illuminate Challenges of Charter School Growth." *Politico*, February 8, 2018. http://politi.co/2EQdcBJ.

Shedd, Carla. *Unequal City: Race, Schools, and Perceptions of Injustice.* Russell Sage Foundation, 2015.

Skiba, Russell J., Choong-Geun Chung, Megan Trachok, Timberly Baker, Adam Sheya, and Robin Hughes. "Where Should We Intervene?" In *Closing the School Discipline Gap: Equitable Remedies for Excessive Exclusion,* edited by Daniel J. Losen, 132–46. Teachers College Press, 2015.

Skiba, Russell J., Robert S. Michael, Abra Carroll Nardo, and Reece L. Peterson. "The Color of Discipline: Sources of Racial and Gender Disproportionality in School Punishment." *Urban Review* 34, no. 4 (2002): 317–42.

Skiba, Russell J., and Reece Peterson. "The Dark Side of Zero Tolerance: Can Punishment Lead to Safe Schools?" *Phi Delta Kappan* 80, no. 5 (1999): 372–82.

Sleeter, Christine E. "Confronting the Marginalization of Culturally Responsive Pedagogy." *Urban Education* 47, no. 3 (2012): 562–84.

Smrekar, Claire. *The Impact of School Choice and Community: In the Interest of Families and Schools*. State University of New York Press, 1996.

———. "The Missing Link in School-Linked Social Service Programs." *Educational Evaluation and Policy Analysis* 16, no. 4 (1994): 422–33.

Sondel, Beth. "'No Excuses' in New Orleans: The Silent Passivity of Neoliberal Schooling." *Educational Forum* 80, no. 2 (2016): 171–88.

———. "Raising Citizens or Raising Test Scores? Teach for America, 'No Excuses' Charters, and the Development of the Neoliberal Citizen." *Theory and Research in Social Education* 43, no. 3 (2015): 289–313.

Sondel, Beth, Kerry Kretchmar, and Alyssa Hadley Dunn, "'Who Do These People Want Teaching Their Children?' White Saviorism, Colorblind Racism, and Anti-Blackness in 'No Excuses' Charter Schools." *Urban Education* (2019): 1–30.

Stengel, Barbara S. "From the Editor: Staying Alive." *Educational Theory* 67, no. 2 (2017): 123–29.

Stitzlein, Sarah Marie, and Craig K. West. "New Forms of Teacher Education: Connections to Charter Schools and Their Approaches." *Democracy and Education* 22, no. 2 (2014): 1–10.

Strauss, Valerie. "The Single Most Telling Sentence Betsy DeVos Said to Congress this Week." *Washington Post*, March 29, 2019. https://www.washingtonpost.com /education/2019/03/29/single-most-telling-sentence-betsy-devos-said-congress -this-week/.

———. "Some 'No-Excuses' Charter Schools Say They Are Changing. Are They? Can They?" *Washington Post*, August 29, 2019. https://www.washingtonpost.com /education/2019/08/29/some-no-excuses-charter-schools-say-they-are-changing -are-they-can-they/.

Streib, Jessi. "Class Reproduction by Four Year Olds." *Qualitative Sociology* 34, no. 2 (2011): 337–52.

Stulberg, Lisa M. *Race, Schools, and Hope: African Americans and School Choice after Brown*. Teachers College Press, 2008.

———. "What History Offers Progressive Choice Scholarship." In *The Emancipatory Promise of Charter Schools: Toward a Progressive Politics of School Choice*, edited by Eric Rofes and Lisa M. Stulberg, 7–51. State University of New York Press, 2004.

Swartz, David. *Culture and Power: The Sociology of Pierre Bourdieu*. University of Chicago Press, 2012.

Swidler, Ann. "Culture in Action: Symbols and Strategies." *American Sociological Review* 51, no. 2 (1986): 273–86.

———. *Talk of Love: How Culture Matters*. University of Chicago Press, 2001.

Taylor, Frederick W. "The Principles of Scientific Management." In *The Sociology of Organizations: Classic, Contemporary, and Critical Readings*, edited by Michael J. Handel, 24–31. Sage, 2003.

Terrill, Marguerite M., and Dianne L. H. Mark. "Preservice Teachers' Expectations for Schools with Children of Color and Second-Language Learners." *Journal of Teacher Education* 51, no. 2 (2000): 149–55.

Thernstrom, Abigail M., and Stephan Thernstrom. *No Excuses: Closing the Racial Gap in Learning*. Simon & Schuster, 2003.

Thomas, Anita Jones, and Sha'Kema M. Blackmon. "The Influence of the Trayvon Martin Shooting on Racial Socialization Practices of African American Parents." *Journal of Black Psychology* 41, no. 1 (2015): 75–89.

Timmermans, Stefan, and Marc Berg. *The Gold Standard: The Challenge of Evidence-Based Medicine and Standardization in Health Care.* Temple University Press, 2010.

Timmermans, Stefan, and Steven Epstein. "A World of Standards but Not a Standard World: Toward a Sociology of Standards and Standardization." *Annual Review of Sociology* 36 (2010): 69–89.

Torres, A. Chris. "'Are We Architects or Construction Workers?' Re-examining Teacher Autonomy and Turnover in Charter Schools." *Education Policy Analysis Archives* 22 (2014): 1–26.

———. "Is This Work Sustainable? Teacher Turnover and Perceptions of Workload in Charter Management Organizations." *Urban Education* 51, no. 8 (2014): 1–24.

———. "Teacher Efficacy and Disciplinary Expectations in Charter Schools: Understanding the Link to Teachers' Career Decisions." *Journal of School Choice* 10, no. 2 (2016): 171–99.

Tough, Paul. "What If the Secret to Success Is Failure?" *New York Times*, September 14, 2011. http://www.nytimes.com/2011/09/18/magazine/what-if-the-secret-to-success-is-failure.html.

Trujillo, Tina, Janelle Scott, and Marialena Rivera. "Follow the Yellow Brick Road: Teach for America and the Making of Educational Leaders." *American Journal of Education* 123, no. 3 (2017): 353–91.

Tuan, Mia. *Forever Foreigners or Honorary Whites? The Asian Ethnic Experience Today.* Rutgers University Press, 1999.

Turco, Catherine J. *The Conversational Firm: Rethinking Bureaucracy in the Age of Social Media.* Columbia University Press, 2016.

Tuttle, Christina Clark, Brian Gill, Philip Gleason, Virginia Knechtel, Ira Nichols-Barrer, and Alexandra Resch. "KIPP Middle Schools: Impacts on Achievement and Other Outcomes. Final Report." Mathematica Policy Research, 2013. https://www.mathematica.org/our-publications-and-findings/publications/kipp-middle-schools-impacts-on-achievement-and-other-outcomes-full-report.

Tuttle, Christina Clark, Philip Gleason, Virginia Knechtel, Ira Nichols-Barrer, Kevin Booker, Gregory Chojnacki, Thomas Coen, and Lisbeth Goble. "Understanding the Effect of KIPP as It Scales: Vol. 1, Impacts on Achievement and Other Outcomes." Mathematica Policy Research, 2015. https://www.mathematica.org/our-publications-and-findings/publications/understanding-the-effect-of-kipp-as-it-scales-volume-i-impacts-on-achievement-and-other-outcomes.

Tyson, Karolyn. "Notes from the Back of the Room: Problems and Paradoxes in the Schooling of Young Black Students." *Sociology of Education* 76, no. 4 (2003): 326–43.

Valenzuela, Angela. *Subtractive Schooling: Issues of Caring in Education of U.S.-Mexican Youth.* State University of New York Press, 1999.

Wacquant, Loïc. "Deadly Symbiosis: When Ghetto and Prison Meet and Mesh." *Punishment & Society* 3, no. 1 (2001): 95–133.

Wallace, Derron. "Reading 'Race' in Bourdieu? Examining Black Cultural Capital among Black Caribbean Youth in South London." *Sociology* 51, no. 5 (2017): 907–23.

Waller, Willard. *The Sociology of Teaching*. John Wiley, 1932.

Warren, Chezare A. *Urban Preparation: Young Black Men Moving from Chicago's South Side to Success in Higher Education*. Harvard Education Press, 2017.

———. "The Utility of Empathy for White Female Teachers' Culturally Responsive Interactions with Black Male Students." *Interdisciplinary Journal of Teaching and Learning* 3, no. 3 (2013): 175–200.

Waters, Everett, and L. Alan Sroufe. "Social Competence as a Developmental Construct." *Developmental Review* 3, no. 1 (1983): 79–97.

Way, Sandra M. "School Discipline and Disruptive Classroom Behavior: The Moderating Effects of Student Perceptions." *Sociological Quarterly* 52, no. 3 (2011): 346–75.

Weenink, Don. "Cosmopolitanism as a Form of Capital: Parents Preparing Their Children for a Globalizing World." *Sociology* 42, no. 6 (2008): 1089–106.

Weiner, Jennie M., and A. Chris Torres. "Different Location or Different Map? Investigating Charter School Teachers' Professional Identities." *Teaching and Teacher Education* 53 (2016): 75–86.

Weinstein, Carol S., Saundra Tomlinson-Clarke, and Mary Curran. "Toward a Conception of Culturally Responsive Classroom Management." *Journal of Teacher Education* 55, no. 1 (2004): 25–38.

Weinstein, Rhona S. *Reaching Higher: The Power of Expectations in Schooling*. Harvard University Press, 2004.

Weiss, Robert S. *Learning from Strangers: The Art and Method of Qualitative Interview Studies*. Simon & Schuster, 1995.

Welch, Kelly, and Allison Ann Payne. "Racial Threat and Punitive School Discipline." *Social Problems* 57, no. 1 (2010): 25–48.

Wells, Amy Stuart, Alejandra Lopez, Janelle Scott, and Jennifer Jellison Holme. "Charter Schools as Postmodern Paradox: Rethinking Social Stratification in an Age of Deregulated School Choice." *Harvard Educational Review* 69, no. 2 (1999): 172–205.

Western, Bruce. *Punishment and Inequality in America*. Russell Sage Foundation, 2007.

Westheimer, Joel, and Joseph Kahne. "What Kind of Citizen? The Politics of Educating for Democracy." *American Educational Research Journal* 41, no. 2 (2016): 237–69.

White, Terrenda. "Charter Schools: Demystifying Whiteness in a Market of 'No Excuses' Corporate-Styled Charter Schools." In *What's Race Got to Do with It?*, edited by Bree Picower and Edwin Mayorga, 121–45. Peter Lang, 2015.

———. "Teach for America's Paradoxical Diversity Initiative: Race, Policy, and Black Teacher Displacement in Urban Public Schools." *Education Policy Analysis Archives* 24 (2016): 1–42.

Whitman, David. *Sweating the Small Stuff: Inner-City Schools and the New Paternalism*. Thomas B. Fordham Institute, 2008.

Whitmire, Richard. *The Founders: Inside the Revolution to Invent and Reinvent America's Best Charter Schools*. BookBaby, 2016.

Whyte, William Foote. *Street Corner Society: The Social Structure of an Italian Slum*. University of Chicago Press, 2012.

Wilcox, Kathleen. "Differential Socialization in the Classroom: Implications for Equal Opportunity." In *Doing the Ethnography of Schooling*, edited by George Spindler, 268–309. Holt, Rinehart and Winston, 1982.

Willis, Paul E. *Learning to Labour: How Working Class Kids Get Working Class Jobs*. Columbia University Press, 1977.

Wilson, Steven F. "Beyond No Excuses: The Promise of Student Agency." *Ascend*, May 16, 2016. http://www.ascendlearning.org/blog/beyond-no-excuses-the -promise-of-student-agency/.

———. "Success at Scale in Charter Schooling." American Enterprise Institute for Public Policy Research, March 2009. https://www.aei.org/wp-content/uploads/2011/10 /03-23948%20EduO%20Wilson-g.pdf.

Wilson, Terri S. "Negotiating Public and Private: Philosophical Frameworks for School Choice." 2008. https://greatlakescenter.org/docs/Research/2008charter /exec_sums/01.pdf.

Woodworth, Katrina R., Jane L. David, Roneeta Guha, Haiwen Wang, and Alejandra Lopez-Torkos. "San Francisco Bay Area KIPP Schools: A Study of Early Imple-mentation and Achievement, Final Report." SRI International, 2008. https:// www.sri.com/publication/san-francisco-bay-area-kipp-schools-a-study-of-early-implementation-and-achievement-final-report/.

Yeh, Stuart S. "A Re-analysis of the Effects of KIPP and the Harlem Promise Acad-emies." *Teachers College Record* 115, no. 4 (2013): 1–20.

Yosso, Tara J. "Whose Culture Has Capital? A Critical Race Theory Discussion of Com-munity Cultural Wealth." *Race Ethnicity and Education* 8, no. 1 (2005): 69–91.

Zappa, Ric. "How We're Shifting School Culture through Restorative Justice." *KIPP: Blog*, April 13, 2015. http://blog.kipp.org/developingcharacter/how-were-shifting -school-culture-through-restorative-justice/.

Zimmer, Ron, Gary T. Henry, and Adam Kho. "The Effects of School Turnaround in Tennessee's Achievement School District and Innovation Zones." *Educational Evaluation and Policy Analysis* 39, no. 4 (2017): 670–96.

INDEX

Page numbers in italics refer to figures and tables.

A NOTE ON THE TYPE

THIS BOOK has been composed in Miller, a Scotch Roman typeface designed by Matthew Carter and first released by Font Bureau in 1997. It resembles Monticello, the typeface developed for The Papers of Thomas Jefferson in the 1940s by C. H. Griffith and P. J. Conkwright and reinterpreted in digital form by Carter in 2003.

Pleasant Jefferson ("P. J.") Conkwright (1905–1986) was Typographer at Princeton University Press from 1939 to 1970. He was an acclaimed book designer and AIGA Medalist.

The ornament used throughout this book was designed by Pierre Simon Fournier (1712–1768) and was a favorite of Conkwright's, used in his design of the *Princeton University Library Chronicle*.